THE FATHERS OF THE CHURCH

A NEW TRANSLATION

VOLUME 43

THE FATHERS
OF THE CHURCH

A NEW TRANSLATION

EDITORIAL BOARD

Hermigild Dressler, O.F.M.
Quincy College
Editorial Director

Robert P. Russell, O.S.A.
Villanova University

Thomas P. Halton
The Catholic University of America

Robert Sider
Dickinson College

Sister M. Josephine Brennan, I.H.M.
Marywood College

Richard Talaska
Editorial Assistant

FORMER EDITORIAL DIRECTORS

Ludwig Schopp, Roy J. Deferrari, Bernard M. Peebles

THE POEMS
OF PRUDENTIUS

Translated by
SISTER M. CLEMENT EAGAN, C.C.V.I.
Incarnate Word College
San Antonio, Texas

THE CATHOLIC UNIVERSITY OF AMERICA PRESS
Washington, D.C.

NIHIL OBSTAT:

> Reverend Henry A. Echle
> *Censor Librorum*

IMPRIMATUR:

> ✠ Patrick A. O'Boyle, D.D.
> *Archbishop of Washington*

August 29, 1962

The *nihil obstat* and *imprimatur* are official declarations that a book or pamphlet is free of doctrinal or moral error. No implication is contained therein that those who have granted the *nihil obstat* and the *imprimatur* agree with the content, opinions, or statements expressed.

Copyright © 1962 by
THE CATHOLIC UNIVERSITY OF AMERICA PRESS, INC.

All rights reserved
Second Printing 1981
ISBN 978-0-8132-2762-7 (pbk.)

TO

MOTHER M. COLUMKILLE
ON THE OCCASION
OF HER DIAMOND JUBILEE

CONTENTS

	Page
INTRODUCTION	ix
PREFACE	xxix

HYMNS FOR EVERY DAY

1. A Hymn for Cock-Crow 3
2. A Morning Hymn 8
3. A Hymn before the Repast 14
4. A Hymn after the Repast 24
5. A Hymn for the Lighting of the Lamp . . . 29
6. A Hymn before Sleep 39
7. A Hymn for the Times of Fasting 45
8. A Hymn after Fasting 56
9. A Hymn for Every Hour 59
10. A Hymn for the Burial of the Dead 69
11. A Hymn for Christmas Day 78
12. A Hymn for Epiphany 83

THE MARTYRS' CROWNS

Hymn

1. Hymn in Honor of the Holy Martyrs Emeterius and Chelidonius of Calahorra 95
2. Hymn in Honor of the Passion of the Blessed Martyr Lawrence 105

CONTENTS—*Continued*

Hymn		Page
3.	Hymn in Honor of the Passion of the Most Holy Martyr Eulalia	128
4.	Hymn in Honor of the Eighteen Holy Martyrs of Saragossa	137
5.	The Passion of the Holy Martyr Vincent . . .	146
6.	A Hymn in Honor of the Most Blessed Martyrs Fructuosus, Bishop of the Church of Tarragona, and Augurius and Eulogius, Deacons	168
7.	Hymn in Honor of the Martyr Quirinus, Bishop of the Church of Siscia	176
8.	On a Spot in Calahorra Where Martyrs Suffered and Where Now is a Baptistery	180
9.	The Passion of St. Cassian of Forum Cornelii . .	182
10.	Discourse of the Martyr St. Romanus against the Pagans	190
11.	To Bishop Valerian on the Passion of the Most Blessed Martyr Hippolytus	240
12.	The Passion of the Apostles Peter and Paul . .	260
13.	The Passion of Cyprian	266
14.	The Passion of Agnes	274

INTRODUCTION

AURELIUS PRUDENTIUS CLEMENS, the greatest of the Latin Christian poets, was born in the year 348 during the consulship of Salia and Philip.[1] The place of his birth is not known with certainty. Three cities of Hither Spain are designated by him as his own: Tarragona, Saragossa, and Calahorra.[2] Partisans of each have claimed him as a native son with convincing arguments. In the case of all three, the expression 'ours,' used by Prudentius in referring to them, may indicate only that they belonged to Spain, or his own section of Spain, the northeast region lying next to the Mediterranean and nearest the center of Roman civilization.

The references to Tarragona in Hymn 6 of the *Peristephanon* may be dismissed as inconclusive, since they probably denote only the importance of that city as capital of the Province of Hispania Tarraconensis.[3] Moreover, the use of the second person in the words, 'Sing the praises of your own Fructuosus,' addressed to the inhabitants of the city seems to indicate that Prudentius did not claim

---
1. *Praefatio* 25.
2. *Peristephanon* 6.143; 4.141-142; 1.116 and 4.31-32.
3. *Ibid.* 6.1, 4-6 and 142-147.

Tarragona as his birthplace.⁴ If the poet is alluding to his native city or region when he laments his separation from Rome by the Vascon Ebro, the Cottian Alps, and the snowy Pyrenees,⁵ he cannot be referring to Tarragona, which lies on the Mediterranean coast between the Ebro and Rome.

Until recently biographers have generally been convinced that Prudentius was born at Saragossa. Bergman and others base their conclusion on the assumption that the Bishop Valerian, to whom the poet addressed Hymn 11 of the *Peristephanon,* occupied the see of Saragossa at the time, and that he belonged to the Valerian family mentioned in the hymn in honor of the martyrs of Saragossa.⁶ Bergman cites Gams, who lists in his *Series episcoporum* a Bishop Valerius among those attending the Council of Saragossa in 380.⁷

The last word on the question of the birthplace of Prudentius is found in an article written by the Benedictine, Mateo Alamo, who presents strong arguments in support of Calahorra.⁸ Alamo cites a hitherto unnoticed manuscript in which the following entry appears: '1. *Valerianus Calagorritane Urbis Episcopus;* 2. *Prudentius Caligorritanus, versificator insignis. . . .*' He shows that this Valerian, and not Valerius of Saragossa, is the prelate addressed by Prudentius in Hymn 11 as his own bishop. Moreover, he strengthens all the previous arguments in favor of Calahorra and refutes those of the Saragossan

---

4. *Ibid.* 6.150.
5. *Ibid.* 2.537-540.
6. *Ibid.* 4.80.
7. Bergman, *Prologomena* X. See also Allard, 'Prudence historien,' *Revue des questions historiques* 35.351.
8. 'Un texte du poète Prudence: *Ad Valerianum episcopum,*' *Revue d'histoire ecclésiastique* 35.750-756.

patriots, leaving little doubt that Calahorra was the birthplace of Prudentius.

Of the life of Prudentius little is known except what he himself reveals in his works. He is not mentioned by any of his contemporaries. The poem that prefaces the collection of his works published in 405 gives a bare outline of his life, which is supplemented by meagre revelations and hints in the works themselves. It is probable that he was born of noble Christian parents, who were Roman citizens of culture and fervent in the practice of their religion.[9] His works give evidence of a profound knowledge of Christian doctrine and a wide acquaintance with patristic literature as well as with the pagan classics.

In the Preface to his poems Prudentius tells us that as a boy in the grammar school he wept under the merciless blows of the teacher's rod,[10] and that later in the school of rhetoric, he learned the lying conceits of classical literature, which he was not the only Christian writer of the period to condemn.[11] Like Cyprian and Augustine he confesses that his youthful years were stained with wanton indulgence.[12] At the beginning of his public life his eloquence and high spirits found ample exercise as well as frequent failures in the law courts.[13] Twice he governed important cities of Spain, and finally he was elevated to a position of trust and dignity close to the emperor himself.[14] What this office was is not known, but it was doubtless conferred by Theodosius and may have been continued under Honorius and Arcadius. The poet praises these rulers

---

9. Cf. Allard, *op. cit.* pp. 347-348; also Ermini, *Peristephanon. Studi Prudenziani* 4-6.
10. *Praefatio* 7-8.
11. Cf. Ambrose, *De Abraham* 1.2; Jerome, *Ad. Rufinum* 1.30; Augustine, *Sermon* 70.2.
12. *Praefatio* 11-12.
13. *Ibid.* 13-15.
14. *Ibid.* 16-21.

in the *Contra Symmachum*.[15] Some commentators hold that he was given a high military post, since he shows a knowledge of the tactics of war in his *Psychomachia;* but it is generally agreed that the office was a civil one and may have been of consular rank.[16] Finally, most probably in his fiftieth year, he realized the vanity of earthly pursuits and resolved to dedicate his talents to the service of God.[17] Some editors have suggested that he may have entered a monastery or attached himself to a group of ascetics living in the world.[18] In the Preface, doubtless written when the poems were ready for publication in 405, and not, as he implies, when he first resolved to consecrate himself to God, he outlines a program of literary activities, including the writing of hymns for the hours of prayer night and day and in praise of the martyrs, and apologetic works in defense of the Catholic Faith. There is no record of the poet's life after the year 405, and the date of his death is not certain. According to the *Chronicon Dextri,* now regarded as spurious, he died in 424 at Saragossa, 'full of years and of illustrious works, after having waged many battles with all the heretics of his time.'[19]

Biographical details found in the works of Prudentius add little to what the Preface reveals. In the *Apotheosis* he records his memories of the time of Julian the Apostate, who became emperor in 361 when Prudentius was a boy of thirteen.[20] He tells of his visit to Rome, probably between

---

15. *Contra Symmachum* 1.1-41 and 524-532; 2.5-11 and 655-665.
16. Cf. Allard, *op. cit.* pp. 351-353; also Bergman, *Prolegomena* VI. Some editors think that the abbreviation V.C. found after the poet's name in certain manuscripts stands for *vir consularis*. The title *vir clarissimus consularis* was given to Roman provincial governors during the fourth century.
17. *Praefatio* 28-35.
18. See *Cathemerinon* 2.45-56.
19. Cf. Bergman, *Prolegomena* VIII, n. 2.
20. *Apotheosis* 450-502.

the years 401 and 403; of stopping at Imola in northern Italy to pray at the shrine of St. Cassian for relief from some distress;[21] of his pilgrimages to the tombs of the martyrs of Rome and his participation in the stations on the feast of St. Peter and St. Paul;[22] of reading the inscriptions in the catacombs and basilicas, including the famous epigrams of Pope Damasus;[23] and of his happy return to Spain and reunion with his beloved Father in Christ, Bishop Valerian.[24] He refers often to his past sinfulness[25] and expresses a humble opinion of his literary merits.[26]

The works of Prudentius as he indicated them in the *Praefatio*[27] include the *Cathemerinon*, a book of hymns for the praise of God; the *Apotheosis*, the *Hamartigenia*, and *Psychomachia*, apologetic works in defense of Catholic truth and morals; the two books of the *Contra Symmachum* and possibly the tenth hymn of the *Peristephanon*,[28] in which he condemns heathen rites and idolatry; and the *Peristephanon*, a book of hymns in praise of the martyrs and Apostles. The *Dittochaeon*, or *Tituli Historiarum*, consisting of forty-nine hexameter quatrains on Old and New Testament scenes, does not find a place in the outline given in the *Praefatio*, but it is generally attributed to Prudentius. The quatrains were probably intended as inscriptions for mosaics or frescoes in some basilica, and may have been inspired by the epigrams of Pope Damasus and the verses composed by Paulinus of Nola to accompany

---

21. *Peristephanon* 9.3-16 and 100-106.
22. *Ibid.* 2.529-584; 11.169-246; 12.55-66.
23. *Ibid.* 11.1-22.
24. *Ibid.* 11.178-182.
25. *Hamartigenia* 931-966; *Peristephanon* 2.573-584; 6.160-162; 10.1136-1140; 11.243-244; 14.124-133.
26. *Contra Symmachum* 1.643-657; 2. Pr. 44-46; *Peristephanon* 10.1-22; *Epilogue* 11-34.
27. *Praefatio* 36-45.
28. Cf. Bergman, *Prolegomena* XIII.

pictures in churches.²⁹ Gennadius, writing at the end of the fifth century, attributes to Prudentius a poem on the creation of the world, *Hexaemeron,* but this is not extant. According to Bergman, Gennadius erroneously referred to a work of the same title by St. Ambrose.³⁰

The chronology of the works of Prudentius has been the subject of much discussion. Some editors think that he may have written earlier poems, not now extant, on pagan themes before he turned his efforts to Christian subjects,³¹ and that some of the works published in 405 may have appeared separately before that date. It seems clear, however, that he published nothing prior to the year 392, since St. Jerome does not mention him in his *De viribus illustribus,* a record of all Christian authors known before the fourteenth year of the reign of Theodosius, that is 392. Ermini, citing earlier critics, concludes that all the poems except the *Psychomachia, Hamartigenia* and *Dittochaeon* were written between 400 and 405, and that these were composed between 405 and 410, the date proposed for the death of Prudentius. A recent discussion of the chronology of the works places all of the literary activity of Prudentius between the years 398 and 405, as the poet seems to suggest in the opening lines of his *Praefatio:* The *Cathemerinon, Apotheosis, Hamartigenia, Psychomachia,* and *Peristephanon* 1 to 7 between 398 and 400; the *Contra Symmachum* 1 and 2 and *Peristephanon* 8 to 10 between 401 and 403 while he was in Rome; and *Peristephanon* 11 to 14 in 404 after his return to Spain. However, this chronology presents two difficulties. In Hymn 2 of the *Peristephanon* Prudentius seems to indicate that the poem was written after his return to Spain;³² and he says definitely at the

---

29. Cf. *Epistle* 32, PL 61.330-343.
30. *Prolegomena* XII.
31. *Cathemerinon* 3.26-30.
32. *Peristephanon* 2.529-544.

end of Hymn 9 that he has returned home. All the hymns of the *Peristephanon* in praise of the Spanish martyrs were probably composed before the journey to Rome, and those which were the fruit of his sojourn in that city were either composed there or after he returned to Spain.[33] The order of the works in the manuscripts of Class A, which may or may not be the order in which they were written, is that suggested by Prudentius himself in the Preface, namely the *Cathemerinon, Apotheosis, Hamartigenia, Psychomachia, Contra Symmachum* 1 and 2, and the *Peristephanon.* This order is followed in most of the editions and in all the translations of the complete works made to date. In the manuscripts of Class B, the *Peristephanon* is joined to the *Cathemerinon* to form as it were one book of hymns in two parts.[34] In the present translation this order has been followed, and of the two books into which the translation has been divided, the first is devoted to the hymns and the second to the apologetic and didactic works.

The *Liber Cathemerinon,* as its name indicates, is a book of twelve 'hymns for every day.' Of these, six were inspired by the nocturnal and diurnal services, or times of private or common prayer observed in the Church from the earliest times: the 'Hymn for Cock-crow,' *Hymnus ad galli cantum;* the 'Morning Hymn,' *Hymnus matutinus;* the 'Hymn before the Repast,' *Hymnus ante cibum;* the 'Hymn after the Repast,' *Hymnus post cibum;* the 'Hymn for the Lighting of the Lamp,' *Hymnus ad incensum lucernae;* and the 'Hymn before Sleep,' *Hymnus ante somnum.* To this cycle are added what might be called the seasonal or occasional hymns: the 'Hymn for the Times of Fasting,' *Hymnus*

---

33. Cf. Ermini, *Peristephanon* 14-22; Bergman, *Prologomena* XIV-XIX; Isidoro Rodriguez Herrera, *Poeta Christianus. Prudentius' Auffassung vom Wesen und uon der Aufgabe des christlichen Dichters* (1936) 16-18.

34. Cf. Bergman, *Prologomena* XX-XXI.

ieiunantium; the 'Hymn after Fasting,' *Hymnus post ieunium;* the 'Hymn for Every Hour,' *Hymnus omnis horae;* the 'Hymn for the Burial of the Dead,' *Hymnus circa exequias defuncti;* the 'Hymn for Christmas Day,' *Hymnus 8 Kal. Ianuarias;* and the 'Hymn for Epiphany,' *Hymnus Epifaniae.* Even though Prudentius may not have intended these hymns for liturgical use, but rather as literary compositions, he was undoubtedly inspired by the liturgical prayer of his day. Fragments of Hymns 1 and 2 are found today in the Roman Breviary: *Ales diei nuntius, Lux ecce surgit aurea,* and *Nox et tenebrae, et nubila* for Tuesday, Wednesday, and Thursday at Lauds; and from Hymn 12 are drawn *Quicumque Christum quaeritis* for the Feast of the Transfiguration of Our Lord, *O sola magnarum urbium* for Epiphany, and *Audit tyrranus anxius* and *Salvete flores martyrum* for Holy Innocents. Other hymns of the *Cathemerinon* found their way, in part or as a whole, into the Mozarabic Breviary. The hymn *Inventor rutilis dux bone luminis* for Vespers of the first Sunday after the Octave of Epiphany is taken from Hymn 5.[35] The hymn *Cultor Dei memento* for Compline is taken from *Cathemerinon* 6, the hymn before sleep.[36] Hymn 7, for the times of fasting, is used in its entirety for the Hours of Terce, Sext, and None during Lent.[37] The hymn *Psallat altitudo coeli* for Vespers of the Sunday within the Octave of Easter consists of twenty-four lines from *Cathemerinon* 9.[38] The rest of this Hymn in sections is used for Vespers from Monday to Saturday of Easter week and for the Feast of the Ascension.[39] The hymn *Deus ignee fons animarum* for the Vespers of the Office of the Dead is composed of

---

35. Cf. PL 86.186.
36. Cf. *Ibid.* 962.
37. Cf. *Ibid.* 269-274.
38. Cf. *Ibid.* 641.
39. Cf. *Ibid.* 898-900.

forty-four lines from Hymn 10, plus an added stanza not found in any of the manuscripts and a doxology.[40] Hymns 1 and 2 are written in the Ambrosian iambic dimeter and the echoes of thought and imagery indicate that Prudentius was acquainted with the hymns of St. Ambrose. In Hymn 9 he was clearly indebted to St. Hilary's *Hymnus de Christo*[41] written in the same meter, the classical trochaic tetrameter catalectic associated with the marching of soldiers. The influence of Vergil, though not as extensive as in the hexameter poems, is evident in all of the hymns, but particularly in the 'Hymn for Christmas Day.'[42] The influence of Horace is shown in the complicated lyrical measures employed in many of the hymns as well as many evident borrowings. Echoes of Seneca and Lucan are found, especially in the 'Hymn for Epiphany.'

The *Liber Apotheosis*, a long apologetic poem of 1084 hexameters in the Vergilian epic manner, is a defense of Christ's divinity and the orthodox doctrine of the Trinity. It is preceded by two prefaces, one a 'Hymn on the Trinity' consisting of twelve hexameter lines, and the other a lyric poem of fifty-six alternating iambic trimeter and dimeter verses on the difficulty of keeping the true faith. Though Prudentius does not mention the Spanish heretic Priscillian, the poem may have been written with the rise of Priscillianism in mind. He refutes all those who deny the divinity of Christ, including the Patripassians,[43] the Sabellians,[44] the Jews,[45] and the Ebionites.[46] He concludes the poem with an attack on the Manichaeans, who by deny-

---

40. Cf. *Ibid.* 978.
41. CSEL 65.219.
42. *Cathemerinon* 11.53-76.
43. *Apotheosis* 1-177.
44. *Ibid.* 178-320.
45. *Ibid.* 321-550.
46. *Ibid.* 551-781.

ing Christ's humanity compromise His divinity.⁴⁷ It is probable that the *Apotheosis* was in part inspired by Tertullian's *Adversus Praxeam,* though Prudentius doubtless was familiar with later apologetic writings. In style the poem is a striking example of the blending of pagan form with Christian thought, with the influence of Vergil predominant.⁴⁸

The *Hamartigenia,* or 'The Origin of Sin,' is a refutation of the Gnostic dualism of Marcion. The poet shows that God is not the Author of evil but that He permits it in order that fallen man may choose freely between virtue and vice and thus merit heaven. The poem of 966 hexameters is preceded by sixty-three iambic dimeters in which the poet compares the heretic Marcion to the murderer Cain. Though Prudentius, in this work, adopts the arguments of Tertullian's *Adversus Marcionem* his treatment is original. His dependence on Vergilian phraseology is even greater than in the *Apotheosis,* especially in the passages in which he describes the torments of Hell.⁴⁹

The *Psychomachia* is an allegorical epic of 915 hexameters representing the contest between the virtues and vices for the possession of man's soul and the triumph of Christianity over paganism. The preface of sixty-eight iambic trimeters tells the story of Abraham's victory over the captors of Lot, symbolic of the victory of the soul in the spiritual combat. The battle is waged between the allegorical characters in the manner of a martial epic. Faith overcomes Idolatry, Modesty conquers Voluptuousness, Patience defeats Anger, Pride is beheaded by Humility, Sobriety overcomes Sensuality, Mercy conquers Avarice, and Concord overthrows Heresy. Though the *Psychomachia*

---

47. *Ibid.* 952-1084.
48. See Albertus Mahoney, *Vergil in the Works of Prudentius* pp. 4-24.
49. *Hamartigenia* 822-838; 922-930.

is the first purely allegorical poem in Latin literature, Prudentius found suggestions in previous classical and Christian writings, notably in the *Metamorphoses* of Apuleius and the *De spectaculis, De patientia,* and *De pudicitia* of Tertullian. In the epic speeches and combats between the virtues and vices he consciously imitates Vergil's *Aeneid.* Mahoney calls the *Psychomachia* the Christian *Aeneid.*[50] The poem was one of the most popular in the Middle Ages and served as an inspiration for mediaeval literature and art.[51]

The *Contra Symmachum* is a refutation of paganism in two books, probably written while Prudentius was in Rome between the years 401 and 403. Twenty years before, the City Prefect Symmachus had made an eloquent appeal to Valentinian II for the restoration of the statue of Victory to the Senate House. The pagan image had previously been removed by Gratian. In a letter to the emperor, St. Ambrose refuted the arguments of Symmachus and the statue was not restored. Some historians have thought that Prudentius was inspired to write the *Contra Symmachum* by a resurgence of paganism under Honorius and Arcadius. It is possible, however, that the poet read the *Relatio* of Symmachus and the letter of St. Ambrose and saw the epic possibilities in the triumph of Christianity.[52] The poem opens with a lyrical preface of eighty-nine asclepiadean verses in which St. Paul's deliverance from the viper on the island of Malta is a symbol of the Church's deliverance from persecution. The first book is an attack against the pagan divinities in the manner of Tertullian and Minucius Felix. The second book is pref-

---

50. Cf. *op. cit.* 47-80.
51. For a detailed discussion of the sources of the *Psychomachia* and its influence on mediaeval thought and art, see Lavarenne, *Prudence* 3.11-45.
52. Cf. Lavarenne, *op. cit.* 89-90.

aced by sixty-six glyconic lines in which the poet calls on Christ to assist him in the struggle against Symmachus as He saved Peter from the stormy waves. He proceeds to refute the arguments of Symmachus' *Relatio* point by point as Ambrose had done in his letter. The poem reveals the patriotism of Prudentius and his love of Rome, destined in God's providence to prepare the way for Christianity by her conquest of the world. The influence of Vergil is clear in this as in the other works in the epic style, but Ovid influenced his descriptions of pagan beliefs and practices and gave him his mythological information.[53]

The *Peristephanon*, 'on the crowns' of the martyrs, comprises fourteen hymns in honor of the 'witnesses' who gave their lives for the Faith during the ages of persecution. Of these, six commemorate Spanish martyrs: Emeterius and Chelidonius of Calahorra, soldiers who died rather than offer sacrifice to pagan gods; Eulalia of Merida, a girl of twelve who gave her life for Christ as did Agnes of Rome; the eighteen martyrs of Saragossa; Vincent, the heroic deacon of Saragossa; Bishop Fructuosus of Tarragona and his deacons Augurius and Eulogius; and the Martyrs of Calahorra above whose tomb a baptistery had been erected. Five hymns celebrate the passions of Roman martyrs: Lawrence, Cassian of Imola, Hippolytus, the Apostles Peter and Paul, and the virgin Agnes. The other three are devoted to Quirinus, Bishop of Siscia (now Susak in Jugoslavia); Romanus, deacon of Caesarea; and Cyprian, Bishop of Carthage and Doctor of the Church. For seven of the martyrs the hymns constitute the earliest extant documents in which the story of their martyrdom is related, namely the Passions of Sts. Emeterius and Chelidonius, St. Lawrence, St. Eulalia, the Eighteen

---

53. For a detailed discussion of the influence of Ovid in the *Contra Symmachum*, see Sister Marie Liguori Ewald, *Ovid in the contra orationem Symmachi of Prudentius* (Washington 1942).

INTRODUCTION   xxi

Martyrs of Saragossa, St. Cassian, St. Romanus, and St. Hippolytus.[54] In writing his hymns in commemoration of the martyrs, Prudentius was inspired by the liturgy of their feasts as celebrated in the churches of the fourth century; by certain historic documents, both those that are now extant and others that may have been lost; by popular tradition; and by his own observations during his pilgrimage to Rome.[55] From the sermons of St. Augustine and other sources we learn that the lections for the offices of the feast days of the martyrs included accounts of their passions.[56] Prudentius was undoubtedly influenced by the epigrams of Pope Damasus, which he read in the magnificent engraving of Philocalus at the shrines of the martyrs. Though the poet may not have intended the hymns of the *Peristephanon* for liturigical use, four of them in their entirety found their way into the office of the feast of the martyr in the Mozarabic Breviary, namely those in honor of Sts. Emeterius and Chelidonius, St. Eulalia, St. Fructuosus and St. Agnes.[57] Four others, those in honor of St. Lawrence, St. Vincent, St. Romanus, and the eighteen martyrs of Saragossa, were used in part.[58]

The *Dittochaeon* or *Tituli Historiarum* is the least important of the works of Prudentius and its authenticity has been questioned. It is not included in the two oldest manuscripts, but it is now generally regarded as genuine. The forty-nine hexameter quatrains are descriptive of scenes from the Old and New Testaments and were doubtless

---

54. Cf. BHL 2532, 4752, 2699, 1502, 1625, 7297 and 3960.
55. Cf. Allard, *op. cit.* 372-385 and 'L'hagiographie au IVe siècle,' *Revue des questions historiques* 37.353-405; also Vives, 'Veracidad historica de Prudencio,' *Analecta sacra Tarraconensia* 17 (1944) 199-204.
56. Cf. PL 38.1252-1268.
57. Cf. PL 86.1106-1111; 1274-1278; 1061-1065; 1050-1054.
58. Cf. *Ibid.* 1179; 901-903 and 1111; 1067-1068 and 1073-1078; 1249.

intended as inscriptions to accompany mosaics in some church.

In addition to the classic dactyllic hexameter used in all of the apologetic works, Prudentius employs in the hymns and prefaces a great variety of lyric metres and several strophes of his own invention. Hymns 1, 2, 11 and 12 of the *Cathemerinon* and Hymns 2 and 5 of the *Peristephanon* are written in iambic dimeter acatalectic, the Ambrosian measure widely used in the hymns of the Church. *Cathemerinon* 6 is the only hymn written in iambic dimeter catalectic. Two hymns, *Cathemerinon* 3 and *Peristephanon* 3, are composed in dactyllic trimeter hypercatalectic. The phalaecian hendycasyllabic metre is employed in *Cathemerinon* 4 and *Peristephanon* 6; the sapphic strophe in *Cathemerinon* 8 and *Peristephanon* 4; the iambic senarius in *Cathemerinon* 7 and *Peristephanon* 10; the minor asclepiad is used in *Cathemerinon* 5, glyconics in *Peristephanon* 7, the fourth archilochian in *Peristephanon* 13, and the alcaic measure in *Peristephanon* 14. Two hymns, *Cathemerinon* 9 and *Peristephanon* 1, are written in trochaic tetrameter catalectic, the metre used by St. Hilary and later in the *Pange lingua* of Fortunatus and also that of St. Thomas. Hymns 8 and 11 of the *Peristephanon* are written in elegiac couplets. The anapaestic dimeter catalectic, suggestive of the movement of the funeral procession, is especially suited to *Cathemerinon* 10, the 'Hymn for the Burial of the Dead.' *Peristephanon* 9 is written in distichs composed of a dactyllic hexameter verse followed by an iambic senarius. The distichs of *Peristephanon* 12 are made up of a grand archilochian line and a line of iambic trimeter catalectic. The stanza of the *Praefatio*, an original creation of the poet, is composed of three lines: the first a glyconic, the second a minor asclepiad, and the fourth a major asclepiad. Metres represented in the lyric prefaces of the hexameter poems include iambic dimeter, iambic trimeter, and asclepiadean and glyconic verses.

Any estimate of Prudentius must include a recognition of certain defects in his works, notably the length and prolixity of his hymns, the crude realism in his descriptions of the torments of the martyrs, the long declamatory speeches, the unreality of his allegory, and his excessive use of alliteration and assonance. Though his writings as a whole cannot be ranked among those of the greatest poets, they do not fall far short of great poetry in many instances. Prudentius has a technical skill surpassing that of the other Christian Latin poets. He is the creator of the Christian ode and the Christian allegory. He has something of the epic power of Virgil and the lyrical beauty and variety of Horace.

Prudentius has still greater claims to greatness, however, in the Christian thought and inspiration of his poetry. A recent critic has declared with truth that Prudentius is 'first a Catholic and only in the second place a poet.'[59] His faith is that of the Nicene Creed. He professes his belief in one God, the Father Almighty, Maker of heaven and earth and all things visible and invisible; in one Lord Jesus Christ, the only begotten Son of God, born of the Father before all ages, God of God, Light of Light, true God of true God, who came down from heaven and was born of the Virgin Mary; and in the Holy Ghost, the Lord and Lifegiver who proceeds from the Father and the Son. He believes in the fall of man, in original sin, and in Christ's death for the Redemption of men. He refers to the Sacraments of Baptism, Confirmation, and the Holy Eucharist, the Sacrifice of the Mass, and the necessity of penance for sin. He believes in the resurrection of the

---

59. F. J. E. Raby, *A History of Christian Latin Poetry from the Beginnings to the Close of the Middle Ages* (2nd ed., Oxford 1952).

dead and the life of the world to come, in heaven, hell, and purgatory, in devotion to the saints and the power of their intercessory prayers. In his poetry, Prudentius celebrates the triumph of Christianity over paganism. He saw the Church emerging from its three-hundred year struggle against the forces of idolatry and heresy, triumphant through its saving doctrine and the blood of its martyrs. He saw the magnificent basilicas, both in Spain and in Rome, rising in the place of the pagan temples. As an historian of Christian thought and culture at the end of the fourth century, Prudentius cannot be overestimated.

The text used in this translation is that of Bergman, Volume 61, of the *Corpus Scriptorum Ecclesiasticorum Latinorum*. The complete translations to date, that of H. J. Thomson in English, of Lavarenne in French, and Jose Guillen in Spanish, have all been examined and in many instances have proved helpful. All of the major translations of individual works and parts of works have likewise been examined. A word of explanation regarding the use of English verse in this translation is necessary. It was felt that the spirit of the lyric poetry of Prudentius might be more faithfully rendered in the English accentual equivalents of the classical metres used in the hymns. The hymns and lyrical prefaces have therefore been translated into unrhymed English verse, following the patterns of the Latin lyric measures, and the apologetic works in blank verse, the best English medium for rendering the Latin dactyllic hexameter. The aim has been to produce a readable verse translation rather than one suitable for singing. An effort was made to keep as close as possible to the original Latin, but in imitating the classical verse forms the exigencies of metre often demanded greater freedom than would be necessary in a prose rendering. Certain of the Latin metres, such as the long archilochian line, and the major asclepiad are difficult to render in English verse.

To give a greater unity to each of the two volumes into which the works of Prudentius have been divided, the hymns have been presented in the first volume and all the remaining poems in the second volume.

SELECT BIBLIOGRAPHY

Texts:

Arevalus, F. *Patrologia Latina* 59 and 60 (Paris 1847).
Aurelii Prudentii Clementis V. C. *opera omnia ex editione Parmensi cum notis et interpretatione in usum Delphini*. Reprinted from the *editio Parmensi* (1788) in 4 vols. (London, Valpy 1824).
Bergman, J. *Corpus Scriptorum Ecclesiasticorum Latinorum* 61 (Vienna 1926).

Translations:

Bayo, M. J. *Peristephanon de Aurelio Prudencio Clemente* (Madrid 1943).
Guillen, J. *Obras Completas de Aurelio Prudencio*, with Introduction and Commentaries by Isidoro Rodriguez Herrera, *Biblioteca de Autores Cristianos*, one vol. (Madrid 1950).
Lavarenne, M. *Prudence*, Société d'Edition 'Les Belles Lettres,' 4 vols. (Paris 1943-1951).
Marchesi, C. *Le Corone di Prudenzio* (Rome 1917).
Planella, S.J., Juan. *El Pindaro Cristiano* (Buenos Aires 1942).
Pope, R. Martin and R. F. Davis. *The Hymns of Prudentius*, The Temple Classics (London 1905).
Smith, E. G. *Songs from Prudentius* (London 1898).
Stam, J. *Prudentius. Hamartigenia* (Amsterdam 1940).
Thackeray, F. St. John. *Translations from Prudentius* (London 1890).
Thomson, H. J. *Prudentius*, Loeb Classical Library, 2 vols. (New York 1949-1954).

Secondary Sources:

Allard, Paul. 'Prudence historien,' *Revue des questions historiques* 35 (1884), 345-385.
―――. 'L'hagiographie au IVe siècle,' *Ibid.* 37 (1885), 353-405.
Ermini, F. *Peristephanon. Studi Prudenziani* (Rome 1914).
Herrera, I. Rodriguez. *Poeta Christianus. Prudentius' Auffassung vom Wesen und von de Aufgabe der christlichen Dichters* (Speyer 1936).
Mahoney, A. *Vergil in the Works of Prudentius* (Washington 1934).
Schanz, M. *Geschichte der römischen Literatur*, 4 Teil, 1 Halfte, 233-258 (Munich 1914).

THE POEMS
OF PRUDENTIUS

VOLUME 1

THE HYMNS

PREFACE

If my memory fails me not,
Through five periods of ten years my life ran its course
And since then seven bright summers have passed, cheering me with their sun.[1]

Life's close draws on apace, and God
To the port of old age steers my declining days.   5
In the time that has passed what have I done worthy of Heaven's smile?

My first years wept beneath the rod[2]
With its merciless blows; soon, in the toga clad,
I was taught to declaim lying conceits, often defiled with sin.[3]

Then an impudent wantoness[4]   10
And indulgence perverse tainted my youthful years
With the canker of vice. Shame and remorse rack me to think of it![5]

---

1. Cf. Lucan, *De bello civili* 7.381.
2. Cf. Horace, *Epistles* 2.1.70; Juvenal, *Satires* 1.15; Ausonius, *Epistles* 22. 24-32.
3. The reference is to the exercises from pagan literature used in the schools of rhetoric. Cf. Jerome, *Adversus Rufinum* 1.30; Augustine, *Sermon* 70.2; Paulinus of Nola, *Poema* 10.33-42 (PL 61.553).
4. Cf. Horace, *Odes* 1.19.3-7.
5. Cf. *Hamartigenia* 948-951 and *Peristephanon* 2.573-576.

Next the forum's contention roused
My impetuous spirit, eager for victory,[6]
And the obdurate wars waged in the law courts led
    to bitter falls.   15

Twice in cities renowned, I held
Reins of government high, ruling with might of laws,
As I rendered to good men their due rights and to the
    wicked doom.

Then the Emperor's kind regard
Advanced me to a post, high in its dignity,   20
When he chose me to stand next to himself in the
    imperial train.[7]

While my life thus engaged flew by,
The gray hairs of old age suddenly stole on me,[8]
Urging me not to lose sight of the years Salia ruled in
    Rome,[9]

When I first saw the light of day;   25
And what winters have passed, what glad springs
    have returned,
Bringing roses to meadows when the ice fled, my
    white head declares.[10]

---

6. Cf. Horace, *Odes* 1.9.24.
7. See Introduction, p. xi.
8. Cf. Juvenal, *Satires* 9.129.
9. Salia was consul with Phillip in 348, the year of Prudentius' birth.
10. Cf. Horace, *Odes* 4.13.12.

What will all these things profit me,
Whether evil or good, after the flesh decays,
When whatever I was, death will efface, blotting out
    all my deeds.   30

To me it must one day be said:
Whosoever thou art, earth, which thy soul held dear,
Is no more. Not of God, who is thy Judge, were those
    pursuits of thine.

And yet now at the end of life
Let my sinful soul cast off its vanities;[11]   35
Let it render to God praise with the voice, even if not
    by works.

Let me link day to day with hymns,
And no night be without homage of song to God;
Let me strive against false teachings, defend Catholic
    Faith with zeal;

Let me trample on heathen rites,   40
Break thy idols, O Rome, ending their evil sway,
Hymns to martyrs devote, lauding their acts, praise to
    Apostles give.[12]

While these verses I write or sing,
O may I wing my flight, free from the body's chains,[13]
To that heavenly sphere, whither my last utterance
    shall be borne.   45

---

11. Cf. Basil, *Epistles* 223.2.
12. In this and the previous stanza, the poet alludes to his various works. See Introduction, p. xiii.
13. Cf. Paulinus of Nola, *Poema* 11.57-60 (PL 61.462).

THE BOOK OF HYMNS FOR EVERY DAY

(LIBER CATHEMERINON)

1. A HYMN FOR COCK-CROW[1]

The winged messenger of day
Sings loud, foretelling dawn's approach,[2]
And Christ in stirring accents calls
Our slumbering souls to life with Him.

'Away,' He cries, 'with dull repose,   5
The sleep of death and sinful sloth;
With hearts now sober, just and pure,
Keep watch, for I am very near.'[3]

---

1. Some commentators think that in this Hymn Prudentius refers to the crowing of the cock shortly before dawn. Isidore of Seville (*Origenes* 5.30) defines the time of cock-crow as midnight. The Hymn undoubtedly has reference to the night office, or vigils, observed by ascetics and the more fervent of the laity during the fourth century. The nocturnal vigils, from which the canonical Hour of Matins later developed, began about midnight after the first crowing of the cock and terminated at dawn with the *hymni matutini*, which Prudentius celebrates in Hymn 2. Frequent mention of these prayers at midnight and at dawn, *media nocte et mane*, are found in the ecclesiastical writings of the third and fourth centuries. Cf. Tertullian, *De Oratione* 29; Cyprian, *De Oratione Dominica* 36; Basil, *Regulae fusius tractatae*, 37.5; Jerome, *Epistles* 130.15; *S. Silviae peregrinatio* 24.1-2 (CSEL 39.71) and 24.8-10 (CSEL 39.73).
2. Cf. Vergil, *Moretum* 2; Ambrose, *Hymn* 1.5-6.
3. Cf. Mark 13.35; Rom. 13.11; 1 Thess. 5.6; 1 Peter 5.8.

After the sunlight floods the sky,
It is too late to spurn your bed,[4]   10
Unless in watching and in prayer[5]
You spend a portion of the night.

The cock's loud voice, which ere the dawn
Awakes the song of noisy birds
That perch beneath the sheltering eaves,[6]   15
A symbol is of our high Judge.

As hid in shadows dark we lie,
Deep buried in the shrouds of night,
He bids us leave our dull repose,
For day's first gleam will soon appear,   20

That when the radiant dawn bestrews
The heavens with her shining breath,[7]
All men worn out by arduous toil
May find new strength in hope of light.[8]

---

4. Cf. Ambrose, *Hymn* 9.2.
5. *Labori.* This is the evident meaning here, as in ll. 23 and 80. Cf. Jerome, *Epistles* 107.9: *et assuescat exemplo ad orationes et psalmos nocte consurgere, mane hymnos canere, tertia, sexta, nona hora ... stare in acie ... sic dies transeat, sic nox inveniat laborantem;* Cassian, *De coenobiorum institutis* 3.9 (PL 49.145): *post vigiliarum laborem; S. Silviae peregrinatio* 35.1 (CSEL 39.85): *Hora prima noctis omnes in ecclesia, quae est in Eleona, conveniamus, quoniam maximus labor nobis instat hodie nocte ista.* See also Niceta of Remesiana, *De vigiliis servorum Dei* 3 (Trans. in Vol. 7 of this series, p. 55).
6. Cf. Vergil, *Aeneid* 8.456; Ausonius, *Ephemeris* 1.2.
7. *Coruscis flatibus.* Though all the MSS read thus, Chamillard (Delphin ed. 57) thinks that *coruscis fletibus*, 'shining tears,' should be read. Arevalus (PL 59.778) shows that *flatibus* is doubtless the correct reading. Cf. Vergil, *Aeneid* 4.584-585.
8. Cf. *S. Silviae peregrinatio* 36.5 (CSEL 39.87): *Postmodum* (the previous vigil) *autem alloquitur episcopus populum confortans*

God gives us in the time of sleep 25
An image of eternal death:[9]
In night of sin's vile durance held,
We lie and groan for light divine.

But out of Heaven's high citadel
The voice of Christ a warning sounds, 30
That dawn is near to free our souls
From bondage to the sleep of sin,

Lest to the very end of life
This leaden torpor may oppress
Our hearts submerged in depths of crime, 35
Oblivious of the heavenly light.

In night's dark shadows, it is said,
The evil spirits in joy may roam,
But at the crowing of the cock
In sudden fear they take to flight. 40

Hateful to them is the near approach
Of light divine, God's saving grace,
Which, breaking through the murky clouds,
Drives far away night's vassal crew.

Forewarned, the fiends know this to be 45
The symbol of our promised hope,
When free from sleep's enthralling chains
We wait the coming of our God.

---

eos, quoniam et tota nocte laboraverint et adhuc laboraturi sint ipsa die, ut non lassentur, sed habeant spem in Deo, qui eis pro eo labore maiorem mercedem redditurus sit.
9. Cf. Vergil, *Aeneid* 6.522.

The Savior once to Peter showed
What hidden power this bird may have,   50
And warned that ere the cock would crow
Himself three times must be denied.[10]

For evil deeds are ever done
Before that herald of the dawn
Enlightens human kind and brings   55
An end to error and to sin.[11]

Forthwith he wept his bitter fall[12]
Who Christ denied with lying lips,
The while his heart was innocent,
And steadfast faith his soul preserved.[13]   60

And never more such word he spoke,
By slip of tongue or conscious fault,
For mindful of the crowing cock,
The just man ceased from ways of sin.

Hence all now hold in firm belief   65
That in the stillness of the night
When loudly crows the joyful cock
Our Lord came back from Hell's dim shore.[14]

---

10. Cf. Matt. 26.34; Mark 74.30; Luke 22.34; John 13.38.
11. Cf. Jerome, *In Isaiam* 7.21.
12. Cf. Matt. 26.75; Mark 15.72; Luke 22.62.
13. Cf. Luke 22.32. Prudentius does not minimize Peter's guilt in the denial of Christ, but he distinguishes between the gravity of the lie that escaped his lips in a moment of cowardice and a complete loss of faith. Peter's denial is the subject of frequent discussion in the writings of the Fathers of the Church. Cf. Augustine, *Contra mendacium* 13, and Ambrose, *Expositio in Lucam* 10.72-93.
14. Cf. Matt. 28.1; John 20.1.

The strength of death was then subdued;
Then Hell's dominion lost its sway;   70
Then day with might more potent far
Compelled the shades of night to flee.

So now let wickedness be still;
Let sin in darkness be at rest;
Let deadly evil languish now,   75
Ensnared within the toils of sleep.

And let the spirit, now awake,
Alert and active vigil keep[15]
Through all the hours that still remain
Until the night attains its goal.   80

To Jesus let us lift our souls
In prayers and tears and holy thoughts;
For fervent supplication keeps
The pure of heart from bonds of sleep.[16]

Too long has deep forgetfulness   85
Oppressed with overwhelming cares
The soul that roams in empty dreams[17]
While limbs lie wrapt in slothful ease.

For vain and fleeting as a dream
Are all the works that we have done   90
For worldly glory and renown:
Awake, my soul, for Truth is here.

---

15. *Stans ac laborans excubet.* See n.5 above.
16. Cf. Ambrose, *Hymn* 2.21.
17. Cf. Vergil, *Aeneid* 10.642.

Delights and gold and earthly joy,
The wealth, success, and honors gained,
Whatever evils nourish pride,   95
All vanish with the morning light.

Come Thou, O Christ, and banish sleep;[18]
Break Thou the chains that night has forged
And wash away our ancient stain;
Renew Thy light within our souls.   100

---

18. Cf. Ambrose, *Hymn* 1.30.

2. A MORNING HYMN[1]

Ye shades of night and turbid clouds,
Confusion of the world, depart,
For light pervades the whitening sky,
And Christ, the Sun of Justice, comes.

---

1. *Hymnus matutinus.* The morning office celebrated in the churches and monasteries during the fourth century was often called *hymni matutini.* Cf. Cassian, *De coenobiorum institutis* 3.5; *S. Silviae peregrinatio* 24.2 (CSEL 39.71) and 24.12 (CSEL 39.74). The present Canonical Hour of Lauds developed from this service, the term being derived from *laudes matutinae,* the name used by authors in the fifth and sixth centuries.

Asunder now earth's gloom is rent,   5
Pierced by the sun's transfixing dart;[2]
The day-star's shining glance restores
The hues of meadow and of plain.[3]

So will our spiritual darkness fade,
When, through the broken clouds of sin,[4]   10
The heart will see its guiltiness,
Made clear in God's all-ruling light.[5]

In vain shall we then strive to hide
The evil thoughts that cloud the mind,
For inmost secrets of the soul   15
In that new dawn will be revealed.[6]

The veil of darkness shrouds the crimes
The thief commits without restraint;
But light, the enemy of guile,
Forbids his cunning to lie hid.[7]   20

In murky shades deceit and fraud
Delight to cloak their subtle arts;[8]
The paramour embraces night,
Most opportune for shameful deeds.[9]

---

2. Cf. Lucretius, *De rerum natura* 1.146-149.
3. Cf. Vergil, *Aeneid* 6.272; Horace, *Odes* 4.5.4-8.
4. Cf. Vergil, *Aeneid* 3.199.
5. Cf. *Ibid.* 1.604.
6. Cf. Vergil, *Georgics* 3.325.
7. Cf. Ambrose, *De Cain et Abel* 2.88.
8. Cf. Horace, *Epistles* 1.16.62.
9. Cf. Ambrose, *Ibid.*

Behold, the fiery sun appears:[10]   25
Disgust and shame now fill his heart,
For in the splendor of the day
No man can persevere in sin.

When morning comes, who does not blush
That cups flowed freely in the night?[11]   30
Then moderation rules desire,
And revelers taste sobriety.

Now life is earnest and austere
And all forsake frivolity;
Now underneath a serious brow
The jester hides his foolish wit.   35

All set about the tasks they love[12]
When morning's golden hour arrives:
The soldier, townsman, mariner,
The craftsman, merchant, husbandman.   40

One seeks the glory of the courts;
Another heeds war's trumpet call;
The tradesman and the countryman
Are eager for their sordid gains.

---

10. Cf. Vergil, *Georgics* 4.426.
11. *Quis mane sumptis nequiter/non erubescit poculis* . . . ? Lavarenne (Prudence 1.9) points out that some commentators are of the opinion that the poet here refers to the violation of a custom among the ancients of not drinking wine in the morning. The context seems to indicate that night carousels are meant. These were common in the decadent society of the Roman Empire. Cf. Ambrose, *De Helia et ieiunio* 12.45 and 15.53.
12. An imitation of Horace, *Odes* 1.2-25 is evident in 11.37-44.

HYMNS   11

But, we, O Christ, who know not wealth,[13]   45
Nor usury, nor eloquence,
Nor daring in the art of war,
Have learned to love but Thee alone.[14]

To Thee, with pure and simple heart,
We raise our voice in holy psalms;   50
On bended knee, we chant Thy praise
And, weeping, cry to Thee for aid.[15]

In this blest service we are rich;
By commerce such as this we live,
And from the rising of the sun   55
These exercises fill the hours.

Into our thoughts now turn Thy gaze;[16]
Examine every word and deed;
Behold the many stains of sin,
Which Thy pure light alone can cleanse.   60

Oh grant that we may ever keep
Our souls as bright and free from soil,
As when the waters on us flowed
From holy Jordan's cleansing stream.[17]

---

13. Lines 45-56 are among those cited as evidence that Prudentius at the time of the writing of the *Cathemerinon* had entered a monastery or attached himself to one of the many groups of ascetics that were formed throughout the Christian Roman Empire during the fourth century. Cf. Jerome, *Epistles* 127.8; Augustine, *De moribus ecclesia* 1.31.67 and 33.70.
14. *Te, Christum, solum novimus.* Cf. 1 Cor. 2.2.
15. Cf. Joel 2.12; Ps. 38.13; Tertullian, *De oratione* 23 (Trans. in Vol. 40, this series, p. 182).
16. Cf. Ambrose, *Hymn* 7.8.
17. Baptism. Early ecclesiastical writers regarded the crossing of the Jordan and the entry of the Israelites into the land flowing with

If by the clouds of earth's black night   65
Our souls since then have been obscured,
Do Thou, O King of the morning star,
Disperse the gloom with Thy bright glance.[18]

O Lord divine, as Thou canst change[19]
Foul pitch to milky white, and make   70
Of ebony a crystal clear,
So wash away our dark misdeeds.[20]

It was beneath night's canopy
That Jacob with the angel fought;[21]
In darkness, the unequal strife   75
Continued till the break of day.

But when the morning sun shone clear,
A lameness struck him in the thigh,
And conquered by his frailty,
He lost the strength and power to sin.   80

---

milk and honey as a figure of baptism. Cf. Origen, *Homiliae in Josue* 4. In the baptismal rites, as late as the sixth century, a drink of milk and honey was given to the newly-baptized after the reception of the Eucharist. Arevalus (PL 59.792) cites evidence that the early Christians were actually baptized in the waters of the Jordan, sanctified by the baptism of Christ. According to Eusebius (*De vita Constantini* 4.62), Constantine desired to be baptized in the Jordan.

18. Cf. Luke 1.78-79; Ps. 79.4.
19. Cf. Isa., 1.18; Ovid, *Ex Ponto* 3.3.97.
20. *Delicta tergens livida.* Several MSS have terge, which Meyer defends. See 'Zu Prudentius,' *Philologus* 93 (1939) 398. The reading *terge* has been followed in the translation.
21. Cf. Gen. 32.24-32.

He tottered from the wounds received
In baser parts of the human frame,[22]
Where vile corruption has its seat,
Far from the reason's high abode.

From this example we can learn   85
That man beset by shades of sin[23]
Is powerless to renew the fight,
Unless perchance he yields to God.

More blessed he whom daybreak finds
A victor in the stern affray,   90
His stubborn passions mortified[24]
And nature overcome by grace.

Let darkness now at length recede,
In which too long our wandering steps
Have led us stumbling on the path   95
Of error and iniquity.[25]

Oh, may the light serenely shine
And make us pure as its own rays;
Let no false word defile our lips,
And no dark thought obscure our minds.   100

So let us live the whole day through
That tongue, or hand, or wandering eyes
May never give offense to God,
And that the body know no stain.

---

22. Cf. Vergil, *Ciris* 69.
23. Cf. Vergil, *Culex* 274-275.
24. Cf. Vergil, *Aeneid* 3.137.
25. Cf. Heb. 12.13.

A Watcher stands above the skies, 105
Who, from the dawn to evening's fall,[26]
Each moment of the passing day,
Beholds us with all-seeing eyes.

Our Witness and our Sovereign Lord,
He keeps creation in His view! 110
He sees the inmost thought of man;
He is the Judge none can deceive.

---

26. Cf. Minucius Felix, *Octavius* 32.9 (Trans. in Vol. 10, this series, p. 390).

3. A HYMN BEFORE THE REPAST[1]

Crucified Savior, the Author of Light,
Source of all things, Word begotten of God,
Born in the Flesh, of the Virgin unstained,
One with the Father in infinite power,
Prior to creation of earth, sea and sky,[2] 5

---

1. In order to complete the sevenfold apportionment of the times for prayer indicated by the psalmist (Ps. 118.164), St. Basil prescribed in his daily *cursus* that the mid-day prayer should be divided, one part being recited before the noon repast and the other afterwards (*Sermo Asceticus* 4, trans. in Vol. 9, this series, p. 212). This hymn and the following seem to indicate that Prudentius had a similar scheme in mind.
2. Cf. Ausonius, *Ephemeris* 3.10-12.

Hither I pray, turn Thy radiant gaze;
Look upon us with Thy favoring smile,
Bringing salvation to mortals below;
Let the fair light of Thy countenance shine[3]
On the repast that we take in Thy name.[4]   10

Lord, there is sweetness in nought without Thee;[5]
What we partake of delights not the taste
If Thy beneficent gifts do not fill
Platters and cups from Thy bounty, O Christ,
Blessings made holy by faith in Thy care.   15

May the refreshment we take in our need
Savor of God and the mercy of Christ;[6]
May our converse, be it serious or gay,
All that we are, every thought, every deed,
By the Triune Love be ruled from on high.[7]   20

Spoils from the rose do not garnish my board,
Nor the aroma exhaled from rich balms;[8]
Heavenly waters from fountains above,
Fragrant with faith, sweet as nectar divine,[9]
Flow from the heart of the Father Himself.   25

---

3. Cf. Ps. 66.2.
4. Cf. 1 Cor. 10.31.
5. Cf. Vergil, *Aeneid* 12.882; Claudian, *In Rufinum* 2.258.
6. Cf. Ambrose, *Hymn* 7.21.
7. Cf. Ausonius, *Domestica* 2.29.
8. Cf. Wisd. 2.7-8; Horace, *Odes* 2.3.13-14; Minucius Felix, *Octavius* 12.6 (Trans. in Vol. 10, this series).
9. Cf. Vergil, *Georgics* 4.415-416.

Scorn the bright leaves of the ivy, my Muse,
That in the past have encircled your brow.[10]
Learn now to weave mystic garlands of verse;
Bind your fair tresses with chaplets of song,
Praising in dactyls the goodness of God.[11] 30

How can the generous spirit of man,
Offspring of heaven and ethereal light,
Render its maker a homage more true
Than to extol in melodious strains
Favors received from His bountiful love. 35

For, from His Providence, man has received
All that he grasps with imperious hand:
All that the sky and the earth and the sea
Yields from the air and the waves and the fields,
This He subjects to me, me to Himself.[12] 40

Birds are entangled in traps or in nets[13]
Skillfully made by the cunning of man.
Flocks of winged creatures are caught in the brush
Smeared with the glue that is made from the bark,[14]
Never to soar through the heavens again. 45

---

10. Cf. Vergil, *Eclogues* 8.12.
11. This stanza has led some critics to believe that Prudentius had previously written poems on pagan themes. Others, including Arevalus, think that the reference is to poetry in general, which Prudentius would devote to religious rather than to profane subjects. Cf. Glover, *Life and Letters in the Fourth Century* 268, n.1 and PL 59.798.
12. Cf. Ps. 8.7-9.
13. Cf. Vergil, *Georgics*, 1.307.
14. Cf. *Ibid.* 1.139.

Lo, through the waters the sinuous nets
Draw in the fish that swim in the sea.
Others are taken with rod and with line;
Trustful, they swallow the coveted bait,
Only to feel the sharp wound of the hook.[15]   50

Natural riches pour forth from the fields,
Bountiful harvests of golden-eared corn.
Here where the vines in luxuriance grow,
Lifting their branches and tendrils on high,[16]
Thrives, too, the olive, the nursling of peace.   55

Servants of Christ in this opulence find
Nurture sufficient for all of their needs.
Far be from them such craving for food
That they find pleasure in gory repasts,
Gorging themselves on the beasts they have slain.[17]   60

Leave to the heathen his barbarous feasts,
Animals slaughtered to satisfy greed;[18]
For us green leaves from the garden's rich store,
Pods filled with lentils of various sorts,
Furnish the viands for innocent cheer.[19]   65

Foaming milk pails bring us liquor like snow,
Beverage drawn from the udders of goats.[20]
Curdled by rennet, the milk becomes firm,
Forming the cheese that is kept for our food,
Pressed down in baskets, of frail wicker made.   70

---

15. Cf. Ausonius, *Mosella* 250-252.
16. Cf. Vergil, *Culex* 74.
17. Cf. Ambrose, *De Helia et ieiunio* 8.25; Jerome, *Epist.* 127.4.
18. Cf. Vergil, *Georgics* 2.537.
19. Cf. Basil, *Epist.* 2.6; Jerome, *Epist.* 22.35 and *Epist.* 43.3.
20. Cf. Vergil, *Georgics* 3.177, 309.

Honey Cecropian distils from the comb
Nectar ambrosial, fresh from the hives,[21]
Made from ethereal dew and the thyme
By bees that labor all day in the fields,
Knowing not wedlock nor carnal delights.[22] 75

From the earth, too, come the mellow windfalls,[23]
Largess of orchards all laden with fruit;
Trees that are shaken rain down their rich load,
Showering apples like hail to the ground,
Scattering heaps of bright red on the grass. 80

What sounding lyre or great trumpet of old,
Famed for the music of wind or of strings,
Could give fit praise to the works of the Lord,
Who is almighty and rich in the gifts
That He provides for the comfort of man.[24] 85

Father, all-gracious, when morning is new,[25]
And when the sun has attained its mid goal;
Then as the daylight grows dim in the west,
When comes the hour for partaking of food,
Thee, we extol in harmonious strains.[26] 90

---

21. Cf. *Ibid.* 4.140,179.
22. Cf. *Ibid.* 4.197; St. Ambrose, *De Virginibus* 1.8.40. See also the *Benedictio cerae* or *Exsultet* ascribed to St. Augustine (PL 72.270 and 365). The passage in praise of bees, evidently borrowed from the *Georgics*, has been omitted in this *Exsultet* as now used in the Roman Rite. Cf. Jerome, *Epist.* 18.1 and Augustine, *De civitate Dei* 15.22. For a discussion of the diction of Prudentius in 1.75 see Meyer, *op. cit.* 401-402.
23. Cf. Vergil, *Eclogues* 1.80.
24. Cf. Horace, *Odes* 1.12.1, 11, 13-15.
25. Cf. Vergil, *Aeneid* 1.555 and *Georgics* 3.325.
26. Cf. Ps. 54.17-18. Many ascetics of the fourth century took only one meal toward evening, the rule for fast days during the first

For the bright spirit that glows in my breast,
For the blood pulsing unseen in my veins,
For the quick tongue that resounds with the voice
As it vibrates in its hollow recess,
Father above, let me sing Thy due praise.   95

Lord, we were fashioned by Thy holy hand,
Formed to Thy image from slime of the earth,
And to make perfect our body of clay,
Thou didst endow it with spiritual life,
Breath of Thy lips, the immortal soul.[27]   100

Then Thou didst give to Thy creature a home,
Leafy retreats in a garden of bliss,[28]
Where the aroma of spring without end
Scented the flowering meadows and glades
Watered by floods from a fourfold stream.[29]   105

---

    centuries of the Church. In some instances a mid-day meal was allowed. In listing the hours for the daily sevenfold praise of God, St. Basil says that the mid-day prayer should be divided, one part being recited before the noon repast and the other afterwards. (*Sermo asceticus* 4, PG 31.878). The reference in 11.86-90 seems to be to the daily ordering of the psalmody rather than to the hours for meals. The Roman custom, which was followed by ordinary Christians, included an early breakfast, a light mid-day lunch, and a sumptuous meal in the late afternoon. Cf. Tertullian, *De ieiunio* 10; Pseudo-Athanasius, *De virginitate* 12-14; Basil, *Regulae fusius tractatae* 37.3-4; *S. Silviae peregrinatio* 28.3 (CSEL 39.80).

27. Cf. Gen. 2.7. Bergman's text based on the oldest MS is *ore animam dedit ex proprio*. For a discussion of the variant reading *flavit et indidit ore animam*, see his *Prolegomena* p. XXXI and note, p. XVI; also J. H. Waszink, *Mnemosyne* 11 (1943) 75-77.
28. Cf. Vergil, *Aeneid* 6.638.
29. Cf. Gen. 2.8-10.

'All these delights you may use and enjoy;
All this domain is for you,' said the Lord,
'But I forbid you to pluck the harsh fruit,
From the fair tree of destruction and death,
That in the midst of this paradise grows.'[30]   110

Then in the form of a serpent, the Fiend
Tempted the woman, unconscious of guile,
Made her through evil persuasion incite
Adam to eat of the pestilent fruit,
Destined to ruin, herself, by the act.[31]   115

When they had eaten, their bodies unclad
Filled them with shame and awareness of sin—
Knowledge contrary to God's holy will:
Garments they made from the leaves of the fig,
Hiding disgrace under modesty's veil.[32]   120

Banished by God for the sin they confessed,[33]
Trembling, they fled from their holy abode.
Doomed was the woman henceforth to bear
Pains of the marriage yoke, not experienced before,
Ruled by her husband in bonds of wedlock.[34]   125

Punishment, too, the vile serpent received:
It was decreed that the woman would crush
Under her heel his triple-tongued head.[35]
Thus did the snake dread the woman's foot,
Just as the woman was subject to man.   130

---

30. Cf. *Ibid.* 2.16-17.
31. Cf. *Ibid.* 3.1-7.
32. Cf. *Ibid.* 3.7.
33. Cf. *Ibid.* 3.23.
34. Cf. *Ibid.* 3.16.
35. Cf. *Ibid.* 3.14-15; Vergil, *Aeneid* 2.264; Horace, *Odes* 3.11.20.

Head these became of a tainted offspring,
Rushing headlong into villainy and crime;
And as posterity mirrored their fall,
Blindly confusing the right with the wrong,
Death was the penalty paid for their sin.[36]   135

Lo, there appears a new scion of our race,[37]
Sent down from heaven, the Second Man,
Not of the earth, like the first of our line;
God, Himself, our humanity assumes,
Free from its frailties and carnal defects.[38]   140

He is the Word of the Father made flesh,[39]
Born of the Virgin, immaculate, fair,
Mother by power of the Spirit of God,
Knowing not man, nor the marriage bond
With its delights and allurements to sin.   145

Here is the cause of that primal hate,
Of the dissension and war to the death,
That has been waged between Satan and man:[40]
Prone on the ground the serpent now lies
Crushed by the feet of the spotless Maid.   150

She who deserved to be Mother of God,
Virgin most powerful, his venom subdues;
Drawing his length into sinuous coils,
Slowly the serpent his poison expels,
Harmless on grass of like hue to himself.[41]   155

---

36. Cf. Vergil, *Aeneid* 11.444.
37. Cf. Vergil, *Eclogues* 4.7.
38. Cf. 1 Cor. 15.47.
39. Cf. John 1.14.
40. Cf. Gen. 3.15.
41. Lines 149-155 have been cited as evidence of the belief in the Immaculate Conception of the Blessed Virgin Mary from the

What hellish fiend does not tremble with fear,
Awed by the whiteness of Christ's shining flock?[42]
Sullen, the wolf in the midst of the sheep
Wanders unfeared and forgetful of blood,
Curbing the might of his ravenous jaws.[43]   160

Lo, by a marvelous change, the mild lamb
Governs the lion, and the gentle dove,
Soaring down from the celestial heights,[44]
Through the storm winds and the wandering clouds,
Drives the fierce eagles in ceaseless pursuit.   165

Thou art my Dove, all-powerful, O Christ,
Dreaded by vultures that feed on our blood.
Thou art the Lamb white as snow that dost keep
Ravening wolves from Thy sheltering fold,
Placing a yoke on the tiger's fierce mouth.[45]   170

Grant to Thy servants, O bountiful Lord,
Blessings we ask on this frugal repast,
Sustenance meet for refreshment and strength;
Let no immoderate banquets induce
Dullness and sloth in the body and soul.[46]   175

---

earliest ages of the Church. Cf. A. B. Heider, *The Blessed Virgin Mary in Early Christian Latin Poetry* (Washington 1918) 42-43.

42. *Grege candidulo,* the newly baptized, who in the early ages of the Church were clothed in white robes. On the meaning of *candidulo* here, cf. Alexander Souter, *A Glossary of Later Latin* (Oxford 1949) 37.
43. Cf. Isa. 11.6; also Vergil, *Georgics* 3.537 and Horace, *Odes* 3.18.13.
44. Cf. Vergil, *Aeneid* 5.216 and 6.202.
45. Cf. *Ibid.* 6.80.
46. Cf. Ambrose, *De Helia et ieiunio* 3.5; Jerome, *Epist.* 22.17; Augustine, *Sermo* 210.8.10

Far from us revels that bitterness bring;
May we refrain from forbidden delights,
Handling no deadly or poisonous thing.
Let the enjoyment of food be in bounds,
And may the passions be tranquil and free.   180

Let the death of men's bodies that came
From the nefarious fruit of the tree
Sate the revenge of the powers of hell.
Let it suffice that the creature of God
Dies only once for the primal offense.[47]   185

Work of God's mouth, the pure spirit that glows[48]
Bright in the being of man cannot die;
Formed by God's breath, and issuing forth
From the Creator's celestial throne,[49]
It is endowed with rational powers.   190

Even the flesh that has perished in death,
Takes on anew the life it has lost.
Members resolved into moldering dust,
Rising again from repose in the tomb,
Mingle to form our original frame.   195

Yes, I believe, and my faith is not vain,[50]
Bodies live always along with their souls;
For I reflect that from Hades' abyss,[51]
Christ in the body came back from the dead,
Mounting with joy to His heavenly throne.[52]   200

---
47. Cf. Ausonius, *Ephemeris* 3.33-36.
48. Cf. Vergil, *Aeneid* 6.730.
49. Cf. Tertullian, *De anima* 4.1 and 24.2.
50. Cf. Vergil, *Aeneid* 4.12; 1 Cor. 15.17.
51. Cf. Acts 2.24,31.
52. Cf. Mark 16.19; Luke 24.51; Acts 1.11.

24 AURELIUS PRUDENTIUS CLEMENS

    Laid up for me is the glorious hope
    That the still body consigned to the tomb,
    Fragrant with funeral balms, will arise,
    Called to empyreal stars by our King,
    Christ, who arose from a similar grave.[53]   205

---

53. If this hymn was written after Prudentius visited Rome, the final stanza may have been inspired by the following epitaph in the Cemetery of St. Callistus:
    Alexander mortuus non est sed vivit
    Super astra et corpus in hoc tumulo
    Quiescit ...
See Pope, *The Hymns of Prudentius* (London 1905) 179.

4. A HYMN AFTER THE REPAST

We have taken this meal by nature sanctioned
For refreshment of bodies faint with hunger;
Let the tongue now give praise to God the Father,[1]

To the Father, who from His throne in Heaven[2]
Holds sway over the mighty hosts of angels,   5
Cherubim and the Seraphim beneath Him.[3]

---

1. Cf. Hymn 3, notes 1 and 26.
2. Cf. Vergil, *Aeneid* 1.506.
3. Cf. Ps. 79.2; Isa. 6.2 and 37.16; Dan. 3.55; Jerome, *In Isaiam* 6.2.

Lord and God of Sabaoth, we invoke Him,[4]
Being infinite, endless and eternal,
Cause and Maker of earth and every creature,[5]

Fount of life from on high serenely flowing,[6]   10
Planting virtue, and holy faith supplying,
Mighty Conqueror of Death, salvation's Author.

From Him have we our life and all our being;[7]
And the Spirit subsists and reigns forever,
One with Father and Son, from both proceeding.[8]   15

Into hearts that are pure the Spirit enters,
And as beautiful temples they are holy[9]
When of God and His grace they have drunk deeply.

But if semblance of guilt or dark defilement
Should appear in the heart now consecrated,   20
Forth He flies from this shrine that is polluted.

For when conscience is seared by fires of passion,[10]
Murky vapors arise, and black corruption
Forces grace to depart from this dark dwelling.

---

4. Cf. Jer. 11.20; Rom. 9.29; James 5.4.
5. Cf. Vergil, *Aeneid* 12.829.
6. Cf. Ps. 35.10.
7. Cf. Acts 17.28.
8. Prudentius here, as in Hymn 5, 1.160, expresses belief in the procession of the Holy Ghost from both the Father and the Son, a doctrine which was maintained by the Fathers of the Church, though the 'Filioque' was not inserted in the Nicene Creed until the year 589, by a decree of the Council of Toledo. Cf. Pohle-Preuss, *Dogmatic Theology* 2 (St. Louis 1946) 168-189.
9. Cf. 1 Cor. 6.19.
10. Cf. Juvenal, *Satires* 1.167.

Not by virtue alone and pure intentions 25
May we build up for Christ a lasting temple
In our hearts and the soul's inmost recesses,

But we must be on guard against indulgence,
Lest the bosom where faith preserves its dwelling[11]
Be oppressed by the weight of sinful gorging. 30

Hearts set free by sobriety and fasting
Taste the sweetness of God's life-giving presence
As the food of the soul and true refreshment.[12]

Loving Father and Guardian, Thou dost strengthen
Soul and body with food divine and earthly, 35
Filling us with Thy grace and holy virtue.

Thus Thy Providence once regaled and rallied,
With a dinner prepared and sent by Heaven,
Him who languished among the roaring lions.[13]

When this hero denounced the molten idol 40
And refused to adore the graven image
Made of metal, refined and smoothly polished,

Cruel Babylon's mob and king condemned him
To a harrowing death, the prey of lions,
Ready with their ferocious teeth to rend him. 45

---

11. Cf. Rom. 10.10.
12. Cf. John 6.56. This is an evident reference to the Holy Eucharist, though some commentators think that the poet refers to the indwelling of the Holy Ghost or to God's Providence. Cf. Arevalus (PL 59.814) and Chamillard (Delphin ed. 1.82).
13. Lines 37-72 are a paraphrase of Daniel 14, of the Septuagint and Vulgate.

HYMNS 27

Oh, how safe is the soul of faith and piety![14]
Round the hero the savage beasts now gambol,
In their reverence for God's unscathed disciple.

Close beside him they stand with manes thrown backward,
Their voracity tamed and stilled their hunger, 50
As they circle their prey with mouths unbloodied.[15]

But when, closely confined and weak from fasting,
He uplifted his suppliant hands to heaven,[16]
Begging God's never-failing help and bounty,

Lo, a messenger sent to earth comes flying 55
Swiftly leaping from favoring heights of heaven,
To bring food to that sorely tested servant.

Soon it chanced that the seraph saw below him
Good Habacuc[17] the prophet as he carried
To the reapers a meal unbought and rustic.[18] 60

Seizing him by the hair, the angel raised him,
And aloft through the air, he swiftly bore him,
Laden as he was with the heaped-up baskets.

Then the prophet, still carrying the viands,
Glided slowly into the den of lions 65
And delivered to Daniel his burden.

---

14. Cf. Vergil, *Aeneid* 4.373.
15. Cf. *Ibid.* 9.63.
16. Cf. *Ibid.* 1.93.
17. *Ambacum*, the form used in the Septuagint. Several MSS have *Abacuc* or *Abbacuc*. Cf. Jerome *Epistles* 22.9, and *In Abacuc* (PL 25.1273).
18. *Dapes inemptas.* Cf. Horace, *Epodes* 2.48; Vergil, *Georgics* 4.133.

'Take this gladly,' he said, 'and eat with joy
These provisions the highest Father sends thee
By the angel of Christ, in this thy peril.'

Strengthened by the repast that he had taken, 70
Daniel lifted his grateful eyes to heaven.
'Alleluia,' he sang and answered 'Amen.'[19]

Thus refreshed by Thy gifts, we sing Thy praises,
Gracious Lord and Dispenser of all bounties,
Rendering thanks from our hearts in tuneful
   worship.[20] 75

Thou dost guard and protect us from the fury,
Of a tyrannous world that holds us captive
Driving from us that hateful foe, the demon,

Who goes roaring around us, raging madly,[21]
As he seeks to entrap us and devour us, 80
When, O infinite God, we praise Thee only.

We are vexed and oppressed by tribulations;
Men harass us and hate us and malign us;
Faith is tested by bitter persecution.

In these trials redress is not wanting, 85
For sweet manna is sent to us from heaven,
When the wrath of the lion has abated.

If man wishes to share this food of angels,
Drinking deeply and savoring its sweetness,
As it saturates every part of his being, 90

---
19. Cf. Deut. 27.15; 1 Cor. 14.16.
20. Cf. Basil, *Sermo Asceticus* 4; also Hymn 3, n.26.
21. Cf. 1 Peter 5.8.

Holy prophets will satisfy his hunger
At the banquet made ready for the just men
Who are reaping the Lord's eternal harvest.[22]

Nought is sweeter to taste nor more delightful,
Nothing gives greater joy to man in bondage, 95
Than the sacred precepts of seers and prophets.[23]

With this nourishment, though the haughty tyrant
May condemn us to death with cruel judgement,
Though the lions, unfed, may rush upon us,

Ever confessing our faith in God the Father, 100
One in Thee, Christ our Lord, we will proclaim Him,
And will carry Thy cross with love unshaken.[24]

---

22. The Apostles and other laborers in the vineyard of the Lord. Cf. Matt. 9.37-38.
23. Cf. Ps. 118. 103-104.
24. Cf. Luke 14.27.

5. A HYMN FOR THE LIGHTING OF THE LAMP[1]

O Christ, heavenly King, Author of shining light,
Thou that rulest our days, fixing the seasons due,[2]
Dark night steals on the world, gone is the glowing sun;
Give Thy glorious light back to Thy faithful flock.[3]

---

1. *Hymnus ad incensum lucernae.* Commentators differ on the

interpretation of this hymn. Some contend that Prudentius had in mind the daily evening office celebrated in the churches and monasteries and designated by such names as *hora incensi* (Ambrose, *De virginibus* 3.4.18), *sacrificium vespertinum* (Jerome, *Epistles* 107.9), *vespertina sollemnitas* (Cassian, De coenobiorum institutis 2.4), *hora lucernarii, lucernarium, hora lucernae* (*S. Silvae peregrinatio* 27.7, 32.2, 39.4, CSEL 39). Ildefonso Schuster (*Liber Sacramentorum*, Vol. 2, p. 247, English trans., London 1925) says that this hymn alone would suffice to prove that Prudentius intended the hymns of the *Cathemerinon* to be used at the daily liturgical prayer of the Church. Arevalus, who entitles the poem *Hymnus de novo lumine paschalis sabbati,* gives lengthy evidence to prove that it commemorates the Easter vigil, with the blessing of the new fire and the paschal candle. Cf. PL 59.677-684. Lesleus, in his edition of the Mozarabic Missal (PL 85.68-69 and 437-446), indicates parallels between passages in the poem and the rites and prayers for the Easter vigil, and concludes that Prudentius wrote the hymn in praise of the paschal candle. The poet in this hymn develops themes found in the *praeconium paschale* attributed to St. Augustine (PL 72.268), for instance the invocation of Christ as the source of light, the flight of the Israelites from Egypt and their miraculous passage of the Red Sea, guided by the pillar of fire, the return of Christ as conqueror from hell to shed His light on mankind, and the offering of the paschal candle to God. Nocturnal vigils held on special feasts and anniversaries of martyrs as well as at Easter began in the evening with the *lucernarium* and lasted until Mass the next morning, which was celebrated before sunrise. Cf. *S. Silviae peregrinatio* 27.7; Jerome, *Contra Vigilantium* 9. Prudentius may have intended this hymn for the evening office and these special vigils on other days as well as that of Holy Saturday. Stanzas 1, 7, 35, and 38-41 are used in the Mozarabic Breviary for Vespers of the first Sunday after the Octave of Epiphany.

2. Cf. Tertullian, *Apology* 18.2; Cyprian, *De oratione Dominica* 35. See also the Preface, *Ab initio noctis sanctae paschae,* of the Missale Gothicum (PL. 72.268).

3. Cf. Horace, *Odes* 4.5.5.

Though Thou paintest the sky, throne of Thy regal
    might, 5
With innumerable stars circling the lunar lamp,
Thou dost teach us to seek light from the solid rock,
Spark that springs from the flint when it is struck by
    steel.[4]

Lest man ever forget that his one hope of light
On the body of Christ has its foundation sure,[5] 10
He desired to be called stone of the Corner firm,[6]
Whence we kindle the flame lighting our little fires.

This we nourish in lamps dripping with dewy oil,[7]
Or dry torches are lit from the celestial fire;[8]
We make candles with wicks dipped in the flowery
    wax, 15
From which honey was pressed, hidden in yellow combs.

Bright the glittering flame, whether a hollow urn
Feeds the oil to the wick thirsting for nutriment,
Or the resin of pine burns on the flaring torch,
Or coarse fiber of flax drinks up the waxen round; 20

Warm nectar from the crown, burning with lively flame,
Tears, sweet-smelling, distils, flowing down drop by drop,
For the force of the heat causes the molten wax
To descend in a shower shed from the taper's point.

---

4. Cf. Vergil, *Aeneid* 6.6.
5. *In Christi solido corpore conditam.*
6. Cf. Isa. 28.16; 1 Cor. 10.4; Eph. 2.20. See also the first collect
   for the blessing of the fire on Holy Saturday in the Roman
   Missal.
7. Cf. Vergil, *Aeneid* 5.854.
8. Cf. *Ibid.* 1.175.

Now our temples and halls shine with Thy gifts, O
    God,   25
Splendid tapers ablaze, praising the Fount of light;[9]
Their rays vie with the day gone with the setting sun,
And dark night, in defeat, flees in her tattered robes.[10]

Who does not recognize God as the source of light,
Flowing swift from on high, heavenly boon to man?   30
He to Moses appeared, clothed in the form of flame
That burned bright in the bush studded with bristling
    thorns.[11]

Blest that man who was deemed worthy to see his Lord,
Heaven's Ruler sublime, present in holy brier;
Unshod bidden to walk over the sacred ground,   35
Lest the place be defiled hallowed by Deity.[12]

That same pillar of fire guided a noble race,
Long accustomed to live under the tyrant's heel;
Freed, though weak, from its chains, saved by its fathers'
    deeds,
It was led by this light shining in desert ways.[13]   40

Its beams, bright as the sun, guided the weary steps
Of the journeying tribes, ever awake to foes,
And illumined the dark when in the midst of night
They continued their march, roused from their peaceful
    sleep.[14]

---

9. Cf. *S. Silviae peregrinatio* 24.4 (CSEL 39.72).
10. Cf. Paulinus of Nola, *De S. Felice natalitium* 3.101-103 (PL 61.467); Eusebius, *De vita Constantini* 4.22.
11. Cf. Exod. 3.2.
12. Cf. *Ibid.* 3.5.
13. Cf. *Ibid.* 13.20.
14. Cf. *Ibid.* 13.21.

But the king of the lands washed by the River Nile,[15] 45
Fired by envy and hate, summons his mighty hosts,
Cohorts swift as the wind, bidding them join in war,
And the blare of the horns sounds in the mail-clad ranks.

Soldiers hasten to arms, girding themselves with swords,
While the trumpet resounds, sadly foretelling doom. 50
Some in javelins trust, others prepare the darts
And the arrows that fly forth from the Cretan bows.[16]

Bands of infantry form, drawn up in seried ranks;
Quick the warriors mount chariots with flying wheels,[17]
While the horsemen aloft govern their prancing steeds, 55
And war's banners advance, proud with the dragon's crest.[18]

Freed at last from the chains forged by the cruel king,
The tribes that had long burned under Egyptian suns
Paused to rest in a land, strange and remote from home,[19]
On the shores of the Red Sea with its purple waves. 60

The foe gains upon them, led by the treacherous king,[20]
And the squadrons attack, strong in battle array.[21]
Moses, calm and unmoved, orders his men to march
Forthwith into the sea, fearless of surging tide.

---

15. Cf. *Ibid.* 14.8-9.
16. Cf. Horace, *Odes* 1.15.17.
17. Cf. Vergil, *Aeneid* 8.433.
18. Cf. Claudian, *De quarto cons. Hon.* 545. Note the anachronism in ascribing to the Egyptians the banners of the Roman imperial armies.
19. Cf. Vergil, *Aeneid* 8.232.
20. Cf. *Ibid.* 9.38.
21. Cf. *Ibid.* 2.50.

Then the waters recede, offering a passage safe   65
To the fugitive race; banks of transparent waves
Stand like ramparts of glass, guarding the sandy path,
While the people of God cross the divided sea.[22]

Yea, the enemy, too, maddened by bitter hate,
Swarthy warriors led by their perfidious king   70
And athirst for the blood flowing in Hebrew veins,
Dared to enter the sea, trusting the furrowed waves.[23]

Through the midst of the flood rushes the royal host[24]
With percipitous haste, like to a hurricane;
But the sundered abyss back on itself now rolls,   75
And impetuous waves join with a mighty roar.

One saw chariots and steeds floating in angry waves,
Shattered weapons of war, princes and peers of rank,
And near, black in the tide, bodies of satellites;[25]
Sad that day was the land mourning the tryant's fall. 80

Who, O Christ, has the power rightly to sing Thy praise?
By calamities dire, Thou with avenging hand
Didst force Egypt to yield, humbled beneath Thy rod,[26]
To the guardian of right, Moses, Thy servant just.

The impassable deep, fierce in its mighty surge,   85
Thou dost curb and restrain, leading Thy people safe
Through the refluent waves,[27] while the rapacious gulf
Soon the impious foe swallows with rabid greed.

---

22. Cf. Exod. 14.21,29.
23. Cf. Ovid, *Heroides* 12.118.
24. Cf. Exod. 14.23
25. Cf. *Ibid.* 14.28.
26. Cf. *Ibid.* 7.12.
27. *Refluo in solo.* Several MSS have *salo* here, a reading which Meyer defends. Cf. 'Zu Prudentius,' *Philologus* 93 (1939) 391-395.

For Thee murmuring springs flow from the desert rocks;[28]
Streams pour forth from the rift made in a stony
    crag[29]   90
And give drink to the throngs, thirsty and sore of foot,
As they travel with haste under the burning sky.

Water tasting of gall drawn from the mournful pool
By the grace of the wood like Attic honey grows.[30]
On account of a Tree bitter is changed to sweet,   95
For hope fixed on the Cross mounts to the skies above.[31]

Then food white as the snow showers on the camp below,
Gliding down from the sky, denser than icy hail;[32]
With this sumptuous feast, banquet divine that Christ
Sent from Heaven above, tables are richly spread.[33]   100

Winds that blow from the south bring with their rainy
    blasts
Flocks of fluttering birds clouding the sky with wings.
Once they glide to the earth, breaking their serried lines,
They are stayed in their flight, never to soar again.[34]

Thus the Father benign signally blessed our sires   105
With miraculous gifts sent from His throne on high;
Now His goodness provides food for our famished souls,
Mystic banquet of love, pledge of eternal bliss.[35]

---

28. Cf. Horace, *Odes* 3.13.15.
29. Cf. Num. 20.11.
30. Cf. Exod. 15.23-25.
31. Cf. Tertullian, *Adversus Judaeum* 13.
32. Cf. Exod. 16.14-15; Num. 11.9.
33. Cf. Vergil, *Georgics* 4.378.
34. Cf. Exod. 16.13; Num. 11.31-32.
35. The Holy Eucharist.

Through the sea of the world rent by the raging winds[36]
His own faithful He leads, guiding their steps aright, 110
And He summons our souls, tossed on the waves of life,[37]
To the heavenly realm where the redeemed abide.

There bright roses exhale fragrance from gardens rare,
And where murmuring springs water the earth around,
Modest violets bloom,[38] crocus and marigold, 115
Lifting radiant flowers, rich in their saffron hues.

There sweet balsams distill perfume from slender trees,
The rare cinnamon breathes spices that fill the air,[39]
And the leaf of the nard floats from the hidden spring[40]
To the mouth of the stream laving the pleasant
   strand. 120

Here the souls of the blest wandering in grassy meads
Blend their voices in song, chanting melodious hymns
That devoutly resound throughout the happy glades,
And with radiant feet they tread the lilies fair.

Even souls of the lost suffering in depths of Hell 125
Have some respite from pain, holding glad holiday
On that night when the Lord came to the world above[41]
Up from Acheron's pool, rising to life again,

Not as Lucifer bright, springing from Ocean's bed,
With his glimmering ray tinges the somber night, 130
But more vast than the sun, shedding the light anew
On the world that had grown dark at the Savior's cross.

---
36. Cf. Ambrose, *De virginibus* 2.2.17.
37. Cf. Vergil, *Aeneid* 1.628.
38. Cf. *Ibid.* 11.69.
39. Cf. Martial, *Epigrams* 4.13.3.
40. Cf. Claudian, *In Eutropium* 1.226.
41. Cf. Augustine, *Enchiridion de fide, spe et caritate* 112.

Hell's fierce torments subside, bringing surcease from pain
To the spirits that live ever in penal fires;
Calm and joy for a while reign in that prison
    house[42]   135
And the sulphurous streams burn not with wonted rage.

Festive vigil Thy flock keeps on this holy night
Through the hours till the dawn, chanting the praise of
    God,
And on altars upraised offer the Sacrifice,
Glad in hope of the grace granted to fervent souls.[43]   140

Ceilings fretted with gold gleam with the brilliant light
Shed from pendulous lamps swaying on supple chains;[44]
The flame fed by the oil languidly swims about,
Casting flickering rays through the translucent glass.

You would think that the sky studded with myriad
    globes   145
Now bent over our heads,[45] bright with the northern
    Bears,[46]
And that evening stars sprinkled their roseate light
On the course of the Wain guiding the team of Dawn.

---

42. Cf. Seneca, *Hercules furens* 57.
43. The reference in this stanza is without doubt to the Easter vigil or the vigils of other feasts which lasted throughout the night and were concluded with the Sacrifice of the Mass at dawn. Cf. Lactantius, *Divinarum institutionum* 7.19; *S. Silviae peregrinatio* 27.7 and 38.1-2 (CSEL 39). On the Christian basilicas of the fourth century see Eusebius, *De vita Constantini* 3.32.36; Jerome, *In Zachariam* 8.6 and *Peristephanon* 12.45-52.
44. Cf. Vergil, *Aeneid* 1.726; Paulinus of Nola, *De S. Felice natalitium* 6.35-37 and 9.389-392.
45. Cf. Paulinus of Nola, *op. cit.* 11.418-20.
46. Cf. Vergil, *Aeneid* 3.516.

Truly meet is the gift offered at dewy eve[47]
By the sheep of Thy fold, Father omnipotent,   150
Light, most excellent boon given by Thee to man,
Light, by which we perceive all Thy remaining gifts.

Thou art light for our eyes, light for our inmost souls,
Thou, our mirror within, mirror also without;
This light deign to receive which, I, Thy servant
   bring,[48]   155
Light imbued with the oil, chrism of holy peace.

Take it, Father Most High, through Thine Anointed Son,
Christ, Thy Splendor revealed, Lord of the universe,
Sole-begotten by Thee, breathing the Paraclete,
Loving Spirit of Truth, from Thy paternal heart.   160

Through Him glory and laud, honor and wisdom high,
Thy benevolent love, goodness and majesty,
Throned in threefold Godhead, reach out from Heaven
   to earth,
Linking age unto age through the eternal years.

---

47. Cf. Seneca, *Agamemnon* 815 and *Octavia* 224.
48. Cf. *Benedictio cerae* attributed to St. Augustine (PL 72.269): *In huius igitur noctis gratia suscipe, sancte Pater, incensi huius sacrificium vespertinum, quod tibi in hac cerei oblatione solemni per ministrorum tuorum manus de operibus apum sacrosancta reddit Ecclesia.* This *Exsultet* is still sung by the deacon on Holy Saturday in the Roman rite.

6. A HYMN BEFORE SLEEP[1]

Be with us, great Creator,
Ne'er seen by eye of mortal,[2]
And Christ, Word of the Father,
With Holy Spirit of comfort!

O Trinity supernal, 5
One in Thy might and power,[3]
O God from God eternal,
And God from both proceeding![4]

The toil of day is ended,
And now the hour of quiet 10
Brings sleep with sweet caressing
To bodies faint and weary.[5]

---

1. Tertullian (*De oratione* 25) speaks of morning and night prayers as obligatory on all Christians. St. Ambrose (*De virginibus* 3.4.18-19) recommends prayer before sleep for virgins consecrated to God. The origin of the Canonical Hour of Compline has been ascribed to St. Benedict in the sixth century. That ascetics of the fourth century observed a prayer of rule before retiring, in addition to Vespers at the ninth or tenth hour, is evidenced by St. Basil's prescription of prayer at the beginning of night that sleep might be sinless and untroubled by dreams. Cf. *Regulae fusius tractatae* 37.5. Lines 125-152 are used as a hymn for Compline in the Mozarabic Breviary (PL 86.962).
2. Cf. John 1.18.
3. *Vis ac potestas una.* Several MSS have *vis una, lumen unum* here, accepted by Arevalus and others.
4. See Hymn 4, n. 8.
5. Cf. Vergil, *Aeneid* 2.253.

The mind by tempests shaken
And racked by cruel anguish[6]
Drinks deep the cup of soothing   15
That stills the voice of memory.[7]

The Lethean streams now stealing
Through every vein of mortal
Dispel the aching sorrow
In hearts forlorn and grieving.[8]   20

This law by God was given
To fragile human bodies
That pleasure, pure and healing,
Might temper labor's harshness.

But while the welcome languor   25
Goes pulsing through our members,
And while the heart is resting,
Bedewed by gentle slumber,[9]

The soul set free flies swiftly
Through the limpid air of heaven.[10]   30
And sees in divers figures
Things veiled from earthly vision.[11]

For freed from care and worry,
The mind, of source celestial
From purest fountain flowing,   35
Is ever alert and active.[12]

---

6. Cf. *Ibid.* 4.1 and 9.798.
7. Cf. *Ibid.* 6.715.
8. Cf. *Ibid.* 6.714 and 2.268.
9. Cf. *Ibid.* 1.691; Ambrose, *De virginibus* 3.4.19.
10. Cf. Tertullian, *De anima* 43.12 (Vol. 10, this series, p. 278); Ambrose, *De Abraham* 2.8.58.
11. Cf. Claudian, *De raptu Proserpinae* 3.124.
12. Cf. Tertullian, *op. cit.* 45.1; Ambrose, *loc. cit.*

A thousand dreams it fashions
Of its own form and substance,
And through this world it wanders,
Pleased with its empty fancies.[13]   40

But in this land fantastic
Oft terror plagues the sleeper.
Sometimes a heavenly splendor
Gives vision of the future.[14]

More often dark phantasms   45
Obscure the truth, misleading
Through black and dreary mazes
The souls whom fear has saddened.

To him who stains but rarely
His soul with sin's offenses   50
A light serene and radiant
Reveals celestial secrets.[15]

But he who has polluted
His heart by impious vices
Is mocked by many terrors   55
And sees appalling phantoms.[16]

Of this our Seer was witness[17]
When to the royal servants,
With him in chains of prison,
He showed their dreams' foreboding.   60

---

13. Cf. Tertullian, *op. cit.* 43.12.
14. Cf. Cicero, *De senectute* 22.81; Tertullian, *op. cit.* 46.
15. Cf. Tertullian, *op. cit.* 47.2.
16. Cf. Job 7.14. Tertullian, *op. cit.* 47.1.
17. Cf. Gen. 40-41.

One to his post returning
Bears cup again to the tyrant;
The other, preying vultures
Devour on a lofty gibbet.

Then that imperious monarch, 65
Perplexed by dubious dreaming,
He warned of coming famine
That harvests might be hoarded.

Soon as a prince and guardian
He ruled throughout the kingdom 70
And shared the royal scepter
In the mighty ruler's palace.

O how profound the secrets
Christ shows to His just servants
When wrapt in peaceful slumber,[18] 75
How dazzling and ineffable!

That faithful friend of the Master,
Evangelist of the Highest,
Saw through the clouds receding
Things sealed from mortal vision: 80

The Lamb of God empurpled
With blood of cruel slaying,
Him who alone can open
The book that holds the future.[19]

His mighty hand is wielding 85
A flaming two-edged saber
Which like the lightning flashes
Its dreadful double menace.[20]

---
18. Cf. Tertullian, *op. cit.* 47.2.
19. Cf. Apoc. 5.6-9.
20. Cf. *Ibid.* 1.16.

He is alone the searcher
Of body and of spirit,[21]   90
And the twofold sword, affrighting,
Is death, the first and second.[22]

But that benign Avenger,
His holy wrath restraining,
Allows but few of the wicked   95
In lasting death to perish.[23]

To Him the eternal Father
Has given the throne of judgment[24]
And Name above all others
As heritage forever.[25]   100

With Antichrist He battles
In conflict fierce and bloody.
And from the raging Monster
Brings back a splendid trophy.

This is the beast stupendous   105
Devouring all the nations,
The whirlpool fell and gory,
Which John declared accursed.[26]

That beast, who with proud daring
Assumed the Name all holy,   110
Is by the true Christ vanquished
And sent to deep Gehenna.[27]

---

21. Cf. Heb. 4.12.
22. Cf. Apoc. 2.11; 20.6,14.
23. Cf. Arevalus, *Prolegomena* 175 (PL 59.701).
24. Cf. John 5.22; Acts 17.31.
25. Cf. Phil. 2.9.
26. Cf. Apoc. 13 and 17.8.
27. Cf. 2 Thess. 2.4,8.

So tranquil was the slumber
Of John, the saintly hero,
That his mind with gift prophetic   115
Through all of Heaven wandered.[28]

We merit not such visions,
Whom frequent faults encumber,
Whom base and earthly longings
For things of evil tarnish.   120

Enough if sleep, refreshing,
Renews our weary bodies.
Enough if no dark shadow
Some future evil threatens.[29]

O Christian soul, remember   125
Baptism's dewy fountain,
The sacramental laver
And holy oil's anointing.

When at the call of slumber
You seek your bed decorous,   130
Then sign on breast and forehead
The Cross of our Redemption.[30]

The Cross dispels all evil,
All darkness flies before it;[31]
With such a symbol hallowed,   135
The mind knows peace and stillness.

---

28. Cf. Lucretius, *De rerum natura* 1.75.
29. Cf. Ovid, *Ex Ponto* 2.7.14.
30. Cf. Jerome, *Vita Hilarionis* 6; *Epistles* 22.37.
31. Cf. Palladius, *Historia Lausica* 2 (PL 73.1094).

Away, away, vile monsters[32]
That haunt the restless sleeper,
Away, hell-born deceiver,
With your infernal malice. 140

O false deluding serpent,
Who in a thousand guises,
With foul and evil promptings,
Disturbs the heart in slumber, [33]

Begone, for Christ is present!
Depart, here Christ is dwelling![34] 145
The sign that you acknowledge
Condemns your hateful army.

Although the weary body
A little while lies sleeping,
Our thoughts shall ever follow 150
Christ in these hours of quiet.[35]

---

32. Cf. Vergil, *Aeneid* 6.258.
33. Cf. Tertullian, *op. cit.* 47.1.
34. Cf. Ambrose, *In Psalmum* 118.8.48.
35. Cf. Ambrose, *De virginibus* 2.2.8; 3.4.19.

7. A HYMN FOR THE TIMES OF FASTING

O Nazarene, the Light of Bethlehem, and Word
Of the eternal Father, born of Virgin's womb,
Be with us in our chaste and holy abstinence
And, gracious King, look now upon this festal day
On which we offer up to Thee our solemn fast.[1] 5

---

1. Cf. Basil, *Homilia de ieiunio* 1.1 and Ambrose, *De Helia et ieiunio* 1.1. In this hymn Prudentius was probably indebted to

Nothing, in truth, is purer than this mystery,
Which cleanses every fiber of the restless heart
And tames the flesh with its unruly appetites,
Lest fumes of gross indulgence rise from heavy meats
And weigh upon the mind with suffocating force.[2]   10

This fast subdues licentiousness and gluttony,
Disgraceful sloth that springs from leaden sleep and wine,
Ignoble lust, salacious wit and pleasantry,
These manifold diseases of disordered sense,
All are restrained beneath the rod of abstinence.   15

For if, abandoned to excess in food and drink,
Man does not curb the body by the holy fasts,
The flame of his high spirit burning bright and pure
Will shrink and pine away, all smothered by delights,
And the soul will fall asleep within his sluggish breast.   20

Then let us check desires of flesh with tighter rein,
And keep the light of wisdom bright within our hearts.
And thus the soul with vision keen will pierce the skies,
And breathing unrestricted Heaven's wider air,
Will praise the Maker of all things more perfectly.   25

Ambrose, as Ambrose was to Basil. From the earliest times Christians fasted on Wednesday and Friday, called 'station' days. Cf. *Didache* 8.1; Hermas, *Sim.* 5.1; Tertullian, *De oratione* 19; *De ieiuniis* 2,10,14. The Lenten Fast of forty days was universally observed in the fourth century. Among ascetics fasting was rigorous. It often extended throughout the year, only one meal being taken during the day after None. Cf. Pseudo-Athanasius, *De virginitate* 8; Ambrose, *De virginibus* 3.4.15; Jerome, *Epistles* 22.35; *S. Silviae peregrinatio* 28.3 (CSEL 39.80-81). Selections from this hymn in its entirety are used in the Mozarabic Breviary for Terce, Sext, and None on all the days of Lent.

2. Cf. Pseudo-Athanasius, *De virginitate* 7; Ambrose, *De Helia et ieiunio* 8.22-23.

Elias, by observance of a solemn fast,
Increased in grace; he was that priest of old who dwelt
In desert wastes far from the world's inane applause,
And it is said he shunned a multitude of sins
Amid the chaste delights of Syrtian solitude.³ 30

But soon to Heaven he was taken through the air,
Borne up in flaming chariot drawn by fiery steeds,
Lest earth's defiling breath should touch that saintly man
Who through long years had lived a life of peace and
    quiet,
Renowned for abstinence that purified his soul.⁴ 35

And Moses, faithful mediator of God's throne,
The King of the seven-vaulted sky could not behold,
Until the sun in its wide circuit through the stars
Had forty revolutions made, and all these days⁵
Had gazed upon the prophet, languishing for bread.⁶ 40

As he communed with God, his only food was tears;
For through the night, with weeping he bedewed the dust,
As bowing low, he pressed his face against the earth,
Until at length aroused by God's forewarning voice,
He trembled at that fire too bright for mortal eyes.⁷ 45

In this observance John the Baptist, too, excelled;
Precursor of the everlasting Son of God,
He straightened out the crooked paths and winding ways,
Correcting devious turns and labyrinthine roads,
To make a highway smooth wherein all men might
    walk.⁸ 50

---

3. Cf. 3 Kings 19.4-9.
4. Cf. 4 Kings 2.11.
5. Cf. Juvencus, *Evangelicae historiae* 1.392 (PL 19.111).
6. Cf. Exod. 24.18; 34.38.
7. Cf. Deut. 5.4; 9.18-19; Heb. 12.18,21,26.
8. Cf. Matt. 3.3.

As messenger of God, who was about to come,
He faithfully observed this law, constructing well,
That every hill might low become and rough ways plain,[9]
Lest when the Truth should glide from Heaven down to earth
It then would find a barrier to its swift approach.   55

Miraculous was his birth, not in the common way;[10]
A late-born child, he swelled his mother's withered breasts
And aged bosom still oblivious of milk;[11]
While yet unborn, of woman far advanced in years,
He recognized his God within the Virgin's womb.[12]   60

Then later he withdrew into the desert wild,
And clothed himself with shaggy skins of savage beasts,
Or bristling camel's hair and wool austere and coarse,[13]
For fear that he might stain and mar his innocence
By taint of cities with their vicious evil ways.   65

A life devoted to strict abstinence that man
Of penance led, with flinty scorn of food and drink
Until the vesper shadows fell upon the earth,[14]
And then it was his wont to take a scanty meal
Of locusts and wild honey flowing from the combs.[15]   70

---

9. Cf. Luke 3.4-5.
10. Cf. Horace, *Epodes* 5.73.
11. Cf. Luke 1.18.
12. Cf. *Ibid.* 41-44.
13. Cf. Matt. 3.1,4.
14. On days of fast the early Christians and ascetics of the fourth century took but one meal toward evening after the ninth or twelfth hour. See n. 1 above.
15. Cf. Matt. 3.4.

First preacher he, and teacher of salvation new,
In sacred flood he washed away the penal stains
Of that primeval sin stamped on the hearts of men,[16]
But when the tainted flesh with water he had cleansed,
The heavenly Spirit poured His light into the soul.[17]   75

From this baptism, freed from guilt's polluting soil,
Men rose reborn, in beauty fair as gold unwrought
Becomes when it is tried again by cleansing fires,
Or as the gleam that shines resplendent from the ore
Of silver purified of dross and burnished bright.   80

Now let me tell the story of an ancient fast[18]
Recorded in the pages of the Book of Truth;
How the all-loving Father's wrathful thunderbolt
Was stayed, its fires extinguished by His clemency,
And the people of a city doomed to ruin were spared.[19]   85

There was in olden days a nation proud and great,
In which the tide of wickedness flowed deep and strong,
And men gave rein to luxury and wanton vice
Until in stubborn pride and scorn of all restraint,
They ceased to worship Heaven's Lord with homage due.   90

---

16. Cf. Luke 3.3.
17. Cf. *Ibid.* 21.22; Acts 19.4-6. For a discussion of the distinction between the baptism of Christ and that administered by John the Baptist, see Pohle-Preuss, *Dogmatic Theology* 8.230.
18. *Referre stemma prisci nunc ieiunii.* Meyer ('Prudentiana,' *Philologus* 87.251) shows that the reading *referre prisci stemma* is to be preferred here.
19. Cf. Jona 3.5-10.

Offended Justice, ever patient, is at length
Provoked to righteous anger, and the God of holiness
Now arms His strong right hand with shining sword of fire;
And wielding crashing storms and roaring hurricanes,
He awes them with the flash of thundering lightning
    flames.[20]   95

But while one little day is given them to repent,
In which they might have willed to tame their sordid lusts
And curb their stubborn follies and their wanton ways,
The awful Judge in mercy stays the threatened blow
And waits awhile to seal the doom He has decreed.   100

The mild Avenger calls that prophet Jonas stern,
And bids him go as herald of the coming woe,
But knowing that the Judge who threatens evils dire
Is prone to pardon rather than to scourge and smite,[21]
The seer to Tharsis turns his steps in secret flight.[22]   105

At shore he mounts the gangplank of a waiting ship,
And soon the anchor on its sodden rope is raised.
The vessel ploughs the deep; the stormy sea grows rough;[23]
And when the lots are cast to find the one to blame
For this sad plight, the number on the fleeing prophet
    falls.   110

---

20. Cf. Ps. 17.15-16; 20.9-10; Exod. 15.6-7; Deut. 32.41; 2 Kings 22.14-16; Vergil, *Aeneid* 7.141-143.
21. Cf. Ezech. 18.23; 33.11.
22. Cf. Jona 1.2.
23. Cf. Seneca, *Medea* 411; Vergil, *Aeneid* 3.374; 4.310.

Alone of all the crew he is condemned to death[24]
Whose guilt the shaking of the urn made manifest,
And he is hurled headlong into the ravenous sea.[25]
A mighty whale receives him in his massive jaws
And gulps him down alive into his cavernous maw.   115

The victim swiftly passing through the monster's jaws,
Escapes the futile sharpness of the teeth, and flies
Unharmed across the bloodless tongue. The molars moist
Are powerless to hold and crush the trembling frame
That journeys through the mouth below the palate's roof.   120

While in the course of three long days and nights the seer
Remained engulfed within the belly of the whale,
He wandered through the shadows of that dark recess
And as he blindly threaded labyrinthine ways,
He panted from the heat inside his prison house.   125

But when the third night rolls around, from thence unharmed
The monster casts him forth with mighty retching throbs;
Where sounding billows break upon the narrow shore[26]
And beat against the briny cliffs with whitening spray,[27]
Disgorged he stands, astonished at his safety.   130

Thus driven back, he turns quick steps to Ninive,
With mind intent on punishing that evil town,
And sternly chides the people for their shameless crimes.
'The wrath,' he cries, 'of Judge supreme hangs over you,
And soon your city will be burned with fire. Believe!'[28]   135

---
24. Cf. Horace, *Epodes* 5.91.
25. Cf. Horace, *Odes* 4.4.65.
26. Cf. Vergil, *Aeneid* 1.160; 10.291.
27. Cf. *Ibid.* 3.534.
28. Cf. Jona 3.3-4.

Then to a lofty mountain peak nearby he climbs
To view from thence the gathering clouds of smoke above
The flaming ruins and dire destruction's crumbling mass;
And there a vine with knotty branches spreading wide,
Upspringing suddenly, provides a grateful shade.[29]   140

But when the wretched city feels the heavy blow
Of coming grief, it is convulsed with deadly fear:[30]
Within the mighty walls the crowds surge to and fro,
The common folk and elders, those of every age,
Youths pale with fright, and women wailing in
  despair.[31]   145

They set a public fast to make amends to Christ,[32]
Whose wrath they would appease; all spurn their wonted
  meals.
The matrons lay aside their jeweled necklaces
And garb themselves in black; they take the silks and gems
From loosened braids, besprinkled now with ashen
  dust.   150

The elders go in squalid robes, of cincture free;[33]
In bristling haircloth clad, the common throng laments;
Fair maids, their tresses all unkempt like shaggy mane,
With sable veils of mourning hide their countenance,
And children roll about upon the dusty sand.[34]   155

---

29. Cf. *Ibid.* 4.5-6.
30. Cf. Vergil, *Aeneid* 12.945.
31. Cf. *Ibid.* 4.667; 9.477.
32. Cf. Jona 3.5.
33. Cf. Juvenal, *Satires* 3.213; Vergil, *Aeneid* 4.578.
34. Cf. Vergil, *Aeneid* 5.336.

The king himself asunder tears the golden clasp
And throws aside his regal robe, aglow with hues
Of Coan purple,[35] precious pearls, and emerald stones;
Then casting from his royal head the jewelled crown,
He soils his hair with ashes, symbol of his shame.[36]   160

Of drinking or of eating no one has a thought;
Observant of the fast, youths turn from tables spread;
Nay, even weeping infants are deprived of milk[37]
And moisten tiny cradles with their flowing tears,
When self-denying nurses bar them from full breasts.   165

The careful herdsmen shrewdly pen the very flocks
Within enclosures strong, lest cattle ranging wide
Touch with their lips the tender grass with showers bedewed,[38]
Or slake their thirst with water from the gurgling springs;[39]
Complaints resound from stables with their empty cribs.   170

Appeased by penance such as this, the loving God
Restrains His short-lived ire and tempers His decree;
For in His mercy God is swift to pardon men
And looks with pity on the tears of penitents
Who humbly beg forgiveness for their evil deeds.   175

---

35. Cf. Jona 3.6; Vergil, *Aeneid* 4.262.
36. Cf. Vergil, *Aeneid* 12.611; Ovid, *Tristia* 1.3.93.
37. Cf. Lucan, *De bello civili* 4.314.
38. Cf. Vergil, *Eclogues* 8.15.
39. Cf. Jona 3.7.

But why record examples from an ancient race,[40]
When lately Jesus, burdened with our mortal flesh,
But pure in heart, abstained and fasted for our sake:[41]
That Jesus whom the prophet's voice once proclaimed
'Emmanuel,' that is the very 'God with us.'[42]   180

The human body, by its nature soft and weak,
Held captive under winsome pleasure's reinless yoke,
He has set free by virtue's stern restraining law;
Emancipator of the flesh enthralled by sin,
He conquered first the tyranny of carnal lust.   185

For in a lonely desert place He dwelt apart
While eight times five recurring days were gliding by,
And all that time He spurned the pleasant taste of food;
Thus by a salutary fast He fortified
Our mortal clay, too frail for holding heavenly joy.[43]   190

The Tempter, marvelling at the hardship and distress
So long endured by creature made of dust,
With shrewd and prying craft invents a subtle scheme
To set at rest his fear that God had come in earthly form;
But foiled and shamed, he fled behind the Savior's
  back.[44]   195

Let us, O Christ, now follow as our strength permits
The way that Thou, the Teacher of all holy truth,
Didst show to Thy disciples by Thy word and deed,
That when the vice of gluttony is overcome,
The flesh may bow beneath the spirit's triumphant
  reign.   200

---

40. Cf. Vergil, *Aeneid* 9.284; Ambrose, *De Helia et ieiunio* 8.22.
41. Cf. Matt. 4.1-2.
42. Cf. *Ibid.* 1.23; Isa. 7.14; Juvencus, *Evangelicae historiae* 1.177.
43. Cf. Lavarenne's note (*Prudence* 1.44).
44. Cf. Matt. 4.2-11.

This is the way that our invidious foe abhors,
Which wins the favor of the Lord of earth and sky
And makes acceptable the Altar's Sacrifice;[45]
Which stirs up living faith within our slumbering hearts
And purifies our breasts of sin's corroding stains.[46]   205

The flowing stream does not more swiftly quench the flame,
Nor heat of broiling sun more quickly melt the snow,
Than fasting with its cleansing power can purge away
The foulness bred by sin and dark concupiscence,
If joined with kindly alms and Christian charity.[47]   210

For these are also virtue's glorious attributes:
To clothe the naked and to feed the hungry man,[48]
To give with generous heart to those who suffer want
And look on all alike, the lowly and the great,
As sharers in the lot of all humanity.   215

Blest truly is the man who stretches out his hand[49]
In meritorious works, unsparing of his wealth,
And does not let his left hand know his charity;[50]
Forthwith eternal treasures shall be his to hold
And fruit a hundredfold will be his rich reward.   220

---

45. Cf. Vergil, *Aeneid* 7.764, 9.585; Matt. 5.23-24.
46. Cf. Horace, *Odes* 3.23.7.
47. Cf. Tob. 4.11, 12.9; Cyprian, *De opera et eleemosynis* 5.
48. Cf. Matt. 25.35-36; 4 Esdras 2.20; Augustine, *Sermon* 93.4 (PL 38.575).
49. Cf. Horace, *Odes* 2.18.14.
50. Cf. Matt. 6.3.

8. A HYMN AFTER FASTING

Christ, the sovereign master of all Thy faithful,
Thou dost rule and guide us with reins that lightly
Curb our wayward tendencies, round us hedging
    Mild regulations.

Though Thou Thyself, laden with mortal body, 5
Didst endure hard labors and racking anguish,[1]
Stern example setting, Thy hand is gentle
    On Thy dear servants.

Now the ninth hour turns the sun to his setting,[2]
Which through scarce three parts of his course has
   glided, 10
Leaving yet one fourth of his shining journey
    Through the heavens.

Brief the fast we break at this hour appointed,
And our vigil ended, we now enjoy
Bounty spread on tables high to replenish 15
    Languishing nature.

Such the gracious love of the eternal Master,
So benign the counsel our kind Teacher gives us,
That observance of His law does not burden
    Man's feeble body.[3] 20

---
1. Cf. Vergil, *Aeneid* 6.437.
2. Cf. Tertullian, *De ieiuniis* 2,10; Pseudo-Athanasius, *De virginitate* 8,12.
3. Cf. Matt. 11.29-30; 1 John 5.3.

Further, He ordains that none with sordid vesture
Clothe himself, nor his comely brow disfigure,
But fair make his face and his head ennoble
    With the hair's glory.[4]

'When you fast,' He said, 'Keep the body stainless;   25
Let no sallow hue on your cheeks appearing
Drive away the roses, and let no pallor
    Whiten your visage.'

It is more just for us to hide with joy
All the good works done for the Father's glory,   30
For God who in secret sees all things hidden
    Will recompense us.[5]

When one ailing sheep lags behind the others
And loses itself in the silvan mazes,
Tearing its white fleece on the thorns and briers,   35
    Sharp in the brambles,[6]

Unwearied the Shepherd, that lost one seeking,
Drives away the wolves and on His strong shoulders
Brings it home again to the fold's safekeeping,
    Healed and unsullied.[7]   40

He brings it back to the green fields and meadows,[8]
Where no thorn-bush waves with its cruel prickles,
Where no shaggy thistle arms trembling branches
    With its rough briers,[9]

---

4. Cf. Matt. 6.16-17; Jerome, *Epistles* 22.27.
5. Cf. Matt. 6.18; also Horace, *Odes* 4.2.20; Vergil, *Aeneid* 5.361.
6. Cf. Vergil, *Georgics* 3.444.
7. Cf. Luke 15.4-6; John 10.11-12.
8. Cf. Ps. 22.1-2; Vergil, *Georgics* 3.13.
9. Cf. Vergil, *Georgics* 1.151-153.

But where palm trees grow in the open woodland, 45
Where the lush grass bends its green leaves, and laurels
Shade the glassy streamlet of living water
    Ceaselessly flowing.[10]

For all Thy gifts, O Shepherd true and faithful,
What service is meet ever to requite Thee? 50
For salvation's cost no devoted worship
    Makes due repayment.

Although by refraining from daily nurture
We should gladly weaken the laggard body,
Night and day spend singing Thy holy praises, 55
    Scorning all comfort,

This atoning service would not be equal
To the gift bestowed by the Heavenly Father,
And severe austerities would but shatter
    Frail earthen vessels.[11] 60

Therefore, lest this fragile clay lose its vigor
And grow faint from watery fluids flowing
In the pallid veins, and the sickly body
    Perish with weakness,[12]

Light and easy is the precept of fasting 65
Laid on all the faithful, and no stern rigor
Impels us; his own capacity urges
    Each to observe it.

---

10. Cf. Vergil, *Aeneid* 7.759, 2.719.
11. Cf. Hymn 7.191.
12. Cf. Horace, *Odes* 2.2.15.

HYMNS 59

Enough, if we sanctify all our actions
By invoking first the divine approval, 70
Whether we accept the food that is given
    Or shun the table.

God of His great bounty bestows these blessings[13]
And with His favoring smile looks upon us,
As we take the bread we have dedicated, 75
    Trusting His goodness.

Grant, I humbly pray, that this food be healthful,
And as it spreads throughout all our members,[14]
May we who adore Thee, O Christ, now nourish
    Body and spirit. 80

13. Cf. Vergil, *Aeneid* 9.106, 10.115.
14. Cf. Lucretius, *De rerum natura* 2.1136.

9. A HYMN FOR EVERY HOUR

    Boy bring my quill of ivory, that I may to
        sounding lyre
    Sing in sweet and tuneful trochees Christ
        and His immortal deeds.
    Him alone my Muse shall honor, Him
        alone my lyre shall praise.

    Christ I sing whom king and prophet, crowned
        with priestly diadem,[1]
    Long ago foretold with voice joined to sound
        of harp and drum, 5
    Drinking of the Spirit from Heaven flowing
        deep into his soul.

1. Cf. Acts 2.30-31.

Tell we now of deeds attested, marvels wrought
    by Hand divine;
All the world is faithful witness, earth denies
    not what it saw,
God in person come from Heaven, teaching
    men His holy way.

Of the Father's love begotten, long before the
    world began,[2]   10
Alpha and Omega titled, fount and term
    of all that is,[3]
All that has before existed, all that shall
    hereafter be.[4]

By His power they were created; at His word
    all things were made,[5]
Earth and sky and ocean's hollow, threefold
    frame of cosmic space,
All that in them live and flourish under
    sphere of sun and moon.[6]   15

He assumed our fragile body, tainted members
    doomed to die,
That the race from Adam springing might
    not perish in the end,
Though a dreadful sentence plunged it
    deep in Hell's profound abyss.[7]

---

2. Cf. John 1.18, 17.5, 24; Hilary, *Hymnus de Christo* 21-22 (CSEL 65.219).
3. Cf. Apoc. 1.8, 21.6. See also the Mozarabic Breviary (PL 86.177): *Benedicat vobis Alpha et Omega cognominatus Omnipotens Dei Patris Unigenitus Filius.* The entire hymn is used in the Mozarabic Breviary for Vespers from Easter to the Sunday within the octave, and on The Feast of the Ascension (PL 86.641, 898-901).
4. Cf. Vergil, *Georgics* 4.393.   6. Cf. Ps. 145.6.
5. Cf. Ps. 32.9, 148.5.   7. Cf. Horace, *Odes* 4.65.

O how blest that Birth supernal, when the
    Virgin Mother bore[8]
Him who is the world's salvation, by the Holy
    Ghost conceived,[9]   20
And the Infant, our Redeemer, showed to us
    His Face divine.

Sing His praises heights of heaven, all ye
    angels sing His praise,
Let the mighty hosts of Heaven, sing in
    joyous praise of God;[10]
Let no tongue of man be silent, let all
    voices join the hymn.

Lo, He comes of whom the prophets sang in
    days of olden time;[11]   25
He who in the faithful pages of these
    seers was once foretold
Now appears, the long expected; let all
    join in praise of Him.

Water poured into the tankards turns
    to rich Falernian wine,
And the waiter claims the vintage from the
    water-pots was drawn,
While the master with amazement tastes   30
    the cups of rosy hue.[12]

---

8. Cf. Hilary, Hymn 1.8 (CSEL 65.209); *Hymnus de Christo* 13 (*Ibid.* 218).
9. Cf. Luke 1.35; Matt. 1.20.
10. Cf. Ps. 148.2.
11. Cf. Juvencus, *Evanglicae historiae* 1.157.
12. Cf. John 2.8-9; Hilary, *Hymnus de Christo* 25-26 (CSEL 65.219).

'Members filled with leprous ulcers, flesh
 corrupted and decayed,
Go and wash them, I command you';
 what He ordered then is done;
Wounds are healed by pious cleansing,
 swollen flesh grows smooth again.[13]

Now on eyes, by lifelong darkness, shrouded
 from the light of day
Thou dost spread a clay of healing, made
 with nectar from Thy lips; 35
Soon the blinded orbs are opened and
 rejoice in late-found sight.[14]

Thou dost chide the angry tempest and
 the savage hurricane,[15]
Which upheave the tossing billows and
 beset the fragile boat;[16]
At Thy bidding winds are subject, and
 the rolling waves are stilled.[17]

Then a woman, weak and timid, touched
 His sacred garment's hem: 40
Instant was His blessed healing, and
 the pallor left her cheek,[18]
As the hemorrhage she had suffered
 through so many years was stopped.[19]

---

13. Cf. Matt. 8.3; Hilary, *op. cit.* 24.
14. Cf. John 9.6-7; Hilary, *op. cit.* 23.
15. Cf. Vergil, *Aeneid* 10.37.
16. Cf. *Ibid.* 2.419.
17. Cf. *Ibid.* 8.86; Matt. 8.26.
18. Cf. Horace, *Epodes* 7.15; Vergil, *Aeneid* 4.499.
19. Cf. Matt. 9.20-22; Mark 5.27-34; Luke 8.33-44.

He beheld the funeral cortege of a youth in
 spring of life,[20]
Whom his widowed mother, weeping, followed
 to his early grave;
'Rise,' He said; then to that mother He
 restored her living son.[21]   45

Lazarus for four days buried, hidden in
 the sunless tomb,
He restores to life and vigor, giving
 power to breathe again,
And the soul returning, enters flesh
 now crumbling to decay.[22]

Lo, He walks upon the waters, treads the
 crests of surging waves,
And the deep in ceaseless motion makes
 a pathway insecure,   50
But the billows dare not open underneath His sacred Feet.[23]

Then a man bereft of reason, dwelling in
 sepulchral caves,
Bound with cruel and grinding fetters and
 with raging frenzy torn,
Rushes forth and kneels in worship, as the
 saving Christ draws near.[24]

---

20. Cf. Horace, *Odes* 1.16.23.
21. Cf. Luke 7.12-15.
22. Cf. John 11.39-44; Hilary, *op. cit.* 24.
23. Cf. Matt. 14.25; Mark 6.48.
24. Cf. Mark 5.2-6.

Driven forth, the wily demons, legion named
    that evil scourge,[25]   55
Seize upon the sordid foulness of a herd
    of filthy swine
And into the muddy waters plunge themselves
    with maddened beasts.[26]

'Place,' He said, 'in these twelve baskets
    all the fragments that remain';
Thousands at that feast reclining, with abundance had been fed
On the five loaves they had eaten and
    two fishes multiplied.[27]   60

Thou, our bread, our true refection, never-failing sweetness art;[28]
He can nevermore know hunger, who is
    at Thy banquet fed,[29]
Nourishing not our fleshly nature, but
    imparting lasting life.[30]

Deafened ears, of sound unconscious,
    every passage blocked and closed,
At the word of Christ responding, open
    all the portals wide,   65
Hear with joy friendly voices and
    the softly whispered speech.[31]

---

25. Cf. Vergil, *Aeneid* 11.792.
26. Cf. Mark 5.13.
27. Cf. Matt. 14.17-20; Mark 6.38-41; John 6.9-13; Hilary, *op. cit.* 27-28.
28. Cf. John 6.56.
29. Cf. *Ibid.* 35.
30. Cf. *Ibid.* 51-52.
31. Cf. Mark 7.34-35.

Every sickness now surrenders, every listlessness departs,[32]
Tongues long bound by chains of silence are unloosed and speak aright,[33]
While the joyful paralytic bears his pallet through the streets.[34]

That the dead might know salvation, who in limbo long had dwelt,   70
Into Hell with love He entered;[35] to Him yield the broken gates,
As the bolts and massive hinges fall asunder at His word.

Now the door of ready entrance, but forbidding all return,[36]
Outward swings as bars are loosened and sends forth the prisoned souls,
By reversal of the mandate, treading its threshold once more.[37]   75

But while God with golden splendor lighted up the halls of Death,
While He shed the dawn's refulgence on the startled shades of night,
Radiant stars grew pale with sorrow in the lurid ashen sky,[38]

---

32. Cf. Luke 6.18-19; Hilary, *op. cit.* 23.
33. Cf. Mark 7.35.
34. Cf. Matt. 9.6-7; John 5.9.
35. Cf. 1 Peter 3.19; 4.6.
36. Cf. Vergil, *Aeneid* 6.126-129.
37. Cf. Seneca, *Hercules furens* 55.
38. Cf. Matt. 37.45.

And the sun took flight from heaven, clad in
    dusky mourning robes,[39]
Left behind his fiery chariot, hid himself
    in anxious grief,   80
While, they say, the whole world shuddered
    with the fear of endless night.[40]

Lift, my soul, your tuneful voice, let
    the tongue be swift to praise,
Tell the victory of the Passion, tell the triumph
    of the Cross,
Sing the Sign that gleams refulgent, marked
    upon the Christian's brow.

O how wondrous and amazing was the wound
    made by the lance!   85
From one side the blood ran downward, from
    the other water flowed:[41]
Truly cleansing is that water, from the blood
    the crown is won.

---

39. Cf. Vergil, *Georgics* 1.466; Hilary, *De Trinitate* 3.10 (PL 10.81).
40. Cf. Seneca, *Hercules furens* 610, *Medea* 9; Hilary, *op. cit.* 43.
41. Cf. John 19.34. Prudentius here, as in *Peristephanon* 8.15 and *Dittochaeon* 165, seems to imply that the lance pierced the body of the Savior from right to left. Arevalus (PL 59.872) cites several early writers, including Cyprian, Gregory of Nazianzus and Leo the Great, who seemed to be of the opinion that Christ received wounds in both sides, either by separate blows of the lance or by a single thrust which entered the right side and passed out through the left.

Then the Serpent saw the Victim, saw the Sacred
  Body slain,[42]
Saw, and straightway lost the venom of his
  bitter, scorching hate,
As his hissing neck was broken, and
  he groaned in frightful pain.[43]   90

What avail, infernal Serpent, were the deep-
  laid, crafty wiles,[44]
By which, in the world's beginning, you
  contrived the first man's fall?
Human nature, God receiving, of its ancient
  guilt was cleansed.[45]

For a while salvation's Leader gave Himself
  to realms of Death,
That He might the dead, long buried, guide
  in their return to light,   95
When the chains that had been welded by that
  primal sin were loosed.

Then, in steps of their Creator, many saints
  and patriarchs,
Putting on their fleshly garments and arising
  from their tombs,
Followed Him, at length returning on the
  third day to the earth.[46]

---

42. Cf. Jer. 11.19; 1 Cor. 5.7.
43. Cf. Vergil, *Georgics* 3.42; *Aeneid* 5.277.
44. *Astutia*. On the reading *hortamine* found in some MSS, see Meyer, 'Prudentiana,' *Philologus* 87 (1932) 340.
45. Cf. Ambrose, Hymn 3.11-12 (PL 16.1474).
46. Cf. Matt. 27.52-53; 1 Cor. 15.20; Hilary, *op. cit.* 44.

You might see the crumbling members
    form again from ashes sear,   100
And the frigid dust grow lively as the
    blood resumed its flow,
All the marrow, bones and sinews, covered
    with the flesh once more.[47]

Then when death He has destroyed and
    mankind restored to life,
That great Victor mounts triumphant to the
    Father's throne above,[48]
And the glory of His Passion bears with
    Him to Heaven's height.   105

Hail! Thou King of all the living; hail! Thou
    Judge of all the dead;[49]
At the right hand of Thy Father, Thou art
    throned in highest power,[50]
And from thence, just Judge of sinners,
    Thou shalt one day come again.

Thee the chorus of the children, Thee the
    old men and the youth,
Throngs of matrons and of virgins, maidens
    young and innocent,[51]   110
Praise with loud concordant voices, all
    uniting in the hymn.

---

47. Cf. Job 19.26; Ezech. 37.6,8; Ambrose, *De excessu fratris* 2.69 (PL 16.1393).
48. Cf. John 20.17; Acts 1.9.
49. Cf. Acts 10.42.
50. Cf. Mark. 16.19.
51. Cf. Ps. 148.12.

Let the streams with running waters, let the
    shores of all the seas,
Snow and frost and summer showers,
    winds and woodlands, night and day,[52]
Join in praising Thee forever, through the
    endless ages long.

---

52. Cf. Ps. 148.8-9; Dan. 3.64-71, 78.

10. A HYMN FOR THE BURIAL OF THE DEAD

O God, of our souls the bright fountain,[1]
Who, mingling in one our two natures,
Pure spirit with clay that is mortal,
Mankind, Thou our Father, didst fashion,

Thine they are, Thine, O Lord, both these natures;   5
In Thee is the bond of their union,
And while living, they flourish together
Both the flesh and the spirit obey Thee.[2]

---

1. Cf. Tertullian, *Apology* 17.6 (Trans. in Vol. 10, this series, p. 53); Augustine, *De quantitate animae* 1.2; Vergil, *Aeneid* 6.730-732.
2. Early Christian philosophers, including St. Augustine, never satisfactorily answered the question of the nature of the union of soul and body. Cf. Augustine, *De quantitate animae* 13.22 and 33.70; *De civitate Dei* 10.29 and 21.10.

But when bonds that unite them are severed,[3]
Each back to its source is then summoned; 10
The bright soul seeks its heavenly fountain,
And the earth claims the dust of the body.

For all things created are destined
To die and to perish forever,
When their elements, parted and sundered, 15
Revert to their primitive substance.

Thou hast willed, O God, in Thy goodness,
To destroy this death for Thy servants,
And to show them a way, sure and certain,
That leads to the body's resurgence. 20

---

3. Cf. Tertullian, *Apology* 48.9. Lines 9-16 vary in the manuscripts. Bergman follows the oldest MS *A*. The text in later MSS, some of which have both versions or the *A* version in the margin, is as follows: *rescissa sed ista seorsum/ solvunt hominem perimuntque;/ humus excipit arida corpus,/ animae rapit aura liquorem;/ quia cuncta creata necesse est/ labefacta senescere tandem,/ compactaque dissociari,/ et dissona texta retexi.* This variant version may be translated thus:

> But when these asunder are riven
> Dissolution and death are man's portion;
> The dry earth claims the dust of the body
> And Heaven receives the pure spirit.
>
> For all things created are destined
> To grow old and at length and to perish,
> What is joined to be parted and sundered
> And dissimilar fabrics unravelled.

Thomson (*Prudentius*, Loeb Classical Library, 1949) thinks that this is a revision by Prudentius himself and not the work of an interpolator.

So that, while the pure spirit is captive
In the chains of its prison terrestrial,[4]
That part of man's being may triumph
Which has its high source in the heavens.

If the will is attached to the earthly   25
And wallows in sordid corruption,
The soul, by this grossness encumbered,
With the body sinks down to its ruin.[5]

But if, of its origin mindful,
The spirit avoids sin's contagion,   30
It carries with it back to Heaven
The flesh of its early sojourning.

For the body we see here reposing,
Bereft of its life-giving spirit,
In the sepulcher stays a brief season,   35
Then rejoins its noble companion.

The swift years will soon bring that moment,
When the soul shall revisit these members[6]
And cherish its earlier dwelling,
Now glowing with life's glad renewal.   40

The motionless corpse, cold and lifeless,
That long in its grave lay moldering,
Will wing its swift flight to the heavens
With the spirit that, time was, informed it.

---

4. Cf. Ambrose, *De bona mortis* 3.9.
5. Cf. Horace, *Satires* 2.2.77.
6. Cf. Vergil, *Aeneid* 9.475.

Hence the care we bestow on the sepulcher, 45
Hence the last solemn rites that are offered
For the body, unfeeling and lifeless,
And the pomp of the funeral procession.

Hence with linen resplendent in whiteness
We are wont to array the dead members, 50
And with Sabaean myrrh we embalm them,
From corruption the body preserving.[7]

For what, pray, is the hollowed stone coffin,[8]
Or the monument rich in its splendor,
Unless we believe the form placed there 55
Is not dead, but is peacefully sleeping?

Enlightened by faith, devout Christians
Thus the dead hold in reverence, believing
That the body enwrapt in cold slumber,[9]
With new life will hereafter be quickened. 60

Whoever in loving compassion
Heaps the earth on corpses neglected
Does this dutiful work of mercy
Unto Christ Himself, the Almighty.

---

7. Cf. Tertullian, *Apology* 42.7; Augustine, *Enarrationes in psalmis* 48.13.
8. Christians of rank in the first centuries followed the ancient Roman custom of burial in sarcophagi, or stone coffins, which were deposited in subterranean vaults or in the catacombs. Above the family vault ornate monuments were often erected. Cf. *Catholic Encyclopedia* 3.424; Augustine, *Sermon* 102.2, *Enarrationes in psalmis* 48.15.
9. Cf. Horace, *Odes* 1.24.5-6.

Since to die is the lot of all mortals, 65
The same law of charity bids us
To mourn for the death of a stranger
As the loss of one of our kindred.[10]

The father of holy Tobias,[11]
That saintly old man of great courage, 70
Though a festive banquet stood ready,[12]
Placed before it the duty of burial.

While his servants around him were waiting,
He forsook the cups and the platters,
And girding himself, he proceeded 75
To inter a sad corpse with much weeping.

His reward comes quickly from Heaven,[13]
With rich wages his goodness repaying,
For his eyes that knew not the sun's shining,
With an unction of gall, God enlightens. 80

Thus the Heavenly Father has taught us
How bitter and sharp is the healing
For the soul immersed in sin's darkness,
When with burning new light it is dazzled.

He taught, too, that to none is it given 85
To behold the celestial kingdom,
Until he has borne earth's affliction
With its wounds and its darkness and sorrow.

---
10. Cf. Lucan, *De belli civili* 6.563.
11. Cf. Tob. 2.1-4.
12. Cf. Vergil, *Aeneid* 4.555.
13. Cf. Tob. 11.13-15.

'Hence death is itself truly blessed,
For its agonies open the gateway 90
To the heavenly heights for the faithful,
Who are led by their sufferings to glory.[14]

The bodies that suffer such torments
Arise to a better existence,[15]
And the frame that regains its lost vigor 95
In the life after death knows no weakness.

The cheeks that disease has now wasted
And darkened with deadly gray pallor[16]
Will then, fairer than any bright flower,
With the hue of the roses be tinted. 100

Old age with its envious gnawing
Will not tarnish the brow's gracious beauty,
Nor the fluid in the members diminish
And leave them all shrunken and withered.

Disease[17] with his deadly contagion, 105
Which now ravages men's weary bodies,
Will then suffer his own bitter torments
As he swelters in harrowing bondage.

The flesh from its seat in the heavens,
Victorious now and immortal, 110
Will behold him eternally bewailing
The pains he himself has engendered.

---
14. Cf. Vergil, *Aeneid* 9.641.
15. Cf. *Ibid.* 6.649.
16. Cf. Horace, *Epodes* 7.15; Vergil, *Aeneid* 8.197.
17. *Morbus* is here personified as in Vergil, *Aeneid* 6.275.

Why does the sad throng of survivors
Unite in lament unavailing?
Why does frantic, unreasoning sorrow   115
Reprove laws so benignly established?

Then let plaintive mourners be silent
And sad mothers refrain from their weeping;
Let none loudly lament their lost pledges,
For this death is but life's glad renewal.   120

Thus the seed in the ground lies decaying,
Ere the plant springs up in green beauty,
And restored from the depths of earth's bosom,
Replaces the previous harvests.[18]

Receive him, O earth, for safekeeping   125
And to thy soft bosom now fold him;[19]
To thy care we confide a man's body;
The remains that we lay here are noble.

This frame was the home of the spirit
That flowed from the Father in Heaven;[20]   130
Holy Wisdom once dwelt in these members,
And Christ was their Head and their Ruler.

Do thou shelter the body we place here;
Its Maker and Author will remember
To seek here the form He has given   135
And made to His image and likeness.

---

18. Cf. John 12.24-25. Tertullian, *De resurrectione carnis* 12; Minucius Felix, *Octavius* 34.11 (Trans. in Vol. 10, this series, p. 393); Ambrose, *De excessu fratris* 2.70.
19. Cf. Vergil, *Aeneid* 5.30-31; Ovid, *Heroides* 17.56.
20. *Cui nobilis ex patre fons est.* Bergman here follows MS *A* and others. Several MSS have *factoris ab ore creatae*, 'created by the breath of God.'

Soon the day that God has appointed
Will bring every hope's fulfillment,
And then thou, O grave, must surrender
This frame that to thee is entrusted. 140

Even though the decay of the ages[21]
Shall resolve the dry bones into ashes,
And the scanty dust that shall linger,
If measured, would be but a handful,[22]

Even though the wandering breezes 145
And the winds every fiber shall carry
With the dust through the empty expanses,[23]
Man shall not know eternal extinction.

But until the perishable body
Thou shalt raise up, O God, and refashion, 150
What mansion of rest is made ready
For the soul that is pure and unsullied?

It shall rest in the Patriarch's bosom[24]
As did Lazarus, hedged round with flowers,
Whom Dives beheld from a distance 155
While he burned in the fires everlasting.

---

21. Cf. Ovid, *Amores* 1.12.29.
22. Cf. Minucius Felix, *Octavius* 34.10.
23. Cf. Vergil, *Aeneid* 12.906, Ovid, *Metamorphoses* 4.718.
24. Abraham. Cf. Luke 16.22. Among the Jews the expression 'the bosom of Abraham' was used to designate the abode of the just after death. Its origin is uncertain, and in Sacred Scripture it is found only in the parable of the Rich Man and Lazarus. It is frequently found in the writings of the Fathers as a synonym for limbo or for Heaven. Cf. Ambrose, *De bono mortis* 12.52 and *De excessu fratris* 2.101. In the *Subvenite* of the present Roman rite for burial, the Church uses the words '*in sinum Abrahae*' to indicate heavenly bliss in company with

We believe in Thy words, O Redeemer,
Which, when triumphing over death's darkness,
Thou didst speak to Thy robber companion,
Bidding him in Thy footprints to follow.[25] 160

Lo, now to the faithful is opened
The bright road to Paradise leading;
Man again is permitted to enter
The garden he lost to the Serpent.[26]

To that sacred abode, O great Leader, 165
Take, we pray Thee, the soul of Thy servant;
Let it rest in its native country,
Which it left, as an exile to wander.

The graves of the dead we shall cherish[27]
And bedeck them with violets and garlands; 170
On the stones with the title engraven
The sweet fragrance of balm we shall sprinkle.[28]

---

    the faithful of the Old and New Law. The expression is found in the earliest burial rites of the Church, with one of which Prudentius must have been acquainted. Cf. P.L. 72.566; 78.217, and 467; 85.1024.
25. Cf. Luke 23.43.
26. The following prayer is found in the Mozarabic *Missa pro defunctorum et pro Episcopo* (P.L. 85.1016): *Fruatur paradisi amoenitate quietis opaca: atque amoenis vegetatus in loca nemoribus laureata.*
27. In the Office of the Dead of the Mozarabic Breviary (P.L. 86.979), for which a part of this hymn was adopted, the following stanza is found instead of 11.169-172: *animas, non immemor ob hoc,/ quorum memores sumus ipsi,/ Deus, sorde rogamus, piatas,/ Erebi rogis fac alienas,* 'Therefore, be not unmindful, O God, of these souls whose memory we cherish; grant, we beseech Thee, that they may be cleansed from stain and preserved from the fires of Hell.' This stanza is apparently not found in any of the MSS of Prudentius.
28. Cf. Horace, *Odes* 1.2.5.

11. A HYMN FOR CHRISTMAS DAY

What means it that the circling sun[1]
Its narrow orbit now forsakes?
Is Christ not born today on earth,
Who widens for us the way of light?

Alas, how fleeting was the smile   5
The hastening day did then bestow!
How dimly glowed her waning torch,
So soon extinguished by the night!

Now let the sky more brightly shine,   10
And joyful earth keep holiday![2]
The radiant sun mounts high again,
Rejoicing in his former course.

Unveil Thy sweetness, Child divine,
The fruit of virgin Motherhood
And chastity inviolate,   15
Our Mediator, God and Man.[3]

Though Thou didst come from the Mouth of God,[4]
Born as His Word on earth below,
Yet as His Wisdom Thou didst live
Forever in the Father's Heart.   20

---
1. Cf. Vergil, *Aeneid* 7.100.
2. Cf. Ps. 95.11.
3. Cf. 1 Tim. 2.5.
4. Cf. Eccli. 24.5.

This Wisdom uttered made the sky,
The sky and light and all besides;[5]
All by the Word's almighty power
Were fashioned, for the Word was God.[6]

But when the universe was formed 25
And ordered by unchanging laws,
The Cause and Architect divine
In the Father's bosom still remained,[7]

Until the slow revolving years
In centuries at length had passed,[8] 30
And He Himself vouchsafed to come
Down to the world grown old in sin.

For men whom passion had made blind
Were led into idolatry
And put their faith in gods of bronze, 35
Or wood, or cold unfeeling stone,[9]

And thus misled by Satan's guile,
They fell beneath his fearful yoke
And plunged their souls, enslaved to sin,
Into the fiery pit of Hell. 40

But such destruction of mankind
The Heart of Christ could not endure;
And lest His Father's handiwork,
Unvindicated, should be lost,

---

5. Cf. Prov. 8.28-30; Col. 1.16.
6. Cf. John 1.1,3.
7. Cf. John 1.18.
8. Cf. Vergil, *Aeneid* 6.748.
9. Cf. Minucius Felix, *Octavius* 22.3-4 (Trans. in Vol. 10, this series, pp. 364-365).

He clothed Himself in mortal flesh,[10] 45
That by arising from the tomb
He might unlock the chains of death
And bring man to His Father's House.

This is Thy natal day, on which
The high Creator sent Thee forth,[11] 50
And gave to Thee a form of clay,
Uniting flesh with His own Word.

Are you aware, O Virgin blest,
As weary months of waiting end,[12]
That your untarnished purity 55
Shines brighter in your Motherhood?

Oh what great joys for the world,
Thy bosom chaste within it holds,
Whence issues forth the golden age
Whose light renews the face of earth. 60

Thy Infant's feeble cry proclaimed
The springtime of the universe;
The world reborn then cast aside
The gloom of winter's lethargy.

The earth, I think, with lavish hand 65
Enameled every field with flowers,
And even Syrtis' desert sands
Were sweet with nectar and with nard.

---

10. Cf. Phil. 2.7.
11. *te spiravit,* literally 'breathed Thee forth.'
12. For a discussion of the influence of the *Fourth Eclogue* of Vergil in 11.53-76, see Brother Albertus Mahoney, *Vergil in the Works of Prudentius* (Washington 1934) 144-147.

At Thy Nativity, O Child,
All hard, unfeeling things were stirred; 70
The unrelenting crags grew kind
And clothed the flinty stones with grass.

Now from the rocks sweet honey flows;[13]
Now fragrant liquor is distilled
From shrivelled trunks of aged oaks, 75
And tamarisks yield ambrosial balms.

How holy, O eternal King,
Is this Thy crib, revered by men
In every age,[14] and even by beasts,
Who hover near in silent awe.[15] 80

Rude cattle at this crib adore,
An ignorant herd, uncouth indeed;
The dull unfeeling tribe adores[16]
Whose strength is found in earthly food.

---

13. Cf. Joel 3.18.
14. For evidences of the veneration of the cave at Bethlehem and the fact that the place was known from the earliest times, see Justin, *Dialogus cum Tryphone* 78; Origen, *Contra Celsum* 1.51; Jerome, *Epistles* 46.10, 58.3, and 108.10. In the year 327 a magnificent basilica was erected over the spot by Constantine and his mother, St. Helena.
15. The belief that the birth of Christ in a stable (Luke 2.7) constituted a fulfillment of Isaias 1.3, either figuratively in the adoration of the shepherds and the Magi, or literally in the presence of the animals, found expression in the apocryphal books and in the writings of the Fathers from Origen onwards. Cf. *Pseudo-Matthew* 14; Origen, *In Lucam* 13 (PG 13.1832); Gregory of Nyssa, *In diem natalem Christi* (PG 46.1142); Ambrose, *Expositio in Lucam* 2.42; Jerome, *Epistles* 108.10, *In Isaiam* 1.3.
16. *adorat haec brutum pecus,/ indocta turba scilicet,/ adorat excors natio* . . . For a discussion of obscurity in 11.81-84, see Lavarenne, *Prudence* 1.65. Cf. Jerome, *In Isaiam* 1.3: *Sapien-*

Though shepherds and four-footed beasts   85
Now hasten in a spirit of faith
To gather round Thy manger bed,
And brutish natures now are wise,[17]

Incensed, the sons of the Patriarchs
Deny their God in human form.[18]   90
You would believe that they were drugged
With venom or with Furies' wrath.

Why hasten thus to ruin and woe?
If in your darkened minds a spark
Of reason's light still faintly glows,   95
Acknowledge now your King of Kings.

This King, bestowed on all mankind,
Now cradled in a dismal stall,
Weak Babe of Virgin Mother born
With humble midwife's zealous care,[19]   100

O unbeliever, you will see
High in the shining clouds of Heaven,[20]
As you, an outcast, then bewail
Your guilt with unavailing tears,

---

    tibus quoque saeculi non recipientibus crucem Christi, indocta nationum turba suscepit.
17. *Sapiatque quod brutum fuit.* Cf. Sulpicius Severus, *Dialogue* 1.14: *cui sapit omne quod brutum est* (Trans. in Vol. 7, this series, p. 180).
18. Cf. Isa. 1.3.
19. Reference is made in the apocryphal narratives and ecclesiastical writings (Cf. Clement of Alexandria, *Stromatum* 7.16) to the presence of a midwife at the birth of Christ. The assumption has no foundation in the canonical Scriptures, however, or in the authentic tradition of the Church. Cf. Jerome, *Adversus Helvidium* 8.
20. Cf. Matt. 24.30; Apoc. 1.7.

When at the awful trumpet's sound[21]   105
The earth will be consumed by fire,
And with a mighty rush the world
Unhinged, will crash in dreadful ruin.[22]

Enthroned on high this powerful Judge
Will grant to each his due reward,   110
Perpetual light unto the good,
And to the lost, Gehenna's fire.[23]

Then trembling at the flaming Cross,[24]
Judea, you will know your God,[25]
Whom at your hands Death once devoured   115
But afterwards gave back again.

---

21. Cf. Matt. 24.31; 1 Cor. 15.52; 1 Thess. 4.16.
22. Cf. 2 Peter 3.10.
23. Cf. Rom. 2.6; Matt. 25.46 and 5.22.
24. Cf. Matt. 24.30. Prudentius, with other Fathers, regards the 'sign of the Son of Man' as the Cross.
25. *Qui sit senties.* Cf. Exod. 3.14; John 19.37; Apoc. 1.7.

12. A HYMN FOR EPIPHANY

All you who look for Christ to come,
Lift up your eyes to heaven above;
There you will see the glorious sign
Of His eternal majesty.

A star that, in its brilliant light, 5
Outshines the dazzling orb of day[1]
Proclaims that God in human flesh
Has come to dwell with men on earth.

No thrall is this of night's domain,
Nor satellite of monthly moon, 10
But sole possessor of the sky,
It rules the shining course of day.

Although the frigid polar stars
That in their circuit backward wheel
Refuse to set, yet veiled by clouds, 15
They oft are hidden from our gaze.

This is an everlasting star
That never sinks beneath the waves;
No cloud that drifts across its face
Has power to hide its beaming light. 20

Let baleful comets now withdraw,
And meteors lit from Sirius' flame,
Confounded by the star of God,
Fall blazing from the heavens above.

---

1. Numerous attempts have been made to explain the star of the Magi as a natural stellar phenomenon. Among the Fathers, Origen expressed the opinion that it was a comet (*Contra Celsum* 1.58). Prudentius follows the generally accepted theory that the star was miraculous, a theory which accords with the literal interpretation of the Gospel and the opinions of most of the Fathers. Cf. Ignatius of Antioch, *Epist. ad Ephesios* 19; John Chrysostom, *In Matthaeum* 6.2,3; Leo, *Sermo* 33.2.

Lo, from the heart of Persian lands,[2] 25
The gateway of the rising sun,
The Magi skilled in astral lore
Behold this star of kingly rank.[3]

As soon as it began to shine,
The other stars put out their lights, 30
And Lucifer then dared not show
The beauty of his radiant face.

'Who is this King,' the Magi cry,
'Enthroned above the starry hosts,
Whom Heaven holds in reverent awe 35
And whom ethereal light obeys?

'We now behold the glorious sign
Of one who never shall have end,
Most high, sublime, and limitless,
More ancient than the earth or sky. 40

'He is the Gentiles' King and Lord,
And Ruler of the Jewish race,[4]
To Father Abraham decreed
And to his seed forevermore.

'Forerunner of all men of faith, 45
Who willed to give his only son
In sacrifice, that sire foresaw
Descendants numerous as the stars.[5]

---

2. Prudentius here follows the most generally accepted tradition regarding the country of the Magi. Cf. Clement of Alexandria, *Stromatum* 1.15; John Chrysostom, *op. cit.* 6.2; Juvencus, *Evangelicae Historiae* 1.276.
3. Cf. Matt. 2.2.
4. Cf. *Ibid.*
5. Cf. Gen. 22.16-18.

'Now blooms the flower of David's race
From root of Jesse springing up,[6]   50
And blossoming on the scepter's rod,
It rules on high the universe.'[7]

With eager gaze fixed on the sky,
The sages followed where the star
Had furrowed out a shining path   55
To guide their hastening steps aright.[8]

But soon above the holy Child
The heavenly ensign took its stand,[9]
And bending down, it cast its light
Upon the Infant's sacred Head.[10]   60

On seeing Him, these Seers bring forth
Their Eastern stores, and as they bend
The knee in worship, offer Him
Incense and myrrh and kingly gold.[11]

O Child, to whom Thy Father gave   65
A threefold dignity sublime,
See in these gifts the mystic signs
Of kingship and unending might.

---

6. Cf. Isa. 11.1. Bergman has *Jessea editus* here, based on MS *A*. Meyer ('Zu Prudentius,' *Philologus* 93.390) thinks that the reading *Jesse aeditus* from MS *O* is to be preferred. Arevalus has *Jesse editus* with the authority of several MSS.
7. Cf. Num. 17.8; Heb. 9.4.
8. Cf. Vergil, *Aeneid* 2.695-698; Juvencus, *op. cit.* 1.279.
9. Cf. Matt. 2.9.
10. Cf. John Chrysostom, *op. cit.* 7.4.
11. Cf. Matt. 2.11.

The gold and Saba's incense sweet[12]
Proclaim Thee to be King and God; 70
The bitter dust of myrrh foretells
The tomb of Thy humanity.[13]

This is that grave where God allowed
His mortal frame to rest awhile,
And raising it to life again, 75
Broke open Death's dark prison doors.

O Bethlehem, of cities great
Thou are the greatest, for in thee
Salvation's Author from on high,
Incarnate, saw the light of day.[14] 80

You nurse the sole-begotten Heir
Of Him who reigns in Heaven above,[15]
His Son made man by the Spirit's power,
Yet very God in human flesh.

His Father's will and testament, 85
By Prophets witnessed and endorsed,
Bids Him to enter His new realm
And take possession of His throne,

A kingdom that embraces all,[16]
The firmament, the sea, and earth 90
From rising to the setting sun,
The depths of Hell and Heaven above.

---

12. Cf. Ps. 71.10; Isa. 60.6.
13. Cf. Irenaeus, *Contra Haereses* 3.9.2; Leo, *Sermo* 31.2; John Chrysostom, *op. cit.* 8.1; Juvencus, *op. cit.* 1.285; Ambrose, *De fide* 1.4.
14. Cf. Mich. 5.2; Matt. 2.6.
15. Cf. Heb. 1.2.
16. Cf. Luke 1.33.

Alarmed, the impious tyrant hears[17]
That now the King of Kings has come
To sit on David's royal throne   95
And rule the race of Israel.[18]

And maddened by the news, he cries,
'This upstart comes to banish me:
Go warriors, unsheathe your swords,
And stain the infants' cribs with blood.[19]   100

'Let all male children be destroyed;
Search out the bosom of each nurse,
And even at the mother's breasts
Let blades be red with infant gore.

'I trust no woman who has borne   105
A son in Bethlehem these days,
For all will strive to steal away
And hide their offspring from your sight.'

Then mad with rage, the torturer draws
His cruel sword and thrusts the blade   110
Into the tender infant forms,
Bereaving them of budding life.

The fiendish slayer scarce can find
On little frames sufficient space
To hold the deadly gaping wound: 115
The blade is wider than the throat.

---

17. Cf. Matt. 2.3.
18. Cf. Luke 1.32.
19. Cf. Matt. 2.16.

O barbarous and inhuman sight!
A head is dashed against a stone
And milk-white brains are scattered round,
While at the blow the eyes leap forth.   120

Again, a trembling babe is plunged
Into a deep, swift-flowing stream,
And water mingling with its breath,
It gasps its fragile life away.

All hail, sweet flowers of martyrdom,   125
Cut down in life's bright dawning hour,[20]
And shattered by the foe of Christ
As rosebuds by the whirling storm.

First victims offered up to Christ,
A tender flock of spotless lambs,[21]   130
Before God's very altar throne,
With martyrs' crowns and palms you play.

Of what avail such wickedness?
What joy in crime does Herod find?
Alone among so many slain,   135
Unharmed and safe, the Christ Child lives.

---

20. Cf. Lucan, *De bello civili* 2.106; Seneca, *Hercules furens* 1132.
21. *Grex immaculatorum tener.* Several MSS and Arevalus have *immolatorum* instead of *immaculatorum*, which Bergman accepts from the oldest MS *A* and others. Meyer ('Prudentiana,' *Philologus* 87, 255-258) thinks that *immolatorum* is to be preferred, since Prudentius knew the teaching on original sin (Cf. *Apoth.* 511-514). Though Bergman himself questioned *immaculatorum*, it seems to me that this reading can be defended. *Immaculatus*, of animals offered in sacrifice, means 'without blemish.' Prudentius here speaks figuratively of the Innocents as lambs sacrificed to Christ. Cf. 1 Peter 1.19.

Amid the streams of blood that flowed
From tender babes of equal age,
Alone, the Virgin's Son escaped
The sword that pierced the mothers' hearts.   140

Thus Moses in a former age
Escaped proud Pharao's foolish law,[22]
And as the savior of his race
Prefigured Christ who was to come.

A cruel edict had been passed   145
Forbidding Hebrew mothers all,
When sons were born to them, to rear
These virile pledges of their love.[23]

Devoutly scornful of the king,
A zealous midwife found a way   150
To hide her charge and keep him safe
For future glory and renown.

And when the boy to manhood grew,
God chose him as His own high priest,
Through whose pure hands He might transmit   155
His law engraved on slabs of stone.[24]

In this great man may we not see
A figure of our Saviour, Christ?
By slaying the Egyptian lord,
That leader lifted Israel's yoke;[25]   160

---

22. Cf. Exod. 1.16-17; 2.2-10.
23. Cf. Exod. 1.16-22.
24. Cf. Exod. 24.12.
25. Cf. Exod. 2.12; Acts 7.24-25.

But when beneath the yoke of sin
We bow in ceaseless servitude,
Our Captain wounds the enemy
And frees us from the shades of Death.

And Moses cheers with waters sweet[26]   165
His people ransomed in the sea,
When led by him through cleansing floods
And guided by the pillar's light.[27]

While Israel's hosts in battle join,
He overwhelms fierce Amalec   170
By lifting up his arms on high,[28]
Prefiguring then the cross of Christ.

A truer prototype of Christ
Was Josue,[29] who led his tribes
With untold cost and sacrifice,   175
Victorious, to the promised lands.[30]

Also, twelve stones from Jordan's bed,
Left dry when waters backward flowed,
He raised and firmly set in place,[31]
The type of Christ's Apostles twelve.   180

---

26. Cf. Exod. 15.25. Lavarenne (*Prudence* 1.73) comments on the obscurity of this and the two following stanzas, and thinks with Arevalus (PL 59.911) that they refer to Christ, 'our Captain,' 1.163, rather than to Moses, 'that leader,' 1.160. That the reference is to Moses as a type of Christ seems apparent.
27. Cf. Exod. 12.21; 1 Cor. 10.1-2.
28. Cf. Exod. 17.11-13.
29. The text here has *Jesus*, the Greek name for Josue found in the Septuagint. Cf. Eccli. 46.1.
30. Cf. Exod. 13.7.
31. Cf. Jos. 4.4-8; 3.14-17.

Then rightly do the Magi hold
That they have seen Judea's King,
For all the deeds of ancient chiefs
In figure told of Christ the Lord.

Of Judges who in olden times 185
Ruled Jacob's race, He is the King;
King now of Holy Mother Church,
Of both the temples, new and old.[32]

The sons of Ephraim worship Him,
With all Manasses' holy house, 190
And tribes sprung from the brothers twelve
All honor Him as Lord and God.[33]

Nay, even children of lost tribes,
Who followed false and shameful rites,
And all who shaped in fiery forge 195
The forms of Baal to adore,

Forsake their fathers' gloomy gods
Of metal, wood, and senseless stone;
Leave idols, hewn and carved by man,
To worship Christ in spirit and truth. 200

Rejoice, all nations of the earth,[34]
Judea, Egypt, Greece and Rome,
With Scythia, Thrace, and Persian realms:
Now over all one King holds sway.

Then praise your Lord, you that rejoice, 205
And all by desolation tried,
In health, affliction or decay:
For none shall taste eternal death.

---
32. Cf. Heb. 9.9-11.
33. Cf. Apoc. 7.4-7.
34. Cf. Ps. 66.5.

THE BOOK OF THE MARTYRS' CROWNS

(LIBER PERISTEPHANON)

1. HYMN IN HONOR OF THE HOLY MARTYRS EMETERIUS AND CHELIDONIUS OF CALAHORRA[1]

Written fair on Heaven's pages are the names of
   martyrs twain;[2]
Christ Himself in golden letters has engraved them
   there on high,
And on earth they are recorded in bright characters
   of blood.

---

1. Little is known of the Spanish martyrs celebrated in this hymn. The poem is, as far as is known, the earliest extant record of their martyrdom. Later martyrologies and the Mass in their honor in the Mozarabic Missal (PL 85.728-733) show indebtedness to the hymn, which is used in its entirety for the Vespers and Matins of the feast in the Mozarabic Breviary (PL 86.1106-1111). According to tradition the martyrs were the sons of St. Marcellus and were serving in the Roman army at Leon when a persecution broke out. They went to Calahorra, where they suffered martyrdom on March 3, a date attested by the martyrology of St. Jerome and other sources. The year is unknown. Allard thinks that they probably suffered under Diocletian in 303 (*Revue des questiones historiques* 39.24). Lesleus (PL 85.729-733) finds reason to think that they were martyred under Nero and not later than Trajan.
2. Cf. Luke 10.20; Apoc. 3.5; 21.27.

Happy Spain this noble garland wears for all the
    world to see;³
In God's eyes that spot seemed worthy to enshrine
    the martyrs' bones 5
Which had to their blessed bodies given kindly
    sepulture.

This land drank the tide warm flowing from the
    twofold martyrdom;
Now the people flock to worship where the sands
    with blood were stained,⁴
And to offer fervent prayers with their gifts and
    holy vows.

Hither comes the foreign pilgrim to invoke these
    blessed saints, 10
For to every land the tidings have been borne on
    wings of fame⁵
That this tomb by throngs surrounded holds the
    patrons of the world.

Not in vain has been the pleading of the souls that
    here have prayed;
Hence the suppliant turns with joy, as he dries his
    anxious tears,⁶
Knowing that his just petitions by the martyrs have
    been heard. 15

---

3. Cf. Seneca, *De beneficiis* 3.28.2.
4. Cf. Vergil, *Aeneid* 12.340.
5. Cf. *Ibid.* 4.173.
6. Cf. Damasus, *Epigram* 61.3-4 (Ihm, *Damasi Epigrammata* p. 627).

Such concern for all our perils do these intercessors
 show,
That no prayer is ever fruitless that to them is
 murmured here,[7]
But straightway is surely wafted to the ear of
 Heaven's King.[8]

Whence from that eternal fountain gifts divine flow
 down to earth,[9]
Bringing to the humble suppliant healing for his
 every ill.   20
To His Martyrs, true and faithful, Christ can never
 ought refuse,

Martyrs who through chains and torture and the
 threat of cruel death[10]
Of the one true God were witness to the shedding of
 their blood,
Yea their blood, but life eternal was the guerdon fair
 they won.

Thus to die is truly splendid, worthy of heroic
 men:[11]   25
To the sword to give the body, but a web of fragile
 veins
Soon devoured by gnawing illness, and to conquer
 thus the foe.

---

7. Cf. Vergil, *Aeneid* 4.210.
8. Cf. *Ibid.* 7.166.
9. Cf. James 1.17.
10. Cf. Vergil, *Aeneid* 10.791.
11. Cf. Horace, *Odes* 3.2.13.

What a glorious boon to suffer at the cruel torturer's
   blow
Mighty wounds that open Heaven to the martyr saints
   of God.[12]
Hither from the hearts' deep dwelling leaps the soul
   baptized in blood.   30

Called to Christ's eternal service, these brave soldiers
   hitherto[13]
Had endured the shock of battle and the rigors of the
   camp;
Valor tried in mortal combat now makes war for holy
   Faith.

They renounce the flag of Caesar for the ensign of the
   Cross;
For the banner they once carried, dragon swelled out
   by the wind,[14]   35
They now choose the Wood as standard, which
   subdued the Dragon's might.

Now they think it vile to brandish javelins with
   skillful hands,
Or to breach the wall with engines and to ring the
   camp with moats,
Or to stain with bloody carnage hands that wield
   unholy swords.

---

12. Cf. Vergil, *Aeneid* 9.401.
13. Lines 31-39 are similar in thought to Damasus, *Epigram* 8 (see Ferrua, *Epigrammata Damasiana* pp. 103-104).
14. Cf. Claudian, *De tertio cons. Hon.* 138-141.

Then it chanced the impious tyrant, ruler of the
    pagan world,   40
To the second race of Israel[15] sent an infamous
    command
To adore at heathen altars and deny their faith in
    Christ.

Malice armed with lethal weapons now assails
    intrepid Faith;
She endures with dauntless courage torments for the
    love of Christ:
Flaying hooks and cruel scourging and at last the
    headman's ax.[16]   45

Pent within the loathsome prisons, Christian necks
    submit to chains;[17]
Every forum reeks with carnage as the torturer wields
    his gear;[18]
Truth is judged as vilest treason, Faith's avowal
    merits death.

Virtue pierced by ruthless iron falls upon the stony
    ground;
Flung amid the blazing fagots, she imbibes the deadly
    flames.   50
In the fires the saints find sweetness; sweetness, too, in
    piercing steel.

---

15. *Secundos Istrahelis posteros*, the Christians, who succeeded the Jews, the first descendants of Israel.
16. Cf. Tertullian, *Apology* 12.4; 30.7 (Vol. 10, this series, pp. 41-42, 87).
17. *Colla bacis inpedit*. Arevalus reads *boiis*, 'collars' instead of *bacis* (PL 60.284).
18. Cf. Horace, *Odes* 3.5.49.

Then the hearts of these two brothers, who in loving
    fellowship[19]
All their days had been united, burn with zeal for
    martyrdom,
And they stand prepared to welcome any death
    reserved for them,

Whether it might be to offer willing necks to public
    ax,   55
After bearing cruel lashes and the fire of searing
    grates,
Or to yield their tortured bodies to the leopards and
    the lions.

'Shall we stoop to sway of mammon who have been
    reborn in Christ?[20]
Formed to God's eternal image, shall we serve the
    fleeting world?
God forbid that flame celestial should be mingled
    with earth's mire.[21]   60

'Tis enough that we, enlisted from the days of
    early youth
In the ranks of Caesar's armies, our due service
    have discharged;
It is now the time to render what is owing unto
    God.[22]

---

19. Cf. Vergil, *Aeneid* 11.215-216.
20. Cf. Matt. 6.24.
21. Cf. 2 Cor. 6.14.
22. Cf. Matt. 22.2. See also Sulpicius Severus, *Life of St. Martin* (Vol. 7, this series, p. 109). Prudentius may have read this work. For its wide diffusion at the end of the fourth century, see Sulpicius Severus, *Dialogue* 1.23 (*Ibid.* pp. 192-193).

'Hence, commanders of the ensigns, and tribunes,
   depart from us;
Take away the golden collars, prizes for the
   wounds received.   65
Henceforth in the splendid armies of the angels
   we shall serve.

'Christ of His own white-robed cohorts is the Ruler
   and the King.
From His throne in highest Heaven He contemns
   your puny gods
And you men who fashion idols, silly monsters to
   adore.'

At these words the valiant martyrs with a thousand
   pains are whelmed.   70
Their two hands are bound with fetters wrought of
   galling links of iron,
And their necks bear cruel bruises from the heavy
   circling steel.

O oblivion of the ages and the silence and neglect
That to us denies the record of their glorious
   martyrdom![23]
Every vestige of the trial by the prefect was
   effaced,[24]   75

---

23. Cf. Vergil, *Aeneid* 6.527.
24. The writings of the Christians were destroyed during the persecution of Diocletian. Cf. Jerome, *In Zachariam* 2.8; Eusebius, *Ecclesiastical History* 8.2 (Trans. in Vol. 29, this series).

Lest in books, all time enduring, should be traced
   in living words
Order, date, and very manner of the pangs they
   underwent,
And on ears of future ages their fair story might
   resound.

But the old times keep unbroken silence on these
   points alone:
Whether endless days in prison saw their unshorn
   hair grow long,[25]   80
Or by what inhuman torments their eternal crowns
   were won.

Of one marvel we have witness, nor has time
   obscured its fame,
That uplifted on the breezes gifts to heaven's
   heights were borne,
Token of the way that opened to a shining Paradise.

On a cloud a ring was wafted, of the faith of one the
   sign,   85
And the wind upraised the kerchief of the other as a
   pledge;
Caught up by a breath supernal, these memorials
   pierced the skies.

In the limpid vault of heaven soon was hid the
   gleaming gold,
But the whiteness of the kerchief longer fled the
   eager gaze;
Then at last the blessed symbols disappeared among
   the stars.   90

---

25. Cf. Vergil, *Aeneid* 7.391.

Those who gathered round the victims saw this
    wondrous miracle;
Saw it, too, the trembling headsman, as he checked
    his hand in fear,[26]
But the cruel blow descended, lest his vile reward be
    lost.

Vascons, once a heathen people, are you not today
    convinced
That you stained your hands unwitting in the blood
    of martyr saints?   95
Do you not believe these victims now enjoy bliss with
    God?

See how many ways fierce demons here are
    vanquished openly,
They who wolf-like break and shatter human forms
    they have possessed,
And the soul itself they torture as with senses they
    unite.[27]

Now is brought a raging creature, by his foe in
    bondage held,   100
Foaming at the mouth and rolling bloodshot eyes in
    his distress,[28]
To be cleansed by exorcism of offenses not his own.

---

26. Cf. *Ibid.* 12.739.
27. Cf. Tertullian, *Apology* 22.4 (Vol. 10, this series, p. 69).
28. Cf. Vergil, *Aeneid* 7.448.

You may hear his doleful shrieking; yet no torturer
   is near;
Now his frame is torn by scourging, but the whip you
   cannot see;
Then he hangs in air suspended, lifted up by
   hidden chains.[29]   105

Thus the virtue of the martyrs persecutes the hellish
   thief,
Vexing him with fiery torments, loading him with
   heavy chains,
Till the foiled and chastened brigand leaves the heart
   he has possessed.[30]

Safe and sound he leaves his victim, flees away with
   thirsty jaws;[31]
He restores him strong and healthy, whole from
   crown of head to foot,   110
As he owns himself a dweller in Gehenna's fiery pit.

Why now speak of pallid bodies healed of lingering
   disease
As the wan and sickly members tremble with an icy
   chill?[32]
See a tumor leave this visage, see the glow of health
   return.

---

29. Cf. Paulinus of Nola, *Poema* 23.61-69, 86-87 (PL 61.609-610); Sulpicius Severus, *Dialogue* 3.6 (Vol. 7, this series, p. 233).
30. Cf. Paulinus of Nola, *Poema* 14.21-40 (PL 61.465).
31. Cf. Vergil, *Aeneid* 2.358.
32. Cf. *Ibid.* 3.29.

God, Himself, bestowed the blessing which we now
    enjoy here,   115
When the bodies of these martyrs He enshrined
    within our town,
Making them the faithful guardians of the lands by
    Ebro washed.

Join, O mothers, in the vigil, raise glad voices in the
    hymns,[33]
Giving thanks for cure of husbands and your children
    raised to life;
Let us with a holy joy celebrate this festal day.   120

33. *State nunc, hymnite, matres.* The reference here is to the stations, or vigils, celebrated at the tombs of the martyrs. For a discussion of the variant *hymnistae* found in the Oxford manuscript, see Ruth E. Messenger, *Speculum* 29 (1947) 83-84.

2. HYMN IN HONOR OF THE PASSION OF
   THE BLESSED MARTYR LAWRENCE[1]

Once mother of unholy fanes,
Rome, dedicated now to Christ,
By Lawrence led to victory,
You trample on the heathen rites.

1. According to the traditions of the fourth century, recorded in authentic sources, St. Lawrence was one of the seven deacons of Rome, who with Pope Sixtus II suffered martyrdom in the year 258 during the persecution of Valerian. See Cyprian, *Epistles* 82 (PL 4.442); Ambrose, *De officiis ministrorum* 1.41 and 2.28; also Mommsen, *Liber Pontificalis* (MGH 1.34-35). When Prudentius was in Rome, he doubtless took part in the celebration of the feast of the martyr and visited the basilica

Proud kings have bowed before your sword,   5
And conquered peoples felt your sway;
Now pagan gods are made to pass,
Beneath the yoke of your empire.

Though savage tribes had been subdued,
The city of the toga lacked   10
One glorious title of renown,
The triumph over wanton Jove,

Not by Camillus' stormy might,
Nor Cossus' arms or Caesar's power,[2]
But by the bloody combat waged   15
By Lawrence in his martyrdom.

Embattled Faith took up the fight,
Of her own blood most prodigal;
For she destroyed death by death
And lost her life to save her life.   20

The Pontiff Sixtus, from the cross[3]
On which he hung, saw at its foot
His deacon Lawrence weeping sore,
And these prophetic words he spoke:

---

on the Via Tiburtina where Pope Damasus had placed one of his inscriptions (Ihm, *op. cit.* n. 2, p. viii and p. 37). St. Augustine in two of his sermons (302 and 303, PL 38.1388-1394) mentions contemporary traditions concerning the martyrdom of St. Lawrence. Several lines of the hymn appear in the Office of St. Lawrence in the Mozarabic Breviary (PL 86.1179).

2. Roman military leaders. For Cossus and Camillus see Livy 4.19-20 and 6.1-13.
3. Sixtus II, who was Pope from August or September 257 to August 258, was beheaded. See Cyprian, *Epistles* 82 and Vol. 15, this series, p. 19. For a discussion of Prudentius' implication here that the Pope was crucified, see Marchesi, *Le Corone di Prudenzio* p. 75.

'Let tears of sorrow cease to flow
At my departure from this life;
My brother, I but lead the way,
And you will follow in three days.'[4]

The holy bishop's dying words
Sure glory for his friend announced,
For Lawrence on the day foretold,
Victorious, won the martyr's palm.

What words, what praises can suffice
To celebrate that hero's death?
How sing his passion worthily
In measured harmonies of verse?

First of the seven ministers[5]
Who nearest to the altar stand,
Levite in holy orders high
And eminent above the rest.

He guarded well the sacred rites
And kept in trust with faithful keys
The precious treasure of the Church,
Dispensing riches vowed to God.

The prefect of imperial Rome,
The agent of an insane prince,[6]
Athirst for money and for blood,
Is driven by his greed for gold

---

4. Cf. Ambrose, *De officiis ministrorum* 1.41, *Liber Pontificalis* (MGH 1.34-35).
5. Cf. Acts 6.1-4.
6. Valerian.

To wrest from sacred shrines by force
Suspected riches lurking there,   50
The talents gathered in vast sums,
And hidden in their secret vaults.

He summons Lawrence to the court
And questions him on coffers filled
With massive ingots of pure gold   55
And hoarded coins in shining heaps.

'You make complaints,' the prefect said,
'When we give vent to lawful ire
By punishing with torments cruel
The Christians who contemn our gods.   60

'To such atrocious punishments
My wrath does not impel me now;
The mild and peaceful claims I make,
You ought to meet with ready grace.

'In your religious rites, they say,   65
It is the custom of your priests,
Ordained by ceremonial laws,
To offer wine in golden cups.

'They say that silver vessels smoke
With blood of victims sacrificed,   70
And tapers at nocturnal feasts
Are fixed in golden candlesticks.[7]

---

7. Cf. Minucius Felix, *Octavius* 8.4 and 9.5 (Trans. in Vol. 10, this series, pp. 335 and 337).

'Then rumor says your brotherhood
Devotes to God with noble zeal
Thousands of sesterces derived   75
From sale of lands and other goods.[8]

'The sons by holy sires disowned,
In abject poverty lament
The sale of vast ancestral lands
Knocked down by heartless auctioneers. 80

'This wealth is hid in secret crypts
Of churches where the Christians meet,
And to despoil your dear offspring[9]
Is deemed the highest piety.

'Bring forth the gold you have amassed 85
By force and evil trickery,
The hoarded treasures you now keep
Enclosed in subterranean vaults.

'The public welfare now demands
That you give up your boundless wealth 90
To fill the coffers of the state
And pay the armies of your prince.

'This is your teaching, so I hear:
"To each man give what is his due."
Look you, great Caesar sees engraved   95
His image on your golden coins.

---

8. Cf. Acts 4.34-35.
9. Cf. Horace, *Epodes* 2.40.

'What you perceive to Caesar due,
To Caesar give;[10] my claim is just.
Unless I err, your God stamps not
His image on your precious gold.   100

'When He came down to earth below
No coins of Philip did He bring,[11]
But without purse, He preached the word
And gave precepts of poverty.

'Put these precepts in practice now,   105
Which you proclaim throughout the world.
Give willingly your minted gold,
And let Christ's words be all your wealth.'

Untroubled, Lawrence made reply
To this perfidious overture,   110
And as if ready to obey,
He gently nodded his assent.

'Our church is very rich,' he said.
'I must confess that it has wealth;
Our treasuries are filled with gold
Not found elsewhere in all the world.   115

'Not even high Augustus holds
Such wealth within his mighty grasp,
Though every silver coin forged
His image and inscription bears.   120

---

10. Cf. Matt. 22.20-21.
11. Gold coins struck by Philip II of Macedon.

'Yet I refuse not to yield up
The riches of our Lord and God;
I shall display for all to see
The treasures that belong to Christ.[12]

'However, one request I make: 125
Vouchsafe to me a short delay
That I may carry out my pledge
With greater ease and richer gain.

'I need this time to take account
Of all the goods possessed by Christ, 130
And then to estimate their worth
And reckon up the total sum.'

The prefect's heart now swelled with joy
At treasure felt within his grasp;
He reveled in the hoarded gold 135
As though it rested in his vaults.

Three days of grace he freely grants,
And Lawrence is dismissed from court,
The trusted bondsman for himself
And for vast stores of hidden wealth. 140

He hastens through the city streets,
And in three days he gathers up
The poor and sick, a mighty throng
Of all in need of kindly alms.[13]

---

12. Ambrose, *op. cit.* 2.28; Augustine, *Sermon* 302.9 (PL 38.1388-1389) and *Sermon* 303.1 (PL 38.1393-1394).
13. *Ibid.*

There one beheld an aged man   145
Uplifting hollow blinded eyes,
And pressing forward with a staff
To guide his faltering steps aright.

The halt and lame were also there.
With stiffened joints or severed limbs   150
Or legs unequal in their length,
They dragged their limping steps along.

From ulcerated members flowed
The foul corruption of disease;
The hands of some were paralyzed,   155
And tendons of the arms were shrunk.

He sought in every public square
The needy who were wont to be
Fed from the stores of Mother Church,
And he as steward knew them well.   160

Then one by one he counted them,
Wrote down the name of every man,
And ordered them to take their stand
In line before the temple gate.

By now the fated day had come: 165
The cruel judge, insane with greed,
Commanded Lawrence angrily
To bring at once the promised gold.

To him the martyr made reply:
'I pray you come with me and view   170
The wondrous riches of our God
Displayed for you in sacred shrines.[14]

---
14. *Ibid.*

'You will behold the anteroom
With golden vases all aglow,
And through the open colonnades   175
The talents ranged in shining rows.'

The prefect deigns to follow him;
The sacred portal soon they reach,
Where stands a ghastly multitude
Of poor drawn up in grim array.   180

The air is rent with cries for alms;
The prefect shudders in dismay,
And turns on Lawrence glaring eyes,
With threats of dreadful punishment.

The saint, undaunted, answers him   185
'Why do you gnash your teeth in rage
At this unwelcome spectacle?
Do you scorn these as foul and mean?

'From rubble of the earth is born
The shining gold for which you thirst,   190
And penal labor quarries it
From veins of ore in sunless mines,

'Or mountain torrents wash it down,
Commingled with their murky sands;
This earthly dross and sordid ore   195
Must be refined in cleansing fires.

'For gold, bright innocence is lost;
For gold, integrity is stained,
Peace is destroyed, faith set at naught,
The very laws abjured and scorned.   200

'Why do you hold in such esteem
This bane of righteousness and truth?
Indeed, the gold that brighter shines
Is light enlightening all mankind.[15]

'These are the foster-sons of light   205
Whom crippled bodies hedge around,
Lest flesh unscathed should shelter souls
Puffed up with pride and insolence.

'When illness racks the human frame,
The spirit burns more ardently;   210
When members glow with health and strength,
The powers of mind and soul are dulled.

'For fiery blood to lust inclined
Feeds passion with diminished strength,
When maladies exhaust its flame   215
And curb its deadly virulence.

'If choice were ever given to me,
I would prefer to suffer woe
From members cruelly crushed and maimed,
And fair within always to live.   220

'Consider all the plagues of man
And match them with his heinous sins:
Are not the ulcers of the soul
More hideous than those of flesh?

'These poor of ours are sick and lame,   225
But beautiful and whole within.
They bear with them a spirit fair
And free from taint and misery.

---

15. Cf. John 1.4,9.

'Your followers are strong of frame,
But marred by inward leprosy.   230
Depravity is halt and lame,
And sightless fraud is blind indeed.

'Your princes clad in splendid robes,
Whose shining faces mirror health,
Are more disabled, I will prove,   235
Than any of these poor of mine.

'The lord puffed up in silk attire,
Who proudly in his chariot rides,
Pale dropsy bloats with poisonous fluid
That lurks within his turgid soul.[16]   240

'The greedy, like one paralyzed,
Has crippled hands and palms so clenched
With claw-like nails, he has no power
His hardened muscles to unbend.

'Another lured by shameful lust   245
Defiles himself with prostitutes,
And wallowing in this filthy mire,
He begs for foul debaucheries.

'Does not the man athirst for show
And burning with desire for fame,   250
Convulsed with fever, rave and gasp
From fire that rages in his veins?

'The gossip itching to divulge
The secrets he would bring to light
Is irritated by a mange   255
That at his heart and liver gnaws.

---
16. Cf. Horace, *Odes* 2.2.13-16.

'Why tell of tumors that infest
The scrofulous hearts of envious men?
Why show the livid, festering sores
Of their ill-will and cruelty?   260

'You, ruler of this mighty Rome,
Who scorn the one eternal God
And fallen hordes of hell adore,
Yourself endure the royal plague.[17]

'These humble paupers you despise   265
And look upon as vile outcasts,
Their ulcerous limbs will lay aside
And put on bodies incorrupt,

'When freed at last from tainted flesh,
Their souls, from chains of earth released,   270
Will shine resplendent with new life
In their celestial fatherland,

'Not foul and shabby, or infirm,
As now they seem to scornful eyes,
But fair, in radiant vesture clad,   275
With crowns of gold upon their heads.

'I would the power were given to me
To bring before your startled gaze
A vision of the doom that waits
For haughty magnates of this world.   280

'You would behold them clothed in rags,
Their nostrils dripping mucus foul,
Their beards with spittle all defiled,
Their purblind eyes made blear with rheum.

---

17. *Morbo regio,* jaundice.

'Than sin-stained soul, nought is more vile   285
Nought is so leprous, nought so sear;
The wound of crime is ever raw
And reeks of Hell's ill-smelling cave.

'These souls, of body once so fair,
Who took delight in splendid mien,   290
Their lot reversed, are now immured
In forms repulsive to the sight.

'See here the gold I promised you,
The coins that no consuming fire
One day to ashes will reduce,   295
Nor thief will ever steal from you.[18]

'Lest you may think that Christ is poor,
I add to these the precious gems
With which this temple is adorned,
Gems of resplendent beauty bright.   300

'The holy virgins here you see;
Chaste widows, too, you may admire,
Who of their first mates now bereft,
A second marriage have renounced.

'These form the necklace of the Church,   305
With these fair gems she is bedecked;
Thus dowered, she is dear to Christ,
Thus she adorns her queenly brow.[19]

'These riches now are yours; take them
To beautify your lofty Rome,   310
To fill the treasury of your prince,
And your own fortunes to augment.'

---
18. Cf. Luke 12.33.
19. Cf. Apoc. 21.2.

'He makes a laughingstock of us,'
The judge cries out in savage rage;
'He mocks us in strange metaphors, 315
And yet the maniac still lives!

'Do you imagine, slippery knave,
That this buffoonery you have staged,
This sanctimonious farce, this hoax,
Will go without due punishment? 320

'Was it a fitting pleasantry
To hold me up to ridicule?
Have I been made the butt of jeers
Like entertainer at a feast?

'Are magistrates no longer grave, 325
Are they no longer obdurate?
Has soft indulgence dulled the edge
Of headsman's ax and torturer's rod?

'You say: "I gladly go to death,
I yearn and sigh for martyrdom"; 330
This folly is, as I have learned
Peculiar to your vain belief.[20]

'But I shall see to it forthwith
That you will quit this earthly life,
Not by the short and easy route 335
Of sudden death, as you desire.

'I will prolong and stay your life
In pains and anguish without end,
And death in lingering agony
Will bar a merciful release. 340

---
20. Minucius Felix, *op. cit.* 8.5 (Trans. in Vol. 10, this series, p. 335).

'Prepare for him a bed of coals,
Lest raging flames that burn too high
May seize too soon the upstart's face
And penetrate his inmost heart.

'Let dying fires exhale dull heat, 345
Diffusing drafts of feverish air
To rack by slow degrees his frame
Already by hot embers seared.²¹

'Well that the chief himself has come
Within my grasp, of all the rest. 350
I will of him an instance make
Of pangs the others must endure.

'Ascend the pyre prepared for you,
Lie on the bed that you deserve.²²
Then argue with me, if you can, 355
That this my Vulcan's power is nought.'

Thus spoke the prefect. At his nod
Forthwith the executioner
Stripped off the holy martyr's robes
And laid him bound upon the pyre. 360

The martyr's face was luminous,
And round it shone a glorious light;
Such countenance did Moses wear
When he descended from the Mount.

His face the Israelites, defiled 365
By worship of the golden calf,
Turned from in fear and could not bear
To see God's glory thus revealed.²³

---
21. *semustulati corporis.* Cf. Vergil, *Aeneid* 3.578.
22. Cf. Augustine, *Sermon* 302.9 (PL 38.1388).
23. Cf. Exod. 34.29-30.

And Stephen, too, a countenance showed
Alight with glory from above, 370
When through the rain of stones he saw
The heavens opened to his gaze.[24]

The face of Lawrence from afar
Was seen to shine by brethren cleansed
But lately in baptism's flood 375
And made for Christ a fit abode.

But in their blindness impious men,
As though the veil of night were drawn
Across their eyes to blot it out,
Saw not the splendor of his face, 380

As when the plague on Egypt fell
And doomed to darkness Pharao's race,
While to the Hebrews it was day,
And all appeared in light serene.[25]

The very odor given forth 385
By holy Lawrence's burning flesh
Was noxious to the unredeemed
And to the faithful nectar sweet.

The same sensation is transformed
So that the fumes inflict on one 390
A vengeful odor, nauseous,
Or soothe the other with delight.

Thus everlasting fire of God,
For Christ is cleansing fire indeed,[26]
Illumines souls of men redeemed 395
And burns the reprobate in hell.

---
24. Cf. Acts 7.55-59.
25. Cf. Exod. 10.22-23.
26. Cf. Mal. 3.2-3.

When slow, consuming heat had seared
The flesh of Lawrence for a space,
He calmly from his gridiron made
This terse proposal to the judge: 400

'Pray turn my body, on one side
Already broiled sufficiently,
And see how well your Vulcan's fire[27]
Has wrought its cruel punishment.'

The prefect bade him to be turned.   405
Then Lawrence spoke: 'I am well baked,
And whether better cooked or raw,
Make trial by a taste of me.'[28]

He said these words in way of jest;
Then raising shining eyes to heaven[29]   410
And sighing deeply, thus he prayed
With pity for unholy Rome:

'O Christ, O Name above all names,[30]
Of God the Father, Light and Power,[31]
O Maker of the earth and sky,   415
And Founder of this city's walls,

'Rome's sceptre Thou didst make supreme,
Subjecting to the conquering arms
Of togaed sons of Quirinus
All nations of the universe,   420

---
27. Cf. Horace, *Odes* 1.4.8.
28. Cf. Ambrose, PL 16.92, 17.1255; Augustine, PL 38.1394. See also Socrates, PG 67.418 and Sozamen, *Ibid.* 1247.
29. Cf. Vergil, *Aeneid* 12.195-196.
30. Cf. Phil. 2.9.
31. Cf. Heb. 1.3.

'That one dominion might unite
The races of the world, diverse
In manners and observances,
In tongues and rites and inborn traits.

'Lo, all the human race has bowed 425
Beneath the rod of Remus' sons;
Dissenting tribes one language speak
And live in peace and harmony.

'This sovereignty was foreordained
That all the world with greater ease,
Might by a single bond be linked 430
Beneath the power of Christian law.

'Grant to Thy Roman people, Christ,
That they may wear the Christian name,
For through their city Thou didst give 435
To others one religious faith.

'All members of this realm are joined
In fealty to this saving creed.
The conquered world has civil grown,
And may the head be tamed at last. 440

'Let Rome behold the lands discrete
Made one in Christ's redeeming grace;
Let Romulus embrace the faith,
And even Numa now believe.

'The Trojan error still confounds 445
The scions of Cato's noble halls,
And on their altars they adore
The exiled gods of Phrygia.[32]

---
32. Cf. Vergil, *Aeneid* 3.11-12, 148-150.

HYMNS

'The Senate two-faced Janus lauds[33]
And Sterculus—I dread to name　　　　　　450
Our fathers' monstrous deities
And Saturnalian festivals.[34]

'Wipe out, O Christ, this infamy;
Send forth Thy angel Gabriel,
That sons of Julus, led astray,[35]　　　　　　455
May learn to worship one true God.

'Two faithful pledges we possess.
That this our hope will be fulfilled;
Two apostolic princes here[36]
Now hold the reins of government.　　　　　　460

'Apostle of the gentiles one,[37]
The other, pontifex supreme,
Unlocks the gates of paradise
Entrusted to his watchful care.[38]

'Begone from us, adulterous Jove,　　　　　　465
Thy sister's vile incestuous mate,
From halls of Rome now take your flight
And set the Christian people free.

'Paul drives you hence, a fugitive,
The blood of Peter thrusts you out;　　　　　　470
The crime of Nero primed by you
Has undermined your baneful power.

---

33. Cf. *Ibid.* 12.198.
34. Cf. *Ibid.* 3.26.
35. Son of Aeneas, from whom the Julii claimed descent. Cf. Vergil, *Aeneid* 1.286-288.
36. St. Peter and St. Paul.
37. Cf. 2 Tim. 1.11.
38. Cf. Matt. 16.19. See also Damasus, *Epigram* 5.3 (Ihm, *op. cit.* p. 9).

'I see in future times a prince,[39]
Adorer of the one true God,
Who will not suffer Rome to serve 475
The idols foul of pagan cults.

'The heathen temples he will close,
Wall up their doors of ivory,
And make secure their brazen bolts,
That none may pass their vile thresholds. 480

'Of bloody sacrifices cleansed,
The marble altars then will gleam,
And statues honored now as gods
Will stand, mere harmless blocks of bronze.'

Thus ended Lawrence's fervent prayer,[40] 485
Thus ended, too, his earthly life:
With these last words his eager soul
Escaped with joy from carnal chains.

Some noble Romans, who were led
By his amazing fortitude 490
To faith in Christ, then bore away
The hero's body from the scene.

A sudden grace inflamed their hearts
With ardent love of God Most High
And made them loathe the mummeries 495
Of their ancestral heathen rites.

From that day forth the worship paid
To sordid pagan gods grew cold;
The temples unfrequented stood,
While people to Christ's altars thronged. 500

---
39. Probably Theodosius.
40. Cf. Vergil, *Aeneid* 10.116.

HYMNS 125

Thus Lawrence in that mighty fray
Had at his side no keen-edged sword,
But seized the weapon of his foe
And on him turned the piercing steel.

When Satan joined in mortal bout 505
With God's unyielding warrior,
He fell, transfixed by his own sword,
And lies prostrate forevermore.

That holy martyr's valiant death
Of pagan temples was the end; 510
Then Vesta saw Palladian fires
Untended with impunity.

The Roman people, who were wont
The cup of Numa to adore[41]
Christ's sanctuaries now frequent 515
And hymn the holy martyr's praise.

Illustrious senators themselves,
Once flamins and lupercal priests,
Now kiss the thresholds of the shrines
Where martyrs and apostles rest.[42] 520

We see patrician families,
The parents, both of noble birth,
Their children dedicate to God,
The dearest pledges of their love.

---
41. Cf. Juvenal, *Satires* 6.343.
42. Cf. Tibullus 1.2.85; Ovid, *Metamorphoses* 1.376; Paulinus of Nola, *Poema* 18.250 (PL 61.496).

The pontiff once with chaplet crowned 525
Is signed now with the cross of Christ,
And, Lawrence, to thy temple comes[43]
The vestal of the Claudian house.[44]

O thrice, nay four and seven times[45]
Are Rome's inhabitants now blest, 530
Who on the very spot, where lie
Thy sacred bones, can honor thee,

Who prostrate at thy nearby tomb
May water with their tears the ground,
Press to their hearts the holy soil, 535
And offer up their murmured prayers.[46]

Removed from thee by mountain heights
And Vascon Ebro's rolling flood,
We dwell across the Cottian Alps,
Beyond the snowy Pyrenees. 540

Scarce is it known in that far land
How rich is Rome in tombs of saints,
How fruitful is her kindly soil
In consecrated sepulchers.

---

43. Constantine had erected a basilica near the tomb of St. Lawrence in the Ager Veranus on the Via Tiburtina. See *Liber Pontificalis* (MGH 1.63-64).
44. An inscription dedicated to a Vestal Virgin in the year 364, with the name beginning with the letter C erased, was discovered in 1883. Lanciani (*Ancient Rome in the Light of Recent Excavations,* pp. 170-171) thinks that the inscription may have been that of the Vestal Claudia referred to here, who had been thus condemned because of her conversion to Christianity.
45. Cf. Vergil, *Aeneid* 1.94.
46. Cf. Paulinus of Nola, *Poema* 18.251-252 (PL 61.496).

But we who lack this precious dower 545
And cannot trace with reverent zeal
The bloody footprints of the saints
Can raise our eyes to Heaven above.

So, holy Lawrence, there we seek
Memorial of thy martyrdom, 550
For in two mansions thou dost live,
Thy body here, thy soul on high.

The heavenly city has enrolled
You as its valiant citizen,
And in its everlasting courts 555
You wear the civic diadem.

Your crown, O Saint, so brightly shines
With sparkling gems, it seems to me
Celestial Rome has chosen you
To hold perpetual consulship. 560

The joy shown by suppliants
Whose prayers for help you kindly heed
Attests the power God grants to you
And wondrous gifts you have received.

Whatever they implore of thee 565
Is to a happy issue brought;
They ask, they plead for what they will,
And none go forth with saddened heart,[47]

For thou are ever near at hand
To aid thy foster-sons of Rome 570
And give to them a father's love,
And mother's tender nurturing.

---

47. Cf. Damasus, *Epigram* 61.3-4 (Ihm, *op. cit.* p. 62).

Among these sons, O saint of Christ,
Give audience to a rustic poet
Who humbly bares his sinful heart   575
And owns his guilt and misery.

I am not worthy Christ Himself
Should hear me, this too well I know,
But martyr advocates can win
His salutary grace for me.   580

O kindly hear Prudentius,
A culprit at the bar of Christ,
And from the bondage of the flesh
And earthly fetters set him free.

3. HYMN IN HONOR OF THE PASSION OF THE MOST HOLY MARTYR EULALIA[1]

Noble by birth and far nobler in death,
Sainted Eulalia, virgin unstained,
Graces the city that claims her its own,
Merida,[2] shrine of her holy remains,
Favored by her with compassionate love. 5

---

1. This hymn of Prudentius is the earliest extant account of St. Eulalia of Merida, who is believed to have suffered martyrdom in the year 304 during the persecution of Diocletian. The following notice appears in the Martyrology of St. Jerome for December 10: *In Hispania, civitate Emerita, passio S. S.*

Nigh to the westering sun lies the land
Where the illustrious martyr was born;[3]
Mighty and populous the city she blessed,
Drenching the soil with her blood there outpoured,
Hallowing it with her virginal tomb.   10

Nine and three years for the maiden rolled by,
Thrice did four winters pass over her head,
When she embraced the fierce tortures of fire,
Making the stern executioner quake,
As he beheld her in anguish rejoice.   15

Offering her heart to the Father above,
Early she showed that no nuptials of earth
Ever would bind her to temporal joys.
When but a child she despised and ignored
Toys and sports with which girls are amused.   20

Trinkets of amber and gold she disdained;
Perfume of roses for her had no charm.[4]
Modest of gait and of countenance grave,
Childlike in ways, even then she possessed
Wisdom that comes with gray hair of old age.   25

Eulaliae virginis. The sermon of St. Augustine for the feast of the martyr indicates how widespread her cult had become at the beginning of the fifth century. Cf. *Revue Benedictine* 9.417-419. The entire hymn of Prudentius is used in the Mozarabic Breviary for Vespers of the feast of the saint on December 10. The similarity of the acts of St. Eulalia of Barcelona, honored on February 12, has led competent authorities to conclude that there was only one St. Eulalia, the martyr of Merida celebrated in this hymn. See Thurston and Attwater, *Butler's Lives of the Saints* 12.121.

2. *Emerita* in Lusitania, now Merida.
3. Cf. Vergil, *Aeneid* 7.473.
4. *flere rosas.* Meyer (*Philologus* 87.346) thinks that *flare* found in one MS is to be preferred.

Dire persecution flared up in the land,
Threatening the servants of God with its wrath.
Followers of Christ were commanded to burn
Incense to idols, and on altars profane
Offer the victims to death-dealing gods. 30

Wroth was Eulalia, soul all afire,
Thirsting to battle the impious foe.
Though a mere girl, she was ready to meet
Weapons of men who were armed against God,
Eager to win her eternal reward. 35

Fearful, her mother with sedulous care[5]
Kept the high-spirited maiden at home,
Far from the town in a rural retreat,
Lest her desire for a glorious death
Lead her to purchase the crown with her blood. 40

Ill did Eulalia brook this repose,
Holding her back from the coveted prize.
Secretly she in the darkness of night
Forces the bars of the portals made fast,
Freeing herself from imprisoning walls. 45

Thence she pursues a circuitous course;
Over sharp brambles that harrow her feet[6]
Onward she goes with angelic escort.
Grim though the darkness and silence of night,
Heavenly brightness illumines her path. 50

---

5. Cf. Vergil, *Aeneid* 1.646.
6. Cf. *Ibid.* 6.462.

Such was the pillar of light that of old
Guided the valiant Israelite throng,
Piercing the shadowy gloom of the night,
Turning the sinister darkness to day,
Where its clear torch shed its gleam on their road.[7]   55

So did the dutiful virgin of Christ
Merit the splendor that lighted her way
Through the dark shades of enveloping night,
Out from the land of Egyptian power
Into the starry abodes of the blest.   60

Many a mile she traversed ere the dawn
Opened the gates of the orient sky.
Scarce had the morning rekindled the earth,
When she appeared at the magistrate's court
Standing among the imperial guards.   65

Boldly she challenged: 'What madness is this
Hurling your souls to destruction and death?
Why do you waste your devotion on gods
Chiselled by you from the indurate crags,
While you deny the Creator of all?   70

'Miserable men, for the Christians you search![8]
Lo, I am one of that odious race,
Foe to your fiendish idolatrous rites.
Witness to Christ with my heart and my lips,
Under my feet I will trample your gods.   75

---

7. Cf. Exod. 13.21; 14.20.
8. Cf. Vergil, *Aeneid* 11.259.

'Isis, Apollo and Venus are nought,
Nought is Maximian,[9] lord of the world;
Nought are those deities fashioned by man,
Nought is the man who pays homage to them—
Vanity all of these, nothingness all.   80

'Mighty Maximian is but a slave
Subject to meaningless idols of stone.
Though at their altars he humbly adores,
Ready to offer his head to his gods,
Why does he harass the servants of Christ?   85

'Sovereign gracious, and eminent judge,
Grimly he revels in innocent blood,
Gorging himself on the bodies of saints;
Flesh undefiled he joys to rend,
Heaping insults on the Christian faith.   90

'Come then, you butcher, and cut, tear and burn
Members compacted of dust of the earth!
Shattered with ease is the vessel so frail,
But on the spirit that lies deep within,
Never can ax of the torturer fall.'   95

Maddened to fury, the prefect cried out;
'Take her, you lictors, and promptly inflict
Punishments dire on this impudent girl.
Teach her to honor the gods of our land;
Make her respect the imperial power.   100

---

9. Ruler of the West under Diocletian, with whom he joined in the persecution of the Christians.

'Nevertheless, ere you go to your death,
Would it were possible, obdurate maid,
I might persuade you to rue your rash words.
Think of the happiness life has in store;
Think of the honor your marriage will bring.   105

'Weeping, your parents are searching for you,
Hearts filled with anguish at thought of the blow
Destined to wreck their illustrious house
If in the sunshine of youth[10] you now die,
Just as the time of your wedding draws near.   110

'Are you not moved by the splendor and pomp
That will attend your espousals one day,
Nor by the pain your rashness inflicts
On the aged parents deprived of your love?
Then, take a look at these instruments of death: 115

'Here is the sword that will sever your head,
There are the beasts that will mangle your frame,
Here are the torches already aflame
That will reduce you to ashes too soon,
Mourned and lamented by all of your kin.   120

'What must you do to escape from these woes?
If you submit to my orders, my child,
And with the tip of your finger you touch
But a few grains of this salt and incense,
You will avoid the torturer's sword.'   125

---

10. *sole . . . in tenero.* Some MSS have *flore . . . in tenero.* Cf. *Psychomachia* 845.

Answer the martyr made not to these words,
But in her heart she was boiling with rage.
Braving the tyrant, she spat in his face,
Upset the idols, and spurned with her foot
Thuribles filled with incense profane.[11]   130

Forthwith two slaughterers seize her and rend,
One on each side, her innocent breasts,
Cutting her virginal flesh to the bone
With clawlike instruments, cruelly sharp.
Counting her wounds, thus Eulalia speaks: 135

'Lo, Thou hast written, O Lord, on my flesh
Beautiful letters I joy to read,
Telling Thy triumph, O Christ, to the world.
Streams of red blood that pour forth from my
    wounds
Utter Thy holy, all-powerful Name.'   140

Such was the paean of joy she sang,
Bravely, with never a tear or a moan.
Torments insufferable touch not her soul.
Blood warm and fresh from the fount of her
    wounds
Stains her fair body with roseate streams.   145

Tortures more fierce she was yet to endure.
Harrowing iron that furrowed her flesh,
Wounding her cruelly, did not suffice.
Now to her bosom and delicate sides
Fiery torches bring anguish anew.   150

---

11. Cf. Vergil, *Georgics* 3.256.

Ringlets, all fragrant with sweet-smelling balms,
Slipped from their bonds in a beauteous shower
Over her shoulders and served as a veil,[12]
Hiding the charms of the virtuous maid
From the irreverent gaze of her foe.   155

Fed by her hair, the enveloping flames
Mount to her face, and surrounding her head,
Blaze up above it in vehement rage.[13]
Thirsting for heaven, the virgin elect
Drinks in the fire with impetuous lips.   160

Then of a sudden a snowy-white dove
Springs from the mouth of the martyr and flies
Forth to the stars in the sight of the crowd.
It was Eulalia's innocent soul,
Winging its way to celestial heights.   165

Fled is her spirit, and her motionless form
Falls to the earth as the fires die away.
Lifeless, her body at last rests in peace,
While in glad triumph her soul takes its flight,
Seeking ethereal mansions above.   170

Clearly the prefect himself saw the dove
Dart from the mouth of the valiant maid.
Stunned at the vision, he fled from the spot,
Far from the scene of his odious crime.
Even the lictor in terror withdraws.   175

---

12. Cf. Horace, *Odes* 4.10.3.
13. Cf. Vergil, *Aeneid* 7.72-75.

Winter with shivering fingers lets fall[14]
Over the forum a mantle of snow,
Covering Eulalia's mortal remains
Lying there under the glacial skies
With a white pall of the crystalline flakes.   180

Let the funereal mourners who stand
Round the sad bier and lament for the dead
Gather not here with their clamorous plaints:
God bids the elements render to thee,
Maiden illustrious, obsequies meet.   185

Merida is where the martyr now rests,
City renowned of Vettonian plain,
Washed by the waters of Ana's green stream
Sweeping along with its turbulent tide
Past the fair walls that encircle the town.   190

Favored indeed is the land that preserves
Safe in its bosom her relics sublime:
There, in a temple agleam with the light
Glancing from marbles of Spain and the world,
Shrined are Eulalia's sacred remains.   195

Overhead shines the glittering dome,
Ruddily gleaming with fretting of gold.[15]
Splendid mosaic the pavement adorns,
So that it seems like a meadow in bloom
Teeming with flowers of manifold hues.   200

---

14. Cf. *Ibid.* 3.285.
15. Cf. *Ibid.* 1.726.

Gather the violets purpling the fields,
Pluck the bright crocus that everywhere grows!
Genial winter, relaxing its frost,[16]
Thaws out the chill of the nurturing clods,
Heaping our baskets with radiant flowers.   205

Offer, O children, as gifts to our saint,
Garlands and wreaths of these blossoms entwined!
Mine shall be dactyls to sing in the choir:
Feeble and dull, they may limp with old age,
Yet they shall gladden Eulalia's feast.   210

Thus we shall honor her relics enshrined
Here in this altar raised up in her name.
She, at the foot of God's heavenly throne,
Touched by our prayers and melodious hymns,
Graciously smiles on her people below.   215

---
16. Cf. Vergil, *Georgics* 1.302.

4. HYMN IN HONOR OF THE EIGHTEEN HOLY MARTYRS OF SARAGOSSA[1]

In one tomb the ashes of eighteen martyrs
My own native country preserves and honors;
Saragossa call we the noble city,
    Guarding these treasures.

---
1. This hymn of Prudentius is the earliest known written account of the eighteen martyrs of Saragossa. According to the Acts they

Home of this great throng of angelic patrons, 5
It fears not the frangible world's destruction,[2]
For it praises Christ with these precious offerings
    Hid in its bosom.

When God will appear in the clouds of heaven,[3]
With His right hand brandishing fiery lightnings,[4] 10
To weigh all the peoples in scales of justice
    Equally balanced,

From the farthest corners of earth each city,
Lifting its bright head, will then go to meet Him,[5]
Bringing precious relics in golden vessels, 15
    Gifts to Him offered.

Afric Carthage proudly will show thy ashes,
O Cyprian, eloquent saint and scholar;
Triple crowns, with Zoilus and Acisclus,
    Cordova will bring. 20

To Christ you will offer a precious garland,
Tarragona, mother of holy martyrs;
Fructuosus wove for you this resplendent
    Crown with three jewels.[6]

---

suffered martyrdom in that city during the reign of Diocletian (BHL 1503-1507). To the eighteen martyrs, Prudentius adds the names of Encratis, or Encratia, Caius and Crementius, who also suffered at Saragossa, and St. Vincent who was born there. Portions of the hymn are used in the Mozarabic Breviary for the feast of St. Engratia and the Eighteen Martyrs on April 16: *In festo Sanctae Engratiae, vel decem et octo Martyrum* (PL 86.901-903; 1111).

2. Cf. Horace, *Odes* 3.3.7.
3. Cf. Matt. 24.30.
4. Cf. Seneca, *Phaedra* 161-3; Vergil, *Georgics* 1.328-329.
5. Cf. Vergil, *Aeneid* 8.180-181.
6. Fructuosus and his two deacons Augurius and Eulogius. See Hymn 6, *infra*.

First of the gems set in your chaplet is he, 25
And near are twin stones that in equal splendor
Send forth double rays in their brilliance flaming
    Bright as the lightning.

Small, but rich in relics of saintly martyrs,
Gerona will bring with her pious Felix; 30
Our own Calahorra will bear its heroes
    Twain whom we honor.[7]

Trusting in great Cucuphas, Barcelona
Will rise to meet Christ, and sunshiny Narbonne
Will present Paul; glorious Arles will have you, 35
    Sainted Genesius.

In haste Lusitania's foremost city
Will bring the remains of its hallowed maiden,
Offering them to Christ on the very altar
    Where she is honored.[8] 40

Bearing in its bosom companion martyrs,
Double gift contained in one reliquary,
Alcala[9] will joyfully bring its treasures,
    Justus and Pastor.

Tangier, ancient tomb of the African monarchs, 45
Will present the ashes of holy Cassian,
Who brought the idolatrous pagan peoples
    Into Christ's service.

Some cities will offer to Christ one martyr,
Some with two or three will give glory to Him, 50
Others even five will present as pledges,
    Victims atoning.

---

7. Emeterius and Chelidonius. See Hymn 1, *supra*.
8. St. Eulalia. See Hymn 3, *supra*.
9. Ancient Complutum.

But you, Saragossa, devoted city,
Eighteen saints will bring as your holy dower,
Lifting your head crowned with the yellow olive,   55
    Symbol of concord.

You alone are ready to meet your Saviour,
Bearing such a numerous host of martyrs;
You alone, lavish in faith and worship,
    Merit such graces.   60

Scarcely can the head of the Punic kingdom,[10]
Scarce can Rome itself on its throne imperial,
Surpass you, our glorious city, in the[11]
    Gifts to God offered.

From every portal the blood here poured out   65
Has debarred the envious race of demons
And has banished far from the chastened city
    Sinister shadows.

Powers of darkness lurk not within its ramparts,
For the vanquished Serpent avoids this people;   70
Christ now dwells in all of its market places,
    Christ everywhere present.

You would think this land whence ascends to heaven
Such a mighty chorus of white-robed martyrs
Had been set apart for the sacred laurels   75
    Won by these heroes.

---
10. Carthage.
11. Cf. Vergil, *Aeneid* 6.546.

It was here, O Vincent, your palm was nurtured,
It was here the priesthood won splendid trophies;
Here was the homeland of the mitred bishops,
  Sons of Valerius.[12]   80

When of old the tempest of persecution
Swept over the earth in its savage fury,
Its wrath always fell with more terrifying
  Rage on that temple.

Nor did the storm ever abate its fury   85
Without bringing fame to our native country
By the noble blood that was always freely
  Shed by its martyrs.

Did you not, O Vincent, heroic witness,
Destined to meet death in a strange arena,   90
Presage your ordeal by blood that moistened
  Streets of this city?[13]

These drops the saint's townsmen preserve and cherish
As though their soil sheltered his very body
And his sacred relics were resting in the   95
  Tomb of his fathers.

---

12. Valerius, Bishop of Saragossa, is mentioned in the Roman Martyrology for January 28. According to the Acts of St. Vincent, he was arrested at Saragossa with his deacon Vincent. See *Acta Sanctorum*, January, 2.394.
13. Reference is made to this tradition in an epigram of Eugene II, Archbishop of Toledo (647-657), *De basilica sancti Vincentii in Caesaraugusta, ubi dicitur cruor eius effluxisse* (PL 87.361).

Ours he is, although in a foreign city[14]
He endured the pangs of his cruel passion,
Favoring with his shrine on the seashore near by
    Lofty Saguntum.[15]   100

Ours he was, a boy in our palaestra,
Where he, with the chrism of faith anointed,
Learned the art of wrestling with powers of evil
    Prompted by Satan.

He knew that in this blessed sanctuary   105
Eighteen famous martyrs had won their trophies,
And stirred by these laurels he soon competed
    For the same glory.

Here, Encratia,[16] is preserved the memory
Of the holy virtues that fortified you   110
In scorning this world and its base allurements,
    Violent maiden.

To no other martyr, life's breath retaining,
Was to dwell on earth again ever granted.
You alone, your terrible throes surviving,   115
    Lived in our country.

You lived and rehearsed step by step your tortures,
And having as token your mangled body,
You told how the blows of the ax and cudgel
    Carved bitter furrows.   120

---

14. Valencia, where Vincent suffered martyrdom.
15. A city about sixteen miles north of Valencia.
16. Encratis is included in the Acts of the Saragossan martyrs, though it is not known whether she suffered with them during the persecution of Diocletian.

Both your sides the torturer sorely wounded,[17]
And the red blood streamed forth from all the gashes.
Heart-deep the blade cut as the breast he severed,
    Baring your bosom.

Less the price of dying in midst of torments,   125
For death brings surcease to the bitter anguish
And gives speedy rest to the aching members,
    Sleep everlasting.

You, Encratia, your deep wound still bleeding,
Lived on, the sharp pangs in your veins abiding,[18]   130
As the fetid humor flowed through your members,
    Causing corruption.

Although the fell sword of the persecutor
Stayed the final blow of your immolation,
Yet the martyr's crown you now merit fully,   135
    Maiden undaunted.

We have seen your flesh torn by cruel pincers,
Lying far off, clutched in the claws of iron.
Pale death had a part of your precious body,
    While you were living.   140

Christ Himself has given this newest garland
For the adornment of our Saragossa,
That it be the home of a living martyr,
    Her holy temple.

City sanctified by eighteen white togas,   145
By Optatus and Lupercus made famous,
Advance, as you praise with loud hymns of joy
    Your chosen senate.

---

17. Cf. Horace, *Odes* 3.5.49.
18. Cf. Claudian, 2 *In Rufinum* 280.

Sing acts of Successus and Martial's glory,
Celebrate the triumph of blessed Urban, 150
Honor Julia and Quintilianus,
    Chanting their praises.

Let Publius be extolled by the chorus,
Tell of trophies that were won by Fronto,
What good Felix suffered and what the gallant 155
    Cecilianus,

How much blood, Evotius, stained your combats,
And yours, too, belligerent Primitivus;
Let hymns never-ending recount your triumphs,
    O Apodemus. 160

It remains for us yet to chant the glories
Of four great heroes, though this line forbids it,[19]
Who under the surname of Saturninus
    Were once remembered.

Love of the bright names of these holy martyrs 165
Makes light of the laws of poetic numbers,
And the bard is never unskilled or errant
    Who sings their praises.

Every measure used by him in reciting
Names written by Christ in the book of heaven 170
That will be unsealed at the day of judgement
    Is full of sweetness.

Then before the Father and Son an angel
Will call out the names of the eighteen martyrs
Who by right of sepulture have dominion 175
    Over one city.

---

19. The poet violates the sapphic metre when he begins line 163 with a spondee: *Quos Saturninos memorat vocatos.*

HYMNS   145

To this honored roll will he add a maiden
Who lived after suffering every torture,
And Vincent whose glory had its beginning
    In the blood shed here.   180

[You, Gaius, will not be omitted, nor you,[20]
O Crementius, (for you both merit mention)
Who brought back with you from a second combat
    Laurels unbloody.[21]

Both of these confessors of God resisted   185
With undaunted courage the fiendish brigands;
Both tasted lightly of the martyr's torments,
    Savored with joy.]

From their place beneath the eternal altar[22]
This mighty throng of empurpled heroes,   190
Cherished by our city, now begs forgiveness
    For our transgressions.

Grant to me, now bathing these graven marbles
With my pious tears in the hope of mercy,
That I may be loosed from the chains that shackle   195
    And hold me captive.

Prostrate yourself here with me, noble city,
At the sacred tombs of your holy martyrs;
Thence you will soon follow them risen once more,
    Body and spirit.   200

---

20. Bergman encloses lines 181-188 in brackets to indicate their omission in *A*, the oldest MS of Prudentius.
21. According to Arevalus, 'second combat' may mean that Caius and Crementius did not die as martyrs, but suffered torments as confessors of the faith in a secondary or less glorious ordeal. The Roman Martyrology for April 16 says that they suffered a second time and tasted the cup of martyrdom. See Paulinus of Nola, *Poema* 21.147-148 (PL 61.573).
22. Cf. Apoc. 6.9.

5. THE PASSION OF THE HOLY MARTYR VINCENT.¹

O holy martyr Vincent, bless
This your triumphant festal day,²
On which you purchased with your blood
The glorious crown of victory.³

The conqueror of a brutal judge, 5
This day, from earth's dark shadows freed,
To highest heaven you advanced
Rejoicing, to the throne of Christ.

---

1. At the beginning of the fifth century the story of the martyrdom of St. Vincent had been transmitted to posterity in three documents or groups of documents: the Passion, or Acts, this hymn of Prudentius, and the sermons of St. Augustine. (See B. de Gaiffier, S.J., 'Sermons latins en honneur de S. Vincent antérieur au Xᵉ siècle,' *Analecta Bollandiana* 67.267). The Passion as it is known today (BHL 8627-8636) may not have antedated Prudentius, though St. Augustine mentions in his sermons on St. Vincent that the Passion of the martyr had just been read (PL 38.1253, 1254, 1255), and this was probably in its main outlines the same as the Acts that are now extant. According to tradition, St. Vincent suffered martyrdom in the year 303 during the persecution of Diocletian and Maximian. Lines 1-288 and 537-576 of the hymn are used in the Mozarabic Breviary for Vespers and Lauds of the feast of the saint (PL 86.1067-1068; 1073-1078). The *inlatio* of the Mass of St. Vincent in the Mozarabic Missal summarizes the details of the Passion as related in Prudentius and in the Acts (PL 85.678-681).
2. Cf. Horace, *Epodes* 8.12.
3. Cf. Apoc. 7.9; James 1.12; Damasus, *Epigram* 39.9 (Ferrua, *op. cit.* 179).

Companion now of angel hosts,
You shine resplendent in the robe[4]   10
That you, undaunted martyr, washed
In rosy streams of your own blood,

When, armed with Rome's atrocious laws,
The satellite of idols false
Strove by the force of iron chains   15
To make you worship pagan gods.

At first he tried to win the saint
By gush of soft, cajoling words,
As ravening wolf, ere it devours
The trustful calf, disports with it.   20

'The king,' he said, 'of all the world,
Who wields the sceptre of the state,[5]
Has now decreed that every man
Observe the cult of ancient gods.

'You stubborn Nazarenes, attend!   25
Renounce your rude, unseemly rites;
These gods of stone our prince adores
Appease with smoke of sacrifice.'

In answer Vincent then cries out,
A levite of the sacred tribe,   30
Who at God's altar stands and serves,
One of the seven pillars white:[6]

'Let these dark fiends rule over you,
Bow down before your wood and stone;
Be you the lifeless pontifex   35
Of gods as dead as you, yourself.

---

4. Cf. Apoc. 3.5, 6.11. Also Eccle. 50.11.
5. Cf. Seneca, *Troades* 771.
6. Cf. Acts 6.3.

'But we, O Dacian, will confess
The Father, Author of all light,
And Jesus Christ, His only Son,
As one true God, and Him adore.'[7] 40

Stirred now to wrath the Prefect roared:
'Do you then dare, unhappy wretch,[8]
To scorn with vile insulting words
This law of gods and lords of earth,

'A law both civic and divine, 45
Which all the human race obeys?
Does not the peril threatening you
Have power to check your youthful rage?

'Give ear to this fiat of mine:
You must now at this altar pray 50
And offer up incense and turf,[9]
Or bloody death will be your lot.'

To him the martyr answer made:
'Come then, put forth your utmost strength,
Use every force at your command, 55
And I will still defy your laws.

'Hear you the creed that we profess:
Christ and the Father are one God,
Him we confess, and Him we serve;
Destroy this faith, if you have power. 60

'Your tortures are to Christians sweet,
The iron hooks and prison chains,
The hissing flames and red-hot grates,
And even death, the final doom.

---

7. Cf. 1 John 1.5,7.
8. Cf. Horace, *Epodes* 12.25.
9. Cf. Horace, *Odes* 1.19.13-14; 3.8.2-4.

'How senseless are your false beliefs,   65
How stupid Caesar's stern decree!
You order us to worship gods
That match your own intelligence,

'Gods hewn by hand of artisan
And by the hollow bellows forged;   70
They have no power to speak or move
But motionless, are blind and dumb.

'For these your costly temples rise
Resplendent with their marble walls;
For these the lowing bullocks yield   75
Their necks to sacrificial ax.

'But in them spirits dwell, you say;
Yes, but infernal powers they are,
Restless, ferocious, and unclean,
Who seek your everlasting ruin.[10]   80

'They trap you in their hidden snares
And lead you into every vice:
To put just men to cruel death
And pious Christians persecute.

'Well do they know and understand   85
That Christ still lives and reigns on high,
And that His kingdom soon to come
Shall to the wicked terror strike.

---

10. Cf. Minucius Felix, *Octavius* 26.8 (Trans. in Vol. 10, this series, p. 378).

'They loudly cry as they confess
That by the power and name of Christ   90
They are cast out of men possessed,[11]
These demons foul, who are your gods.'[12]

No longer could the wicked judge
Endure the martyr's ringing words.
'Silence the wretch,' he madly cries;   95
'Stop his contemptuous blasphemies!

'Come, stifle his malicious words,
And to the lictors give him up,
Those Plutos of condemned outlaws
Who feed on torn and mangled flesh!   100

'Now I shall make this railer feel
The force of our praetorian law;
Due punishment he shall receive
Who mocks and ridicules our gods.

'Do you think, rogue, that you alone   105
May trample on Tarpeian rites,
That you alone may disobey
The Senate, Caesar, mighty Rome?

'Come tie his hands behind his back
And on the rack his body turn,   110
Until you break his tortured limbs
And tear asunder every joint.

'When this is done, flay him alive
With piercing blows that bare the ribs,
So that through deep and gaping wounds   115
The throbbing entrails may be seen.'

---
11. Cf. Matt. 8.28-29.
12. Cf. 1 Cor. 10.20.

At these torments God's soldier laughed,
As he rebuked the bloody crew
Because the clawing iron hooks
Did not more deeply pierce his flesh.   120

Meanwhile the executioners
Were wholly spent in rending him,
And breathless labor had worn out
The muscles of their weary arms.

The martyr now in ecstasy,   125
No shadow of his bitter pain
Upon his shining countenance,
In vision, saw Thee near, O Christ.

'O shame! What face the man puts on!'
Cried Dacian in an angry voice.   130
'More ardent than his torturers
He beams with joy and courts their blows!

'None of the blows so often dealt
In punishing these miscreants
Have power to hurt in this combat,   135
And all their lethal strength is foiled.

'But you, brought up in prison keeps,
A pair I've never seen outdone,
Leave off and rest your hands awhile,
That your tired sinews may revive.   140

'Then when his open wounds are dry,
And clotted blood has formed hard scabs,
Your hands may plough them up again
And rend anew his tortured frame.'

To him the levite makes reply: 145
'If now you see that all the strength
Of your vile dogs is giving way,
Come, mighty slaughterer, yourself,

'Come, show them how to cleave my flesh
And my inmost recesses bare; 150
Put in your hands and deeply drink
The warm and ruddy streams of blood.

'You err, unfeeling brute, if you
Imagine that you punish me
When you dismember me and kill 155
A body that is doomed to die.

'There is within my being's depths
Another none can violate,[13]
Unfettered, tranquil and unmarred,
Immune from pain and suffering. 160

'This body that you seek to maim
With such a show of frenzied strength
Is but a fragile vase of clay
That must be shattered in some wise.[14]

'Nay rather strive to lacerate 165
And smite with cruel stinging lash
The spirit that within me dwells
And tramples on your senseless rage.

'This spirit strike, this spirit crush,
This being free, invincible, 170
And subject to no violent storms,
Subservient to God alone.'

---
13. Cf. 2 Cor. 4.16.
14. Cf. 2 Cor. 4.7.

Thus spoke the saint, and once again
The grinding hooks tear at his flesh.
Then serpent-like, with crafty lips,   175
The prefect hisses forth these words:

'If such headstrong perversity
So steels that thick-skinned heart of yours
That you disdain to touch the couch
On which our sacred gods recline,[15]   180

'Show us your scriptures and the tomes
That you conceal in secret nooks,
That we may give to vengeful fires
Your creed that sows such evil seeds.'

On hearing this the martyr cries: 185
'You threaten, wicked judge, to burn
Our mystic books,[16] but far more just
Will be the fire prepared for you.

'For God's avenging sword will smite
The tongue that speaks such baneful words   190
Against our scriptures, heaven-sent,
And sear it with a lightning flash.

'You see the embers that bespeak
Gomorrha's crimes and shameless sins,
And ashes strewn on Sodom's ground   195
Are witness of eternal death.[17]

---

15. In the *lectisternium* the images of the gods were placed upon a couch as guests of the feast. Cf. Horace, *Odes* 1.37.3-4.
16. In 303 Diocletian ordered the sacred books of the Christians to be burned. See Hymn 1, n. 24, *supra*.
17. Cf. Gen. 19.24-25.

'This, serpent, shadows forth your doom,
The fumes of sulphur, black and foul,
The mingled pitch and tar that soon
Will wrap you in the depths of hell.' 200

The tyrant, maddened at these words
Turns pale, then red with burning rage;
He rolls his frenzied blood-shot eyes,[18]
Foams at the mouth, and grinds his teeth.

Then after some delay, he roared: 205
'Let trial by torture now be made,
The crown of all our punishments,
The gridiron, flames, and red-hot plates.'

The martyr hurries with swift steps
To undergo these torments fierce; 210
On wings of joy he flies ahead
Of hastening ministers of pain.

They reach the glorious wrestling-ground,
Where faith contends with cruelty,
Where martyr and tormentor join 215
In fearful hand to hand conflict.

A gridiron with its cruel spikes,
Set far apart, a rough bed makes,
And under it the glowing coals
Breathe forth the fumes of torturing heat. 220

No trace of fear upon his brow,
The holy man now mounts this pyre,
As though ascending upon high
To take possession of his crown.

---
18. Cf. Vergil, *Aeneid* 7.448-449.

Bestrewn with salt, the crackling fire 225
Sends forth bright sparks from underneath
That here and there implant themselves
With sizzling punctures in his flesh.

The wounds made by the blazing darts
Are bathed in fat that oozes forth 230
And slowly covers all his frame
With copious dew of smoking oil.

Unmoved amid these sufferings,[19]
As though unconscious of his pain,
The saint to Heaven lifts his eyes, 235
For heavy fetters stay his hands.[20]

Then from his fiery bed of pain,
More brave than ever, he is raised
And cast into a dungeon foul
Lest light sustain his lofty spirit. 240

There is within the prison hold,
Deep down, a place of blacker shades,
And here low-hanging stones enclose
A stifling subterranean crypt.

Eternal night lurks in this place[21] 245
That never sees the star of day,
And it is said this dungeon holds
A dread inferno of its own.

The angry foe now hurls the saint
Into this pit of deepest woe 250
And thrusts his feet in wooden stocks
With tortured limbs set far apart.

---
19. Cf. *Ibid.* 4.449.
20. Cf. *Ibid.* 2.405-406.
21. Cf. Seneca, *Hercules Furens* 610.

The monster skilled in penal art
Then adds a torment new and strange,
To no oppressor known before,   255
Recorded in no previous age.

He orders broken earthenware,[22]
Sharp-cornered, jagged, piercing keen,
Spread out upon the dungeon floor
To make for him a painful bed.   260

Fierce torments arm this resting place,
Set everywhere with cruel spikes
That stab his body from below
And render vain all hope of sleep.

The clever tyrant had devised   265
This scheme with diabolic skill,
But Christ frustrates the cunning plan
Concocted by Beelzebub.

The darkness of the prison cell
Now glows with strange refulgent light,   270
The stocks fly open as the bolts
Leap forth from out their double holes.

And then does Vincent recognize
That Christ, the Source of light, has come
To bring the promised recompense   275
For all the pangs he has endured.

He sees the broken earthenware
Now clothe itself with tender flowers
That fill the narrow prison vault
With fragrance like to nectar sweet.   280

---
22. Cf. Damasus, *Epigram* 27.5 (Ihm, *op. cit.* p. 32); also Paulinus of Nola, *Poema* 15.185 (PL 61.472) and *Epistola* 18.7 (PL 61.241).

And then around the martyr throngs
A host of angels greeting him,
Of whom one of majestic mien
Accosts the hero in these words:

'Arise, O glorious martyr saint, 285
Arise, set free from all your chains,
Arise, now member of our band,
And join our noble company.

'You have already run your course
Of frightful pain and suffering; 290
Your passion's goal is now attained,
And death now gives you kind release.

'O dauntless soldier, unsubdued,
The bravest of all warriors brave,
Your very torments, fierce and grim 295
Give way before your conquering arm.

'Christ, God, who watched your gallant fight,
Rewards you with eternal life
And crowns you with His own right hand
As sharer of His bitter cross. 300

'Forsake this fragile earthly vase,
This mortal fabric shaped from dust
That soon will crumble and decay
And, free at last, mount to the skies.'

The angel ceased; the light within 305
Then penetrates the bolted doors,
And through the narrow crevices
Its hidden splendor is revealed.

The guardian of the dim threshold,
Who had been stationed there to watch   310
The lethal chamber through the night,
Awed at this marvel, stands aghast.

He hears, besides, the tuneful hymn
The martyr in his prison sings,
And echoing from the hollow cell,   315
A voice chanting in response.

Then, trembling, he draws near the door
And plants his eyes against the jamb
That he may through the narrow slit
Explore the room as best he can.   320

He sees the bed of potsherds bloom
With fragrant flowers of many hues,
And, singing as he walks about,
The saint himself with fetters loosed.

The prefect of this wonder hears;   325
Enraged, he weeps at his defeat,
And mulling over his disgrace,
He groans with anger and chagrin.

'Remove him from his cell,' he cries,
'And bathe his wounds with healing balms,   330
That when he is somewhat restored,
He may be food for further pangs.'

From all the city you might see
The faithful thronging to the scene
To make for him an easeful bed   335
And wipe the blood from gaping wounds.

They kiss the double furrows made
By cruel lacerating claws,
And even lick with pious joy
His body stained with purpling gore.   340

And many moisten linen cloths
With blood that oozes from his wounds
To keep as relics in their homes
For generations yet to come.

The warden of the prison cell   345
And keeper of its bolted doors,
As old tradition witnesses,
Accepted Christ with sudden faith.

He in amazement had beheld
Through doors fast-locked by iron bars   350
The darkness of that dungeon glow
With brightness of unwonted light.

Soon as the holy martyr tastes
The soothing quiet of his couch,
Worn out by tedious delays   355
And burning with a thirst for death—

If that should be accounted death
Which sets the fettered spirit free
From its dark prison house of flesh
And gives it back to God, its Source,   360

That spirit purified by blood
And washed in death's baptism clean,
Which gave itself, its very life,
To Christ in willing sacrifice—

The saint now rests his weary head 365
Upon the silken coverlets;
His soul soon quits his mortal frame
And mounts in triumph to the skies.

A way is opened straight for him
That to the Father leads on high, 370
The way which holy Abel trod
When by his brother he was slain.[23]

As he ascends, around him throngs
A white-robed company of saints,
And John the Baptist summons him, 375
Like to himself from prison freed.[24]

The hater of the Christian name,
His bitter venom foiled at last,[25]
Was now consumed with furious ire
That burned within his vengeful heart. 380

As serpent of its fangs bereft
The madman raged in frenzy wild.
'The rebel has evaded me
And carried off the palm,' he cries.

'Though he be dead, I still can wreak 385
One last outrage upon the wretch:
I'll throw his body to the beasts,
Or give it to the dogs to rend.

---

23. Cf. Gen. 4.8.
24. Cf. Matt. 14.10.
25. Cf. Vergil, *Aeneid* 12.857; Damasus *Epigram* 46.7 (Ihm, *op. cit.* p. 49).

'His very bones I shall destroy,
Lest in an honored tomb they rest,   390
Where vulgar crowds may worship him
And name of martyr there inscribe.'

Thus raved the sacrilegious judge,
And then (O crime unspeakable!) [26]
The sacred body he exposed,   395
All naked in a sedgy marsh.

But neither ravening beast nor bird,
In hunger, dared to desecrate
With gnawing teeth and claws unclean[27]
The glorious relics of the saint.   400

When at a distance some foul hawk
Flew round about with raucous cries,[28]
A savage bird with fierce onslaught
Drove it away in craven flight.

It was a raven, bird once sent   405
To bring Elias food and drink,[29]
That did this service to the saint
And stood on guard with tireless zeal.

Out of a thickset copse nearby
It drove a huge ferocious wolf,   410
Attacking him with noisy wings
And blinding him with pinions strong.[30]

---
26. Cf. Vergil, *Aeneid* 4.563.
27. Cf. *Ibid.* 3.216-218, 262.
28. Cf. *Ibid.* 3.226, 233.
29. Cf. 3 Kings 17.6.
30. Cf. Vergil, *Aeneid* 12.876-877.

Which of those butchers would presume
To think that such a ravenous beast,
With power to conquer savage bulls,   415
Would yield before a feather's touch?

The wolf skulked off with sullen growl,
Browbeaten by the swooping wings,
And left his hoped-for prey behind
At threats from that unwarlike guard.   420

What, Dacian, did you feel, when news
Of these great wonders reached your ears?[31]
What hidden arrows pierced your heart
And made you groan with bitter rage,

When by the power of a corpse   425
You saw yourself outwitted so,
A match not even for dead bones,
And subject to the lifeless clay?

Will any sign from Heaven sent
Avail, mad tyrant, to arrest   430
That headstrong violence of yours?
Will nothing break your stubborn will?

'No, never will I stay my hand,
For even if the fierce wild beasts
Grow tame, and raven cormorants   435
Become benign and merciful,

'I'll plunge the body in the sea;
The raging billows never spare
The shipwrecked sailors of the main;
The foaming deep is pitiless.   440

---

31. Cf. *Ibid.* 4.408.

'There drifting ever with the tide,
It will be tossed about by storms,
The plaything of the wandering winds[32]
And food for shoals of hungry fish,

'Or underneath the rugged cliffs 445
That rise around a distant bay,
The jagged points of flinty rocks
Will tear and rend his harrowed flesh.

'Is there some man among you here
Who, skilled in piloting a boat 450
With oar and rope and hoisted sail,
Can briskly plow the open sea?

'Go, take the body that now lies
Unharmed among the marshy reeds
And, in a wherry light and swift, 455
Bear it away through surging tides.

'Wrap up the corpse and then enclose
It in a sack of rushes made,
To which a heavy stone is tied,
That it may sink into the deep. 460

'Push out across the ocean waves,
With dripping oar-blades flying swift,
Until the distance hides from view
The shore that you have left behind.'

And then a soldier, moved by hate, 465
Makes haste to carry out the charge,
A fierce, hot-headed ruffian,
Who bore the name Eumorphio.

---

32. Cf. Lucan, *De bello civili* 708-710.

Straightway he weaves a net of ropes,
In which he sews the lifeless form; 470
Then to mid-sea he steers his course
And hurls it out into the waves.

O mighty is the power of God,
The power that all things did create,
That calmed the waters of the sea 475
When Christ upon its surface walked,[33]

So that in treading on the waves,
He moved dry-shod across the deep,
Nor ever did He wet his soles
As light He skimmed the surging flood.[34] 480

That same almighty Power enjoined
The Red Sea once to open wide,
The while the people fearless trod
A pathway dry upon its bed.[35]

And now this Power commands the sea 485
To serve the body of the saint
By moving with unruffled tide
Directly toward the curving shore.

The heavy millstone swims along
As lightly as the snow-white foam; 490
The bag that holds the sacred pledge
Is borne on top of swelling waves.

---
33. Cf. Mark 6.48-49.
34. Cf. Vergil, *Aeneid* 7.810-811.
35. Cf. Exod. 14.21-22; Ps. 77.13.

Aghast, the baffled mariners
Behold it floating calmly back
Across the level, shining sea, 495
Sped on by favoring tide and wind.[36]

With rapid oars they cleave the main,
As wroth they urge their vessel on,
But far ahead the body flies
Into a quiet, secluded bay. 500

And so at last the peaceful earth
Again receives the sacred form
Before the skiff can touch the shore,[37]
Though driven at its utmost speed.

How happy was that friendly beach 505
Which cherished in its mellow sands
The martyr's consecrated flesh,
And gave it place of sepulture,

Until the saints with pious care
Could raise with tears a splendid mound 510
And place the body in a tomb
To wait in peace for future'life!

But when the foe at last was quelled,
And peace was granted to the just,
A temple gave the blessed bones 515
The resting-place that was their due.

Within the sanctuary laid
And buried at the altar's foot,
They breathe the sweet incense exhaled
Before the holy sacrifice. 520

---
36. Cf. Vergil, *Aeneid* 10.687.
37. Cf. Vergil, *Georgics* 1.303.

Such was the body's destiny,
But in the house of God the soul
Now dwells with brothers Maccabees[38]
And near Isaias, sawed apart.[39]

But these a single crown obtained 525
For all the pains that they endured,
Because the final blow of death
Released them from their cruel pangs.

Did he who once asunder cut
Isaias' body with a saw 530
Dare throw the segments to wild beasts
Or give them to the ocean's waves?

Or did the tyrant, who plucked out
The Maccabean martyr's tongue
And tore the scalp from off his head,[40] 535
These relics fling to cruel birds?

O doubly noble, you alone
Have won a glorious two-fold crown;
Two laurels you alone have twined
As trophies of your victory. 540

A conqueror first in cruel death,
You afterwards like triumph gained
When with your lifeless frame alone
You trampled on the wicked fiend.

Be with us now and hear the prayers 545
We raise with humble voices here;
Ask pardon for our grievous sins,
Our advocate at God's high throne.

---

38. Cf. 2 Mach. 7.
39. Cf. Tertullian *De patientia* 14 (Trans. in Vol. 40, this series, p. 218); also Jerome, *Commentaria in Isaiam prophetam* 15.57.
40. Cf. 2 Mach. 7.4.

By your own self, by prison cell
In which your glory was enhanced, 550
By galling chains and fires and hooks,
By shackling stocks that held you fast,

By keen-edged broken earthenware
That made your halo brighter still,
And by the bed that in this age 555
We kiss with reverential awe,

Have pity on our fervent prayers,
That Christ in mercy may incline
His ear to us, his followers,
And charge us not with all our sins. 560

If we with joyful heart and tongue
Observe your feast with solemn rites
And kneel before this holy shrine
Where your exalted relics lie,

Come hither for a little while 565
And win for us the grace of Christ,
That souls oppressed by sin may feel
The solace of His pardoning love.

So may the time be not far off
When your undaunted spirit will wear 570
Its glorious risen flesh once more,
Which equal martyrdom endured;

And as the body shared in pains
And bore in common every storm,
So may it be coheir in bliss 575
While never-ending ages run.

6. A HYMN IN HONOR OF THE MOST BLESSED MARTYRS FRUCTUOSUS, BISHOP OF THE CHURCH OF TARRAGONA, AND AUGURIUS AND EULOGIUS, DEACONS[1]

Tarragona, O Fructuosus, raises
High its fortunate head agleam with splendor
From the fires lit for you and your two deacons.

God regards with benevolence the Spanish,
For the Trinity singularly honors   5
This Iberian city with three martyrs.

Bright Augurius seeks the highest heavens,
And Eulogius shining not less brightly
Takes his flight to the throne of Christ supernal.

---

1. Both Prudentius and Augustine were evidently acquainted with the Acts of Fructuosus, which hagiographers agree in considering authentic (BHL 3196). See J. Serra-Vilaro, *Fructuos, Auguri i Eulogi, Martirs Sants de Tarragona*, 35-50 and Augustine, *Sermon* 273 (PL 38.1247-1252). All the episodes related in the Acts are found in this hymn, and St. Augustine in his sermon for the feast of the martyrs, which followed the reading of their Passion, quotes directly from the Acts in two instances (*Sermon* 273.2-3). According to these Acts St. Fructuosus and his two deacons suffered martyrdom at Tarragona in the year 259 during the persecution of Valerian and Gallienus. The entire hymn of Prudentius is used for Matins and Lauds of their feast in the Mozarabic Breviary (PL 86.1061-1065).

Their guide, Master, and teacher, Fructuosus,   10
To the heavenly heights advanced in glory,
Dignified by the holy name of bishop.

Summoned all of a sudden to the forum
By command of the judge, the holy prelate
Had appeared with his levites as companions.   15

As the butcher, who fed on blood, was dragging
These heroes to the galling chains of prison,
Fructuosus ran hence with eager joy.

Lest with fear his companions should be stricken
Their courageous instructor urged them forward,   20
Kindling in them the love of Christ the Savior.

'Stand you firm with me, men. The bloody serpent
Calls the servants of God to cruel sufferings.
Be dauntless in death. The palm awaits you.

'For Christ's followers prison leads to victory,   25
Prison wafts them up to the heights of heaven,
Prison wins for them God's eternal blessings.'

At these words they approached the prison
   stronghold,
Where, performing baptism's mystic cleansing,[2]
They confounded the darkness with its waters.   30

For six days in this prison they lay hidden;
Then they stood at their cruel foe's tribunal,
And the gridirons shuddered at the trio.

---

2. According to the Acts Fructuosus baptized a neophyte named Rogatianus while he was in prison.

With a menacing look, Aemilianus,[3]
The proud, impious prefect, fierce and brutal, 35
Bade them worship at altars of the demons.

'You, false teacher, who sow this modern fiction,
This new doctrine that makes your fickle maidens
Forsake Jupiter's sacred groves and forests,

'If you now have good sense you will relinquish 40
This old woman's belief,[4] for Gallienus
Has decreed that all worship as he worships.'

At this mandate the gentle prelate answers:
'The eternal monarch of days I worship,
The Creator and Lord of Gallienus, 45

'And Christ, Son of the everlasting Father.
His servant, of His flock I am the shepherd.'
The judge smiled on him:[5] 'You are that no longer.'

Mad with passion, he cannot curb his anger,
And ordains cruel fires for the martyrs. 50
They, rejoicing, restrain the tearful mourners.

Certain ones from the crowd a cup presented
For the bishop to quaff, but he refused it,
Saying, 'I will not drink, for we are fasting.

---

3. Governor of Spain under Valerian and Gallienus.
4. Cf. Horace, *Satires* 2.6.77-78.
5. Cf. Vergil, *Aeneid* 1.254. See Mahoney, *Vergil in the Works of Prudentius* 165.

'The ninth hour has not freed us from this duty;[6] 55
Never will I transgress this sacred precept,
Nor will death itself slacken my observance.[7]

'Thus did Christ in the hour of crucifixion
Spurn the cup that was offered when He thirsted,[8]
And refusing to drink, prolonged His anguish.' 60

Now at last they approach the vast arena,
By its circular tiers of seats surrounded,
Where the mobs drunk with blood of wild beasts
  gather

And applaud with delight the gory pageants
During which gladiators, held as nothing, 65
Fall beneath the keen thrust of cruel sabers.

Here a swarthy assassin had made ready
For their torture a pyre of blazing fagots,
And was laying the last brands on the altar,

Where their bodies would be consumed by burning, 70
And their souls now aflame with love of Heaven
Would be freed from their shattered carnal prison.

Pious friends now came forward to assist them:
One would take off the sandals of the bishop,
Bending low to untie the throngs that bound them. 75

---

6. The fast on Wednesday and Fridays ended at the ninth hour, or about three o'clock in the afternoon. Cf. Tertullian, *De ieiuniis* 10.
7. Cf. Vergil, *Aeneid* 4.27.
8. Cf. Mark 15.23.

But forbidding him, holy Fructuosus
Said to him, 'Do not show us such compassion;
Leave us now, lest you make our death more painful.

'Behold, I myself will unloose my sandals,
That with feet unimpeded by the latchets   80
I may run with swift steps into the furnace.

'Why this grief and cheeks wet with weeping?
Why implore me to keep you in remembrance?
I shall pray unto Christ for all the faithful.'[9]

Scarce these words of assurance had he spoken,[10]   85
When the ties of his sandals he unfastened
As did Moses when he approached the thorn-bush.[11]

For to tread on that fire was not permitted,
Or to draw near to God there truly present,
Till his footmarks were free of all defilement.   90

As with bare feet the martyr there was standing,
Lo the voice of the Spirit from Heaven sounded,
Uttering words that astonished all the hearers:

'This, believe, is not punishment you witness,
These fierce torments that pass in one brief moment   95
And deprive not of life, but recreate it.

'Blest indeed are these souls to whom is given[12]
To mount upwards through fire to heights celestial;[13]
Fires eternal shall flee from them hereafter.'

---

9. Cf. Augustine, *Sermon* 273.2 (PL 38.1249).
10. Cf. Vergil, *Aeneid* 5.693.
11. Cf. Exod. 3.2-6.
12. Cf. Vergil, *Aeneid* 6.669.
13. Cf. Damasus, *Epigram* 33.4 (Ferrua, *op. cit.* p. 168).

At these words with quick steps the martyrs enter   100
The hot furnace of flames that crackle round them
And recoil before them, all atremble.

Soon the fetters that bound their hands behind them[14]
Were consumed in the blaze and quickly falling,
Left the flesh of the holy ones uninjured.   105

For the penal thongs did not dare to hinder
Palms that they would fain lift up to the Father,
Arms in form of a cross in prayer extended.

You would think that you looked upon the trio
Who in midst of the Babylonian furnace   110
Once astounded the tyrant with their singing.[15]

But the reverent flames spared those heroes,
For the era of martyrs was still distant,
Nor had Christ yet revealed that death's rich merit.

While these saints, when the blazing fires retreated,   115
Prayed to God that the flames might rush upon them
And soon bring to an end their dreadful peril.

Sovereign Majesty heard these faithful servants,
And releasing them from their fragile bodies
Bade them come to Himself by death's sure pathway.   120

Then a guard from the palace of the prefect
Saw the heavens stand open for the martyrs,
And the heroes borne through the starry spaces.

---

14. Cf. Vergil, *Aeneid* 2.57.
15. Cf. Dan. 3.23-24.

Nay, he showed to his master's little daughter
This clear sign of her father's reprobation,   125
That those slain in his forum lived in Heaven.

Thus the maiden was favored with the vision,[16]
From her parent enshrouded all in darkness,
That the crime of its lord might warn this household.

Then men sprinkled with wine the sacred relics,   130
And collecting the bones and glowing embers[17]
Each one claimed for himself some precious token.

So intent were the brethren in obtaining
For their homes these blest gifts of holy ashes,
Or to bear them as pledges in their bosoms.   135

But lest sacred remains that soon were destined
To arise and to live with God in Heaven
Should in realms far apart be given burial,

Now appeared the three saints in snowy garments,[18]
And enjoined that their hallowed dust be gathered   140
And enshrined in a sepulchre of marble.

O distinction threefold, O triple glory
That lifts high the proud head of our fair city,
Far above all Hiberia's cities rising!

Let us honor the names of our three patrons   145
Who now cherish and protect the people dwelling
In the lands of the Pyrenean mountains.

---

16. *videre per sudum.* Cf. Vergil, *Aeneid* 8.529.
17. Cf. *Ibid.* 6.227-228.
18. Cf. Apoc. 7.9.

Let a chorus come forward of both sexes:
Youth and maidens and children, men and women,
Sing the praises of your own Fructuosus! 150

Let a psalm now resound to your Augurius,
And Eulogius be praised in equal measures;
Let us raise hymns alike to both these heroes.

In this city let gilded domes re-echo,
Let melodious song rise from the seashore 155
And the billows unite in festal praises.

On that day when the universe will crumble,
Fructuosus will shield you, Tarragona,
From the fires and the terrors of the judgement.

Then perchance he may deign with Christ's
    indulgence 160
To look kindly on me and soothe my torments,
My sweet hendecasyllables recalling.[19]

---

19. The hymn is written in Phalaecian hendecasyllabic verse, or trochaic pentameter with a cyclic dactyl in the second foot. The translation is written in the English accentual equivalent of the classical meter.

7. HYMN IN HONOR OF THE MARTYR QUIRINUS, BISHOP OF THE CHURCH OF SISCIA[1]

Siscia's ramparts enshrine a saint
Cherished with a paternal love,
Quirinus, that illustrious hero,
Whom the Father was pleased to grant
As a martyr to bless that town.   5

In the reign of Galerius
Of Illyrian shores the lord,[2]
Who held sway with oppressive hand,
He enhanced by his glorious death
The renown of the Catholic faith.   10

---

1. St. Quirinus, Bishop of Siscia, now Susak in Yugoslavia, suffered martyrdom under Galerius between the years 305 and 310. The Acts (BHL 7035-7038), which are regarded as substantially genuine, were probably compiled after the time of Prudentius. The poet omits all the details of the arrest, imprisonment and trial of the martyr and confines his narrative to the final episode of his death by drowning. St. Jerome (*Chron. Eusebii*) summarizes in a brief notice for the year 312 all the incidents related by Prudentius. According to the Acts and Martyrology of St. Jerome, St. Quirinus was buried in Sabaria in Hungary. Later the remains were brought to Rome, but the date of the translation is uncertain. Some think that it occurred during the pontificate of Pope Damasus, and that Prudentius in the first stanza of the hymn refers to the tomb of the martyr as preserved in Rome. See Marchesi, *op. cit.* 125.
2. Cf. Vergil, *Aeneid* 1.243.

Not by stroke of relentless sword,
Nor by fire or ferocious beast
Did he suffer a cruel death,
But the tide of a surging stream
Laved him clean as it bore him down.[3]   15

Little matters it whether blood
Or the waves of a glassy stream
Bathe the martyr in death for Christ;
Equal glory adorns his crown
In whatever flood he is washed.   20

Shepherd he, of a holy flock,
From a bridge he was cast headlong
Straight into the tempestuous tide;[4]
By a cable around his neck
Was suspended a heavy stone.   25

But the river received the saint,
As he fell, in a quiet pool,
And it suffered him not to sink,
But miraculously afloat
It upheld the enormous rock.   30

On the ground far above, the crowd
Watched their master with trembling gaze,[5]
For the people of Christ had swarmed
On the banks of the winding stream
In a myriad, anxious throng.   35

---

3. Cf. *Ibid.* 4.635.
4. Cf. Vergil, *Georgics* 1.203.
5. Cf. Vergil, *Aeneid* 9.168-169.

But as Quirinus raised his head,
He beheld with regret the fear
Of that timorous multitude,
While amid the encircling flood
He was heedless of threatening doom. 40

He consoles their devoted hearts,
As he begs them in gentle words
By his plight not to be dismayed,
To their faith to be staunch and true,
Nor to think it an ill to die. 45

While he speaks, the meandering stream
Bears him safe on its tranquil breast,
And the depths that beneath him roll
Dare not yawn to engulf the man,
Or the stone and its dangling rope. 50

Then the bishop and martyr felt
That the merited palm of death
Was about to be snatched from him,[6]
And that stayed was his upward flight
To the Father's eternal throne. 55

'Jesus, Sovereign Lord,' he cried,
'Not to Thee is this wonder new
Or unwonted to tread the sea,
With its turbulent sounding waves,
Or to curb the impetuous stream. 60

'Well we know Thy disciple true,
Peter, who was afraid to plunge
Mortal feet in the surging tide,
Stood secure on the billows' crest
With the help of Thy strong right hand.[7] 65

---

6. Cf. Damasus, *Epigram* 13.5 (Ihm, *op. cit.* p. 20).
7. Cf. Matt. 14.29-31.

'We have heard this example too,
Of the Jordan, that vagrant stream,
Which abruptly reversed its course,
As it rapidly flowed along,
And fled back to its source again.[8]

'Thou, O Lord, dost reveal Thy might
In this miracle witnessed now:
Thou hast willed that I keep afloat
On the top of these surging waves,[9]
Though a stone from my neck is hung.

'Now Thy glory is manifest
And the power of Thy name declared,
While astounded the heathen stand.
Free my soul, O good Lord, I pray
From the bonds that delay its flight.

'By upholding this heavy stone
Do these waters display Thy power.
Grant me now this most precious boon
Still remaining to prove Thy love,
That for Thee I may die, O Christ.'[10]

Thus he prays, and his breathing fails
With his voice and vital warmth;
Then to Heaven his soul ascends
As the weight of the stone bears down,
And the waters receive his form.

---
8. Cf. Jos. 3.13-17.
9. Cf. Vergil, *Aeneid* 9.23.
10. Cf. Ps. 115.6.

8. ON A SPOT IN CALAHORRA WHERE MARTYRS SUFFERED AND WHERE NOW IS A BAPTISTERY[1]

This is a spot that was chosen by Christ for uplifting
  to Heaven
Souls that are tested by blood, souls that are cleansed
  in this font.

Here two brave soldiers once gave up their lives for the
  name of the Savior,
Winning the martyr's bright crown blazoned with
  purpling blood.

Here, too, the mercy of God in a limpid stream
  from this fountain[2]   5
Flows in a healing flood, washing away
  old sins.

---

1. This hymn is written in the manner of the epigrams of Damasus and the inscriptions found on baptisteries of the fourth and fifth centuries. See Schuster, *The Sacramentary* 1.23-25 and Ihm, *op. cit.* 101 and 103; also Paulinus of Nola, *Epistles* 32 (PL 61.332). The fact that the name of the place is omitted in some manuscripts has led editors to see in the hymn a reference to the legend of the baptism of the two soldiers Processus and Martinian by St. Peter in the Mamartine Prison at Rome. The general opinion however is that the martyrs mentioned in lines 3 and 4 are Emeterius and Chelidonius of Calahorra, celebrated by Prudentius in Hymn 1.
2. Cf. Vergil, *Georgics* 2.200.

Let him who fain would mount to the
   lasting kingdom of heaven[3]
Come in his thirst to this font opening
   a luminous way.

Once victorious martyrs to heights celestial
   ascended,
Now from baptismal floods souls to heaven
   take flight.[4]   10

Here the Spirit eternally flowing down on these
   waters,
As He once gave the palm, now gives remission
   of sin.

Be it water or blood, the earth drinks in
   the heavenly shower,[5]
Ever bedewed by this stream, which is poured
   forth to her God.

He of this place is the Lord from whose wounds
   two fountains once issued.   15
Water from one distilled and from the other
   blood.[6]

You will go hence, as to each is the grace,
   through the wounds of the Savior;
One by the way of the sword, one by the water
   will rise.

---
3. Cf. Damasus, *Epigram* 53.8 (Ihm, *op. cit.* p. 55); Juvencus, *Evan. Hist.* 3.400.
4. Cf. Vergil, *Aeneid* 7.343.
5. Cf. *Ibid.* 12.339-340.
6. Cf. John 19.34; also *Cathemerinon* 9, n. 41.

9. THE PASSION OF ST. CASSIAN OF FORUM CORNELII[1]

There is a town where Cornelius Sulla[2]
   established a Forum;
Hence the Italians call it by its founder's name.[3]

There, when to thee, O Rome of the world the mistress,[4] I journeyed,
   Hope in my heart was born that Christ would prosper me.

Prone on the ground I was praying in front of the tomb of the martyr   5
Cassian, who consecrates that soil by his remains.

---

1. This hymn of Prudentius is the oldest extant document concerning the martyrdom of St. Cassian (BHL 1625). The Martyrology of St. Jerome has this entry for August 11, *In Nicopoli, passio multorum martyrum, quorum nomina Deus scit: et passio S. Cassiani*, and it lists the feast of the martyr as occurring on August 13. In lines 17-20 the sacristan tells the poet that the story of St. Cassian is recorded in ancient writings, possibly the original acts no longer extant. Hagiographers list the Passion of Cassian among the Acts possessing some degree of authenticity. Some think that the saint suffered martyrdom during the persecutions of Valerian or Diocletian, while others suggest the time of Julian the Apostate (361-363), who forbade Christians to teach the classics. See Julian, *Epistles* 36 (Wright).
2. Roman dictator, 138-78 B.C.
3. A town in north Italy, now Imola.
4. Cf. Vergil, *Aeneid* 7.602-603.

HYMNS 183

As I was weeping and in my heart I was sadly
    reflecting
On all the sins and griefs and labors of my life,

Towards Heaven I lifted my gaze and beheld
    there before me
A picture of the martyr painted in bright hues,   10

Bearing a thousand wounds that pierced
    every part of his body[5]
And showing all the little gashes in his flesh.

Round him a troup of boys (a pitiful scene!)[6]
    were uniting
To prick and pierce his body with the little styles[7]

They were accustomed to use in imprinting
    the wax of their tablets   15
As they wrote down the humdrum lessons
    of the school.

When I questioned the sacristan, he replied:
    'This, O stranger,
Does not depict a foolish woman's empty tale.[8]

'Pictured here is a story in ancient writings recorded,
    Which manifests the steadfast faith
        of olden times.   20

---

5. Cf. Claudian, *In Rufinum* 2.431.
6. Cf. Vergil, *Aeneid* 6.706; 1.111.
7. Instruments used for writing on tablets of boxwood covered with wax. One end was pointed and the other was flattened for erasing what had been inscribed on the wax.
8. Cf. Horace, *Satires* 2.6.77; also Augustine, *De utilitate credendi* 1.2 (Trans. in Vol. 2, this series, p. 392).

'Cassian conducted a school for boys
    and round him had gathered
  A throng of pupils whom he taught the learned arts.

'Skillful was he in shorthand, a rapid method of
    writing
  Dictated words with symbols pricked upon the
    wax.[9]

'Harsh at times were his rules, and the
    wearisome lessons   25
  Aroused the dread and anger of the youthful mob.

'For the teacher is ever abhorred by beginners
    in learning,
  And discipline is never sweet to any child.[10]

'Then came a tempest that lashed at the faith,
    a dire persecution
  Harassing all the champions of the
    Christian name.   30

'From the midst of his circle of pupils the diligent
    master
  Was dragged because he spurned the pagan
    sacrifice.

'When he who metedced out punishments asked
    what kind of profession
  The rebel of such contumelious spirit pursued,

---

9. A system of shorthand was invented by Tiro, the secretary of Cicero.
10. Cf. Ambrose, *Hexameron* 6.6.38 (PL 14.271).

'One responded, "A band of callow boys
    he teaches,[11]   35
  Instructing them in clever signs for writing words."

' "Take him away," cried the judge; "remove him hence
    as a culprit
  And give him to the children he was wont to flog.

' "Let them make sport of him as they will;
    let them torture him freely,
  And in their master's blood make red
    their truant hands.   40

' "It is a joy to think that the harsh schoolmaster
    will furnish
  Amusement for the pupils he so often curbed."

'Having stripped him, they tie his hands
    securely behind him
  And then the youthful band approaches,
    armed with styles.

'All the anger that they had harbored
    in silent resentment   45
  They now are free to vent on him with bitter gall.

'Some at him hurl their tablets; against his face
    these are shattered,
  And flying wooden splinters penetrate his brow.

'Loudly the wax-covered boxwood breaks
    on his cheeks all abloodied,
  And from the blow the page is wet
    with ruddy dew.   50

---

11. Cf. Vergil, *Aeneid* 5.548-549.

'Others dart at him styles made of iron,
    sharp-pointed and cruel,
  One end of which they use to carve the words in
    wax,

'And the other to blot out the letters engraved
    on its surface
  And make the furrowed tablet bright and
    smooth again.

'Christ's confessor is stabbed with the one
    and rent with the other;   55
  One end impales the tender flesh, one cleaves
    the skin.

'Hands, two hundred, have pierced at one time
    all parts of his body,
  And blood from every gaping wound at once distils.

'Greater torments that child inflicted who pricked
    the skin's surface.
  Than he who penetrated deep into the flesh;   60

'For the former with feeble onsets that are not fatal
  Has skill in giving pain by means of puny darts,

'While the latter by piercing the vital organs more
    deeply
  Gives greater solace, for he hastens death's
    approach.

' "Be unflinching" the judge cries; "let your years
    be belied by your vigor,   65
  And what you lack in age make up in cruelty."

'But in their evil emprise the youthful assassins
    grow weary;
  The torments multiply as energy declines.

' "Why do you groan" exclaimed one of them;
    "you yourself as our master
  Have given us this iron and armed
    our childish hands.   70

' "Lo, we give back the thousands of ciphers
    you taught us to sculpture,
  As we in tears gave heed to your dictated words.

' "You should not be displeased at our marks;
    it was you who commanded
  That never in our hands we hold an idle style.

' "We do not ask for the holiday now you
    so often refused us,   75
  O grudging teacher, when you kept us in your
    school.

' "We like pricking these signs, entwining furrow
    with furrow,
  And making chains by interlacing curving strokes.

' "You may look over the long-drawn series of
    lines and correct them,
  If any hesitating hand perchance has erred.   80

' "Exercise your dominion;[12] you may upbraid us
    for blunders
  If any pupil makes on you a heedless mark."

---

12. Cf. Vergil, *Georgics* 2.370.

'Thus these boys amused themselves on the
  body of Cassian,
   But lingering anguish did not free their weary
    guide.

'Finally Christ from Heaven looks down on his
  combat with pity   85
   And orders that his soul be loosed from earthly
    bonds.

'He cuts short for his spirit the time of dolorous
  waiting
   And opens wide the narrow lurking-place of life.[13]

'From the deep-seated fount of the veins the rosy
  blood follows
   The pathways opened up and quits the
    inmost heart.   90

'Through the myriad outlets made by the wounds
  in his body
   The vital warmth from every fibre is exhaled.

'Here is depicted in radiant colors this marvelous
  story,
   Here, stranger, you behold the laurels Cassian won.

'Offer him now your pious prayers and fervent
  petitions   95
   If any hope or care now burns within your heart.[14]

---
13. Cf. Vergil, *Aeneid* 4.693-695.
14. Cf. *Ibid.* 11.373-374.

'You may be sure that the martyr will listen
    to every entreaty
  And grant all prayers he finds deserving
    of God's grace.'

I obeyed and embraced the tomb with
    disconsolate weeping,
  While from my lips and breast the
    altar stone grew warm.   100

Then I reflected on all my pent-up worries and
    sorrows
  And softly whispered all my needs and all my
    fears:

Prayers for the home I had left behind in a
    difficult crisis[15]
  And doubtful hope of future bliss and happiness.

I was heard; I arrived at Rome; heaven smiled
    on my mission:
  At home once more, I sing the praise of Cassian.

---
15. Cf. Claudian, *In Rufinum* 2.245.

10. DISCOURSE OF THE MARTYR ST. ROMANUS AGAINST THE PAGANS[1]

Romanus, champion staunch of Christ's divinity,
Come, make my silent tongue vibrate within my
  mouth;
Bestow on me, though mute, the gift of tuneful song
And grant that I may hymn thy glorious miracles,
For thou dost know the dumb are given power
  to speak.   5

---

1. The fact that this hymn is found either before or after the other martyr hymns in all the manuscripts has led some editors to believe that it was written as a separate book and that it is the work to which Prudentius refers in line 40 of the Preface: *conculcet sacra gentium*. See Bergman, *Prolegomena*, pp. XII and XIII. The poem appears first as Hymn 10 of the *Peristephanon* in the edition of Sichard published in 1527, and this order has been retained by subsequent editors. St. Romanus was a deacon of Caesarea, who suffered martyrdom at Antioch during the persecution of Diocletian, probably during the year 304. The earliest extant account of him is found in the *Martyrs of Palestine* by Eusebius. Between the years 387 and 398 St. John Chrysostom preached several panegyrics on the martyrs, among which are two sermons on St. Romanus (PG 50.605-618). The details of the passion as recounted by Prudentius are in the main those related by Eusebius and St. John Chrysostom. St. Romanus is listed in the Martyrology of St. Jerome on November 17. The Roman Martyrology mentions him on November 18 with the boy martyr Barula, who is mentioned, but not by name, by St. John Chrysostom and Prudentius. The

HYMNS 191

The cruel butcher tore from out thy throat the tongue
That made sweet music on thy palate's sounding
    strings,
But could not render mute the lips that praised their
    God.
The voice that testifies to truth cannot be stilled,
Though it be forced to gasp through severed
    passageways.[2]   10

I stammer out my halting words with feeble tongue[3]
And strain at measures harsh and unmelodious,
But if thou dew supernal on my heart wilt shed
And inundate my thirsty soul with spiritual milk,[4]
My grating voice then will breathe sweet
    harmonies.[5]   15

These precepts the Messias to his apostles gave,
As written down for us by the Evangelist:
'When driven to declare my sacred mysteries,
Be not solicitous beforehand for your words;
That moment I will give you all that you shall say.'[6] 20

    Mozarabic Missal contains a Mass for St. Romanus on November 18, in which reference is made to the traditional incidents of his martyrdom and the boy is honored by the name of Theodulus (PL 85.914-926). A saint named Theodota is listed with St. Romanus in the Martyrology of St. Jerome. Twelve lines from the poem of Prudentius are found in the hymn for Vespers of the martyr's feast in the Mozarabic Breviary (PL 86.1249).
2. Cf. Lucan, *De bello civili* 2.181-182.
3. Cf. Ps. 21.16.
4. Cf. 1 Cor. 10.4.
5. Cf. Vergil, *Aeneid* 11.458.
6. Cf. Matt. 10.19.

Of myself I am dumb, but Christ most eloquent
Will use my tongue to speak words full of light and
  power.
He will describe the roaring tempests Satan raised
In final throes of rage as he was being quelled,
A scourge in his last frenzy viler than before. 25

Thus does a serpent wounded by a spear
Gnaw at the steel, and made more savage by his pain,
He grips it with his teeth and shakes it back and
  forth;
But driven farther in, the lance remains secure,
Unconscious of the futile threats of mordant fangs. 30

Galerius, so it happened, ruled the Roman world,
A tyrant cruel, as the ancient records tell,
Relentless, obdurate, implacable, and vile.
An edict he had sent throughout his wide domain
That any man who wished to live must Christ deny. 35

Then, through the Roman emperor's mouth
  that Serpent spoke
Who, coming from the sepulchers, once cried aloud:
'Why comest Thou before the time to end my rule?
Spare me, O Son of God Most High, or give
  command
That I possess the bodies of this herd of swine.'[7] 40

The prefect Asclepiades with energy
Directed that his minions go and carry off
The people of the Church from holy shrines of prayer
And cast them into prison, bound with heavy chains,
Unless they spurned the doctrines of the Nazarene. 45

---

7. Cf. *Ibid.* 8.28-31.

Then he himself, intending to invade the church
And eager to profane the sacred mysteries,
Fiendlike made ready with ungodly armament
To overthrow the altar of the sacrifice
And smash the very doors from off their hinges torn. 50

But learning suddenly of these unholy schemes,
Romanus, hero for his holiness renowned,
Gives warning in advance of the oncoming foe
And urges timorous souls with suasive words of power
To stand prepared and not to yield before the storm. 55

United in one spirit is the Christian flock,
A company undaunted, bold and resolute,
Of mothers, husbands, little children, virgin maids;
All are resolved with valiant hearts, steadfast and true
To bear firm witness to the faith or for it die. 60

The soldiers, driven back, inform the magistrate
That of the stubborn band Romanus is the chief,
And that all burn with resolution obdurate
To meet the charge unflinchingly with throats laid bare
And die a glorious death with holy fortitude. 65

Command is given that Romanus now be seized
And brought to trial to answer for that scornful mob,
As firebrand that alone inflamed and led them all.
He goes without resistance, asking to be bound,
And gladly turns his willing hands behind his back. 70

His passion for the crown outruns the lictor's art,
As he without demur presents his naked ribs
To be severely gashed by double iron claws.
He rushes through the high doorway, and after him
He drags the torturer, as ushers stand amazed. 75

He stands before the tyrant, who upbraids him thus:
'You vile unruly monster, base and lost to shame,
Disturber of our city, like a raging storm
You sway the fickle minds of this inconstant horde
And urge the ignorant rabble to despise our laws. 80

'The unlettered multitude has been led to believe
A vulgar doctrine, through the hope of glory vain.
They think that immortality awaits all those
Who as the Giants of old make war against the gods,
And overcome, 'neath fiery mountains
    are entombed.[8] 85

'You, villain, have prepared this spectacle
Presented by the slaughter of poor citizens,
Who by their sacrilege have stained this age with sin
And for your precepts must be put to cruel death:
You are the author of their death and of their
    crimes. 90

'If I mistake not, it is only just and fair
That what you as their guilty head made many bear
Should fall on you, their bloody executioner,
And in the carnage soon to come you should be first
To feel the tortures you persuaded them to seek.' 95

To this tirade Romanus boldly made reply:
'With joy unshrinking I embrace your sentence,
    judge,
That for the faithful people I alone shall die,
A victim meet, in my esteem, to suffer all
The torments your inhuman malice may devise. 100

---

8. Cf. Vergil, *Aeneid* 3.578-580.

'The servants of the devils and the pagan gods
May never enter our salvation's holy house,
Lest that abode of pious prayer should be defiled;
For this I firmly trust the Holy Spirit's might,
That on its blest threshold you never will set foot,   105

'Unless one day converted you may be received
Into our fold, which may the Father bring to pass.'
Beside himself with fury, Asclepiades
Gave orders that the body of the saint be hung
Upon the rack and torn and stretched with hooks
   and cords.   110

But his attendants mentioned to the irate chief
That the accused was of a long and noble line
And worthy, as a citizen, of highest praise.
He bade them take away the instrument of death,
Lest he condemn a peer to vulgar punishment.   115

'Let him be flogged with ceaseless blows upon his
   back,'
He cried, 'and let his shoulders swell with leaden
   thrusts.
Each person must receive appropriate penalties,
And whether he be slave or lord is of import;
The prisoner's rank decides the form the tortures
   take.'   120

And then the martyr, quivering from the hail of
   blows,
Intoned a hymn amid the strokes of leaded thongs,
And afterwards with head erect he thus declaimed:
'Believe not that my parents' blood or curial law[9]
Ennoble me; Christ's lofty precepts make men
   great.   125

---

9. Cf. Horace, *Odes* 2.20.6.

'If by unraveling man's descent and pedigree,
You seek the source and first beginnings of our race,[10]
You find that we from God the Father's mouth
   came forth.[11]
Whoever serves the Father is a nobleman.
He who rebels against Him is degenerate.   130

'And then a new distinction glorifies our line,
A splendid honor like a civil post of rank,
When wounds inflicted by tormenting fire and sword
Sign him who witnesses the Name with dauntless faith
And bring an end to tortures in a glorious death.   135

'Take care lest you mistaken mercy show to me,
And do not spare me with indulgent tenderness.
Torment my flesh, assassin, and ennoble me.
If in this conflict I am rendered glorious,
The birth of father or of mother will be nought.   140

'Why do you set such value on the dignities
You have attained? Will all not quickly pass away,
The rods, the axes, chair of state, and bordered
   robe,[12]
The lictor, judgement-seat, and badges numberless,
At which you swell with pride and then you are
   brought low?   145

---

10. Cf. Vergil, *Aeneid* 7.371.
11. Cf. Gen. 2.7.
12. Cf. Juvenal, *Satires* 10.35.

'When you begin the consulship, as slaves are wont,
You feed the sacred chickens, I confess with shame;[13]
He who advances with the ivory eagle high[14]
Assumes an air of haughtiness and prides himself
On tusk of brute wrought in the shape of bird
   of prey.   150

'When you prostrate yourselves before your pagan
   shrines,
Inclining at the foot of statues carved from oak,
Than your abasement, what can I esteem more vile?
I know that togaed princes, in the hollow rites[15]
Of Idaean Mother, bare their feet before her car.   155

'The sooty image of a woman is encased
In silver and is seated in a chariot
To be devoutly carried to the cleansing pool.[16]
With shoes removed you lead the way to Almo's
   stream
And bruise your feet upon the hard and stony
   ground.   160

'But what about that other shameful pagan rite?
How vile you show yourselves in the Lupercal race![17]
Must I not reckon him the meanest slave of all
Who naked runs through every public thoroughfare,
Belaboring girls in sport with blows of leathern
   strap?   165

---

13. Feeding the sacred chickens was a method of divination used by Roman magistrates at their inauguration and by military leaders in the conduct of wars. Cf. Cicero, *De Divinatione* 2.34.
14. Cf. Juvenal, *Satires* 10.43.
15. Cf. Vergil, *Aeneid* 9.619; Ovid, *Fasti* 4.181-186.
16. Cf. Lucan, *De bello civili* 1.600.
17. During the Lupercalia, a Roman festival held on February 15, youths ran naked through the streets, striking all they met,

'Your cults, your rulers, and your gross observances
Fill me with pity, Rome, thou head of all the world.
Come, prefect, let me bring to light your mysteries.
Now, willing or unwilling, you must hear from me
What base divinities you worship and adore.   170

'That frantic rage with which you boil affrights me not,
That scowling look, that head in air, that angry mien,
With which you threaten me with pains and cruel death.
Exchange with me the blows of reason, not of rage.   175

'You ask me to renounce the Father and His Christ
And with you to adore a thousand deities,
Females and males, satanic gods and goddesses,
The children, grand and great-grand children born to them
Of either sex, offspring of base adulteries.   180

'Their maidens wed, and victims often of deceit,
They are seduced by snares that cunning lovers set.
The flames of lust and fornication rage apace;
A husband is unfaithful and his wife abhors
His mistress, while adulterous gods are bound with chains.[18]   185

'Tell me, I pray you, at what altars you require
My turf to smoke in sacrifice of slaughtered ram.
Shall I to Delphi go? The ill repute forbids
Of him who in the flower of youth your god made soft
Through shameful licence in gymnastic exercise.   190

---

especially women, with strips of goat-skin. Cf. Ovid, *Fasti* 2.283-284, 425-428.
18. Cf. Ovid, *Metamorphoses* 4.171-184.

'The lustful god soon mourned his favorite done to
   death
By heavy quoit and deified the wanton youth.[19]
Employed as the shepherd of a mortal's flock,
He let a robber carry off the sheep and lost
His weapons, too, the lazy fellow that he was.[20]   195

'Or shall I go to Cybebe's fair grove of pines?
The lad unmanned because of her foul lust forbids,
Who by a shameful mutilation saved himself
From that immoral goddess' passionate embrace,
A eunuch by the Mother mourned in many rites.[21]   200

'Perhaps I should elect the shrine of mighty Jove,[22]
Who if he were now brought to trial by your laws,
Entangled in the meshes of the Julian code,
Would have to pay the stern Scantinian penalty,[23]
And you would judge him worthy of imprisonment.   205

'What? Do you think the founder of the golden age[24]
Deserves my adoration? You will not deny
That fearing injury the outcast hid himself;
If Jupiter should hear that he is still alive
He would not fail to punish all who sheltered him.   210

---

19. Cf. *Ibid.* 10.162-185.
20. Cf. *Ibid.* 2.683-688; Horace, *Odes* 1.10.9-12.
21. Cf. Catullus 63.
22. Cf. Vergil, *Aeneid* 3.351.
23. The *lex Iulia* and the *lex Scantinia* were laws enacted by Augustus against adultery and unnatural vices.
24. Saturn. Cf. Vergil, *Aeneid* 8.319-320.

'How think you can a witless mortal make a choice
Between the altars of unfriendly deities?
The warlike Mars will be incensed if Lemnius
Is praised,[25] and Juno's wrath will fall on him who rears
For mighty Hercules a statue or a shrine.[26]   215

'You say that these are fictions poets create at will,[27]
But of these mystic cults they too are votaries,
And they adore gods they invent. Why do you find
Such pleasure in the reading of these sinful tales
And cheer them when you see them acted on the stage?   220

'The wanton swan performs his sinful pantomime,
A dancer acts the Thunderer as a horned bull:
You as the high priest sit and watch these evil scenes,
You laugh at them and question not their verity,
Although the name of that great deity is soiled.'[28]   225

'Why, pontiff, do you split your sides with loud guffaws,
When Jove the husband of Alcmena feigns to be?[29]
And when a harlot mourns Adonis in a scene
Suggestive of a passion frankly dissolute,
Does not this scorn of holy Cypris anger you?[30]   230

---
25. When Vulcan was hurled from heaven by Jupiter, he landed on the island of Lemnos. Vulcan was the husband of Venus, whose intrigues with Mars caused the enmity between the two gods. Cf. Ovid, *Metamorphoses* 4.171-189.
26. Hercules, the son of Jupiter and Alcmena, was hated by Juno for his mother's sake. Cf. Ovid, *Metamorphoses* 9.23.
27. Cf. Lactantius, *Institutiones divinae* 1.11 (PL 6.169-170).
28. Cf. Tertullian, *Apology* 15.1-3 (Vol. 10, this series, p. 47).
29. Amphitryon. The story is told in Plautus' play of this name.
30. Venus. For the story of Venus and Adonis, see Ovid, *Metamorphoses* 10.525-559 and 708-739.

'Is not the truth revealed in statues of these gods
By emblems of wrongdoing graved on them in brass?
What means the image of the bird affixed to Jove?
It is the armor-bearer swift, the panderer
Who to the tyrant brought his youthful favorite.[31]   235

'With robe ungirded, Ceres holds a torch outstretched:
Why, if a god did not a maiden carry off,
In seeking whom the sleepless mother spends the
    night?[32]
We see Tyrinthius revolve a spinning wheel:
Why, if a mistress did not make a fool of him?[33]   240

'What? Must I brand those monstrous rural deities,[34]
Priapus, Faunus, him who plays upon the pipes,[35]
The nymphs who swim about in oceans and in streams
Like frogs, abiding at the bottom of deep pools,
Divinity enthroned amid the vile seaweed.   245

'Are these the gods you call on me to worship,
    honored judge?
Can you, if you are sane, regard such myths divine?
When you reflect on these inane absurdities
Are you not moved to laughter at the monstrous
    powers
Which old wives, drunk with wine, imagine in their
    dreams?   250

---

31. Ganymede was carried off by the eagle, the armour-bearer of Jupiter, to be the cup-bearer of the god. Cf. Vergil, *Aeneid* 5.252-255.
32. Proserpina, the daughter of Ceres was carried off to the underworld by Pluto. Cf. Ovid, *Metamorphoses* 5.391-424; 438-445.
33. Hercules, sold as a slave to Omphale, queen of Lydia, became so infatuated with her that he wore woman's apparel and spent his time spinning wool. Cf. Ovid, *Heroides* 9.53-118.
34. Cf. Vergil, *Aeneid* 3.59.
35. Pan.

'If every false religious rite we must observe,
Be you the first to lead the way: without demur
Adore all gods held sacred everywhere on earth,
The Latin gods and Egypt's alien gods as well,
Those Rome invokes and those Canopus supplicates.   255

'You pray to Venus; venerate the ape also;
The sacred asp of Aesculapius you bless:
Why not the crocodile, the ibis, and the dog?
Extol the leeks on holy altars raised to them,
Revere the fiery onion and the garlic rank.[36]   260

'Are grimy household gods appeased with incense sweet,[37]
And consecrated herbs abjured and set aside?
Why do you deem the hearth of greater majesty
Than plants that in the cultivated gardens spring?
If godhead dwells in pottery, it dwells in leeks also.   265

'But molten images of bronze are beautiful.
What curses shall I wish upon the studios of Greece
That fashioned deities for foolish pagan tribes?
The tongs of Myron and Polyclitean maul[38]
Are source and substance of your celestial gods.   270

'Art is an instrument for spreading false beliefs.
When mighty Jupiter's unshaven beard it curls,
When Liber's flowing hair it twines in ringlets soft
And polishes his locks and bunch of purple grapes,
And when it makes Minerva's bosom fierce with snakes,[39]   275

---

36. Cf. Juvenal, *Satires* 15.2-11.
37. Cf. Horace, *Odes* 3.23.3-4.
38. Myron and Polyclites were celebrated Greek sculptors. Cf. Juvenal, *Satires* 8.102-103.
39. Cf. Vergil, *Aeneid* 8.435-438.

'It fills men's hearts with deadly fear and cowardice.[40]
They shudder at the Thunderer's brazen lightning flash
And at the hissing Gorgon's venom are appalled.
They think the youth just come from Indian victories[41]
Can strike them with his thyrsus in a drunken rage. 280

'And when they see Diana with her robe girt up,
They are affrighted at the huntress-maiden's bow;
Or if from molten metal with its quivering flood
A Hercules with gloomy countenance is cast,
They think he threatens unbelievers with his club. 285

'What terror fills the hearts of trembling worshipers
If Juno's wrath has by the artist been portrayed?
It is as though she looks on them with angry eyes
And turns her face away from victim sacrificed,
When graven stone depicts her with a sullen brow. 290

'I am surprised that Mentor was not deified,
And that no temple has been raised to Phidias,[42]
They are the makers and the fathers of the gods,
And if they had not plied their forges with such zeal
No Jupiter would ever have been cast in bronze. 295

'Do you not blush, you shallow-brained idolater,
To think what loss of victuals you always incurred
When you devoted them to these divinities
Made out of worn utensils melted in a forge,
Your broken ladles, cauldrons, bowls, and frying pans.[43] 300

---
40. Cf. *Ibid.* 12.335.
41. Bacchus, god of wine.
42. Mentor and Phidias were Greek sculptors. Cf. Juvenal, *Satires* 8.103-104.
43. Cf. Tertullian, *Apology* 12.2 (Vol. 10, this series, p. 41).

'I overlook these vagaries in common folk,
Who take alarm at party-colored wool on stumps[44]
And are deceived by every charlatan.
They think all things are holy that the idle talk
Of toothless hags has prompted them to dread and
    fear.   305

'I marvel that you erudite and learned men,
Who regulate your lives by well-considered laws,
Know not the power that rules things human and
    divine,
How great the majesty of Him who made all things
And governs all creation as its Lord and King.   310

'This power is God, eternal and ineffable,
A being thought or sight can never comprehend,
Surpassing all the reaches of the human spirit.
Not seen by mortal eyes,[45] he fills and penetrates
All things, the heart within and universe without.   315

'Eternally existing ere the first day was,
The state of being and of always having been
Belongs to Him alone. True light and source of light,
Because He was the light, His own light He diffused:
This splendor born of light is His begotten Son.   320

'One in their might are both the Father and the Son,
And that one splendor generated by one light
With all the Godhead's plenitude of brightness
    shone.
In God one undivided being operates,
And by one power was created all that is,   325

---

44. Cf. Ovid, *Fasti* 2.641-644.
45. Cf. 1 Tim. 6.16.

'The sky above, the earth and ocean's mighty depths,
The orbs presiding over day and over night,[46]
The winds and tempests, lightnings, showers of rain
   and clouds,
The polar stars, the star of evening, heat and snow,
The fountains, hoarfrosts, precious veins of ore and
   streams,   330

'The rugged cliffs and level plains and mountain
   dells,
Wild beasts, the fowls of air and reptiles, all that
   swim,
The beasts of burden, cattle, oxen, mammoth brutes,
The flowers and shrubs, the vines, the herbs and
   woodland groves,
All plants that shed their fragrance, plants that
   food supply.   335

'All these God made, not by laborious art or skill,
But by His soverign word He ordered them to be;[47]
Then was created all that had not been before.
This diverse fabric He created by the Word,
And in the Word the Father's power ever dwelt.   340

'Our God has been revealed to you: learn now
   from me
How He must be adored and what His temple is,
What gifts He has commanded us to offer Him,
What prayers He enjoins, what priesthood He
   would have,
What nectar He requires there to be sacrificed.   345

---

46. Cf. Ps. 135.7-9.
47. Cf. Ps. 148.5.

'His temple He has founded in the soul of man,[48]
A spiritual temple, living, fair, and sentient,
Not capable of dissolution or of death,
A structure bright and graceful, raised to heights
    sublime,
And gilt with ornaments of variegated hues.   350

'A priestess at the consecrated threshold stands,
The virgin Faith, who guards the entrance to that
    shrine,
Her queenly head adorned with royal diadem.
She asks that offerings to the Father and to Christ
Be chaste and pure, such as she knows acceptable: 355

'Decorous bearing and an innocence of heart,
Tranquility of peace, a body pure and chaste,
The fear of God, the measure of enlightenment,
Sobriety of fasting and of abstinence,
A hope that never faints, an ever open hand.   360

'From offerings such as these the clouds of incense
    rise
Sweeter than the scent of saffron or of balm,
Or breezes redolent of spices from the East.
The fragrant fumes are wafted straight to Heaven's
    throne
And giving joy to God, they win His holy grace.   365

'The hostile foe who puts a ban upon this creed
Bans virtuous living and pursuit of sanctity,
Forbids us to uplift our minds to heavenly things,
Inclines the fire of intellect to things of earth,
And does not suffer wisdom's spark to be inflamed.   370

---

48. Cf. 1 Cor. 3.16, 6.19; 2 Cor. 6.16; Eph. 2.21-22.

'How blind and buried in the mire are pagan tribes!
How carnal are the hearts of heathen multitudes!
How dense their ignorance! How darkened is the
 race
Devoted to the earth and bodies soon to die,
Regarding always things below, not those above!   375

'Is it not height of folly and insanity
To think that creatures born of nuptial ties are gods,
To look for immaterial being in the earth
And mundane things upon the altars consecrate,
That which was once created its creator deem,[49]   380

'To pray to trunks of trees that by the ax are hewn,
With blood of filthy swine to sprinkle graven stones,
To offer on your altars scraps of quartered beef,
And when you know that those you deify are men,
To kiss the funeral urns of mortal criminals?   385

'Cease, worldly-minded judge, to force such
 wickedness
On men who are courageous, generous and free.
Nought can be higher than the love of truth and
 right.
Those who confess the everlasting name of God
Have nothing they should fear, not even death itself.'   390

While thus the martyr reasoned, Asclepiades
Had burned within with sullen rage he scarce could
 hide,
And as in silence he had swallowed mounting ire,
His indignation grew deep-buried in his breast;
He now gave vent to all the force of pent-up wrath: 395

---

49. Cf. Rom. 1.25.

'By Jupiter, what do I hear from this vile wretch?
Amid the altars and the statues of the gods
He stands in open court, while I forced silence keep,
And villain that he is, pours forth a foul tirade,
Defiling all that is divine with impious lips.   400

'Alas for ancient laws and stable usages!
Our age condemns the rites ordained by former
    kings,
Such as Pompilius, for the welfare of the state.[50]
What modern heresy impels these casuists
To argue that the gods ought not to be adored?   405

'We see today the flowering of the Christian cult,
Now when a thousand consulships have glided by
Since Rome began, not to revert to Nestor's times.[51]
This novelty that now springs up was not before.
Ask Pyrrha if you wish to know how things began.[52]   410

'Where was that highest God of yours in that far
    time
When Romulus, the son of Mars by aid divine,
Was building up the citadel of seven hills?[53]
If Rome, divinely founded, now is flourishing,
She owes her power to stayer[54] Jove and other gods.   415

---

50. Numa Pompilius, according to tradition, the second king of Rome and founder of Roman religious institutions.
51. Greek hero of the Homeric age.
52. Pyrrha and her husband Deucalian, the only survivors of the flood, repeopled the earth by throwing stones behind them, which turned into men and women. Cf. Ovid, *Metamorphoses* 1.350-415.
53. Cf. Vergil, *Aeneid* 6.777-783.
54. *Iovi Statori.* Cf. Livy 1.12.6.

'Since time began this by our fathers was enjoined:
We ought to offer prayers for our prince at shrines
That he may win in battle glorious victories,
And having overcome his foes, he may subject
A peaceful world to law and order as its king. 420

'Prepare, most wicked man, whoever you may be,
To beg the gods with us according to our rites,
To give our emperor long life and happiness,
Or as a common traitor you must shed your blood:
To spurn the temple is to scorn the prince himself.' 425

The saint replied: 'No other favor will I ask
For our great emperor and his intrepid hosts
Than that they may become the soldiers of the faith
And in Christ's waters to the Father may be born,
Receiving from on high the Paraclete himself, 430

'That they may spurn the darkness of idolatry
And see the radiance of everlasting hope
That does not penetrate the lymph of mortal eyes,
Nor through the open windows of the body shine,
But lights up from within the innocent of heart. 435

'The gross eye of the flesh sees only what is gross,
And passing, it perceives that which must pass away;
The spirit is capable of seeing spiritual things;
This glowing principle alone can comprehend
The dazzling strength of brightness in divinity. 440

'I long to have the emperor discern this light,
Your lord and mine, if he is willing to be mine,
For if he stands against the holy Christian name,
My emperor one such as he will never be;
I shall not serve, believe me, one who bids me sin.' 445

'How can you stand there, slaves?' the prefect
   loudly cries,
'Do you stand still and hold in check avenging
   hands?
Why do you not dismember him and carve his flesh,
Pluck out the spirit that lies hid within the man,
Whence come these impious words against the
   emperor?'   450

With cleaving sword the wicked soldiers tear both
   sides
Of that undaunted saint as in the air he hangs,
And slowly trace upon his members furrowed
   wounds
That cross each other as they pierce his trembling
   frame,
Till soon his breast is white where all the bones are
   bare.   455

The butchers now are out of breath and drenched
   with sweat
While he on whom they vent their rage remains
   unmoved.
Romanus in the midst of torture freely speaks:
'If you, O cruel prefect, seek to know the truth,
The wounds that you inflict on me distress me not.   460

'What grieves me is the error seated in your hearts,
Through which you lead with you great numbers
   of lost souls.
They run from every side to view this spectacle,
A vulgar heathen throng, lamentable, alas,
Who tremble at the harsh example of my bitter
   doom.   465

'Hear, all of you. Afar I cry and I proclaim,
From this high gibbet I send forth my flaming word:
The splendor of the Father's glory,[55] Christ, is God,
Creator of all things and sharer of our lot,
Who to the faithful promises eternal life,   470

'Salvation of the soul, the spirit that never dies,
But lives forever in the one or other state;
It either shines in light or in dark night is sunk;
When it has followed Christ, it enters Heaven
   above;
Cut off from Christ, it is consigned to lowest Hell.   475

'What should concern me is the kind of recompense
That my immortal soul will merit to receive;
To me it matters little how my body dies,
Since by the law of its own nature it must die.
Let what is doomed to perish crumble into dust.   480

'It does not matter whether fire or chains torment,
Or whether cruel sickness racks the weakened frame,
For grave disease is often armed with greater pangs.
The iron claws that penetrate into the side
Cause not such piercing darts of pain as pleurisy.   485

'The red-hot plates that sear the skin burn not so
   deep
As fever that consumes the veins with deadly plague,
Or inflammation from within that chafes the flesh
And breaks out on the body in a violent rash,
More painful, you would feel, than hissing branding
   irons.   490

---

55. Cf. Heb. 1.3; 2 Cor. 4.4.

'You think me wretched that I am suspended here,
With arms behind my back and feet wrenched out of
   place,
And that my joints creak as breaking tendons snap;
But those tormented by arthritis or by gout
Cry out in pain as though their bones were rent
   apart.   495

'You shudder at the blows of executioners.
But are the hands of doctors more considerate
When they make use of Hippocratic butchery?
The living flesh is cut and blood, fresh-flowing, stains
The scalpels when the tainted members
   are removed.   500

'Consider that the surgeons thrust their cruel knives
Into my ribs and that to heal they cut my flesh.
That which restores our health is not injurious:
These butchers seem to rend and tear my putrid
   limbs,
But they give healing to the living spirit within.   505

'And yet who does not know how subject to decay
Is mortal flesh, polluted and ephemeral.
It is unclean and bloated, rheumy, fetid, sore;
It is puffed up with anger, gives free rein to lust,
And often wears the livid marks that gall effects.   510

'Is not the shining gold amassed but for the flesh?
Embroidered robes and jewels, purple cloth and silks
By myriad wiles are sought to gratify the flesh;
Excess in eating pampers flesh and makes it fat,
And pleasures of the flesh give rise to every
   crime.[56]   515

---
56. Cf. Horace, *Odes* 1.3.26.

'I pray you, O assassin, heal these mighty ills,
Cut off and tear asunder that which leads to sin,
Remove the gangrene from the flesh that now decays,
In order that my soul may live secure from pain
And wearing nought by tyrant to be cut away.   520

'Be not affrighted, you that press around me here;
I lose that only which all men must one day lose,
The king with all his subjects, the rich as well as
    poor.
The flesh of slaves and senators will waste away
Alike when it is buried in the sepulcher.   525

'A trifling loss or injury distresses us
If we have fear of losing what we must forsake.
Why does the will resist what is inevitable?
Why not transform the natural to a glorious thing?
Let us account as gain the doom by law ordained.   530

'But let us see the recompense the brave receive,
A true and certain recompense that never ends.
The spirit released from earth will fly to heaven
    above,
And by the splendid light of God the Father blest,
Will dwell forever in the realm of Christ the King.   535

'One day the heavens will be rolled up as a book,[57]
The sun's revolving orb will fall upon the earth,
The sphere that regulates the months will crash in
    ruin,
And God alone, together with the souls redeemed
And hosts of everlasting angels, will remain.   540

---

57. Cf. Isa. 34.4; Apoc. 6.14.

'Despise the joys of this life, O prudent man,
The joys that must end, that you must leave behind,
Cast off the body that is destined for the grave,
Direct your course to future glory and to God.
Know what you are and overcome the world
    and time.' 545

The fervent martyr scarce had ended this discourse,
When Asclepiades in fury cut him short:
'Come, let the executioner transfer his blows
To this glib ranter's mouth; let him direct all hands
With piercing blade and stinging lash
    upon his jaws. 550

'Destroy the organ of his galling verbiage,
Transpierce his bloated cheeks, that his loquacity
May be deprived of wind that gushes forth in speech,
For no restraint avails to stop this flow of sound;
The driveler's very words I charge you to torment.' 555

The impious lictor executes the prefect's words;
He draws deep lines upon both cheeks
    with keen-edged hooks,
And traces bleeding furrows on the martyr's face;
He tears in shreds the skin with rough unshaven
    beard,
And cleaves his countenance down to the very chin. 560

Amid the flowing blood the martyr calmly speaks:
'Abundant thanks I owe to you, O magistrate,
That now through many open mouths
    I may preach Christ.
One passage dwarfed the praises of His mighty
    name
And was too narrow for the glories of our God. 565

'The voice I now send forth finds open crevices,
And flowing from these many lips, produces sounds
More numerous as it proclaims on every side
The lasting glory of the Father and of Christ.
As many mouths now utter praise as I have wounds.' 570

Confounded by such constancy, the angry judge
Commands the punishments to cease, and thus he speaks:
'I swear by flaming fires enkindled in the sun,[58]
Which governs by alternate rounds our passing days,
And whose return brings back again the light and year, 575

'A blazing funeral pyre shall be prepared for you
On which your body will be burned as it deserves,
For it persists in scorning all our ancient rites,
Nor is it spent or overcome by pain's fierce darts,
But even bolder grows in frightful agonies. 580

'What stoicism prompts this constancy of heart?
Your mind is obstinate, your body steeled to pain,
Such is the folly that inspires this modern creed:
Indeed, this Christ you worship lived not long ago,
And you confess that He was nailed upon a cross.' 585

'It is that cross which brings salvation to us all,'
Romanus cried, 'through it all mankind is redeemed.
I know you cannot grasp this doctrine, impious judge,[59]
That you cannot imbibe our sacred mysteries,
For night can never comprehend the light of day.[60] 590

---
58. Cf. Juvenal, *Satires* 13.78.
59. Cf. 1 Cor. 2.14.
60. Cf. John 1.5.

'Yet in this darkness I shall hold a gleaming torch.
The innocent will see, purblind will veil their eyes.
"Remove the light," the soul beyond recall will say;
"The brightness dazzles one who cannot bear its
    gleam."
Give ear, unholy man, to that which you detest.   595

'The King eternal an eternal King begot,
In Him abiding, and not after Him in time,
For He exists outside of time; Christ is the source
Of all beginnings, of the days and of the years;
Born of the Father, Christ the Son is one with Him.   600

'The Son revealed Himself to eyes of mortal man;
His immortality took on a mortal frame,
That God by putting on a body doomed to die,
Might give our bodies power to rise to Heaven's
    height:
As man He died for us, as God He rose again.   605

'With God incarnate, Death engaged in conflict fierce;
It struck our flesh, but yielded to the deity.
All this is foolishness to you, O worldly wise,
Yet did the Father choose the foolish of the earth,
That weak ones of the world might be
    the wise of God.[61]   610

'You talk about antiquity of Romulus,
The wolf of Mars, the vultures' primal auguries.
If modern times you spurn, nought is more new
    than these.
The march of days fills up with scarce a thousand
    years.
The epoch since the time our founding augur lived.   615

---
61. Cf. Matt. 11.25; 1 Cor. 1.27-28.

'A thousand kindgoms I could count, if I had time,
That were established in the world and won renown
Long ere the Gnosian she-goat, as the story goes,
Gave suck to Jupiter,[62] the sire of warlike Mars.
But these are gone, and soon this realm
    will pass away.   620

'The cross of Christ, which you have said
    is something new,
Was shown in figures and set forth in sacred books,
When man was first created in the birth of time.
Christ's coming through a thousand marvels was
    foretold
By holy prophets who agreed in all their words.   625

'Kings, prophets, judges, all the rulers of those days
Through their exploits, wars, religious rites, and pen
Continued to portray the figure of the cross.
The cross was heralded, the cross was shadowed
    forth,
Those ancient times drank in the image of the cross.   630

At last the words of all the prophets were fulfilled,
And in our age tradition has been verified,
Appearing to us in a shining countenance,
Lest faith should stumble in uncertainty and doubt,
Unless the Truth itself were seen by human eyes.   635

'With steadfast faith we hold the body will not die,
Though it is given to the tomb to be devoured,
For Christ raised up His body, dead upon the cross,
And carried it with Him back to the Father's throne,
Thus opening a way for all to rise again.   640

---

62. As an infant Jupiter was nursed by the she-goat Amalthaea on the island of Crete.

'The cross is ours, that gibbet we also ascend;[63]
For us Christ died, for us as God Christ rose again;
In dying He is man, His nature is twofold.
He dies and triumphs over all-devouring death,
Then He returns to that existence without end.   645

'Let it suffice that I have spoken these few words
About the mysteries of our faith and way of hope.
I shall be silent now: it is forbidden us
To scatter pearls of Christ among the filthy swine
Lest what is holy they should trample under foot.[64]   650

'Since I cannot convince you with deep arguments,
Let us appeal to what is not beyond your reach,
Let us find out the sentiments of one naive,
With understanding simple and without deceit.
Let one be arbiter who has no thought of guile.   655

'Bring me a boy seven years of age, or less,
One free from prejudice and with ill-will toward
   none,
Who does not fall into the snares of sophistry.
Let us see what this tender child will have to say,
Let us behold the wisdom of the artless mind.'   660

Accepting readily the holy martyr's word,
The prefect straight directs that from the infant
   band[65]
One be selected not long weaned and brought to
   him.[66]
'Inquire of him whatever you may wish,' he said;
'Then let us follow what this little lad approves.'   665

---

63. Cf. Gal. 2.19.
64. Cf. Matt. 7.6.
65. Cf. Vergil, *Aeneid* 11.533-535.
66. Cf. Horace, *Odes* 4.4.15.

Romanus, eager that the candor of the child,
A suckling still, should now be tested, said to him:
'My little son, come tell me which is right and just,
To worship Christ and God the Father in His Christ,
Or offer prayers to idols of a thousand shapes?' 670

The boy smiled and instantly he made reply:
'The entity that men call God must needs be one,
And what belongs to that one God is also one.
Since this is true of Christ, He therefore is true God.
Why, even children doubt that many gods exist.'[67] 675

The tyrant stood aghast, beside himself with shame;
It was not proper for the law to use its power
Against a little child so young and innocent,
But towering rage forbade the pardon of such words.
'Who taught you, boy, to say such impious
   things?' he asked. 680

The child replied: 'My mother, who was taught by
   God.
Enlightened by the Spirit, from God Himself she
   drew
That which she fed me when I in my cradle lay.
When from the fountains of her breasts the milk I
   drank
While yet a babe, I drank belief in Christ also.' 685

'Then go and bring the mother here; let her
   approach,'
Cried Asclepiades; 'Let the teacher see
The bitter sequel of her godless discipline.
Let her be tortured by this ill-bred infant's death,
Let her bewail the loss of him she has misled. 690

---
67. Cf. Juvenal, *Satires* 2.152.

'A good-for-nothing woman shall not tire the arms
Of our assistants. Death will quickly bring relief,
And trifling blows will serve to break the tender
    frame,
But at the sight the mother will endure more pain
Than if her flesh were mangled by the
    bloody claws.' 695

No sooner had he spoken than he bade his crew
To lift the child on high and spank him lustily,
Then strip him of his clothes and lash him with a rod,
Until his tender back was cut with cruel blows,
And from his many wounds more milk
    than blood distilled.[68] 700

What adamantine rock could bear this spectacle,
What iron or unfeeling bronze could suffer it?
Each time the willow lashed the body's helpless form,
The dripping withes were reddened with the
    drops of blood
That trickled in a livid shower from every wound. 705

They say the floggers' surly cheeks were wet with tears,
And spreading drops fell down unchecked upon the
    lips[69]
Of those uncouth assassins, grumbling at their task;
That no dry eyes were seen among recording scribes
Or common folk and peers of rank who gathered
    round.[70] 710

---

68. Cf. *Ibid.* 11.68.
69. Cf. Vergil, *Aeneid* 11.90.
70. Isidoro Rodriguez sees a parallel between this passage and the description of the death of Astyanax in Seneca's *Troades* 11. 1098-1114. (*Obras Completas de Aurelio Prudencio* p. 698).

The mother only gave no sign of plaintive grief;
Her brow alone was luminous with joy serene,
For piety is stronger in the hearts of those,
Who for the love of Christ stand firm in suffering
And steel themselves to sentiments of tenderness.   715

The child cried out, complaining of a burning thirst.
His breath grew hot as agonizing pains increased
And forced him now to call for water's cooling
   draught.
Not far away, his mother sadly looked on him
And thus upbraided him in words austere and stern: 720

'My son, I feel that you are moved by childish fears,
And that the dread of torture overpowers you.
I did not promise God the offspring born of me
Would so behave. I bore you in the glorious hope
That you would never bend before the threat
   of death.   725

'You ask a drink of water, when within your reach
A living fountain rises that forever flows,
A font unique that waters all who live on earth,
Within, without, the body and the soul alike,
Bestowing everlasting life on all who drink.[71]   730

'This fountain ever flowing you will soon attain
If only in your soul and inmost being burns
An ardent longing to see Christ. A single draught
So quenches all the fires enkindled in the breast
That in the life of blessedness no thirst is known.   735

---

71. Cf. John 4.14.

'This is the chalice that you now must drink, my
    son,[72]
Of which a thousand babes in Bethlehem once
    drank:[73]
Their tender years, unmindful of the flowing breasts,
Were fed from bitter cups that soon to nectar
    changed,
Partaking of the blood as sweet as honey dew.   740

'Essay to follow that example, valiant child,
The noble scion of your race, your mother's pride.[74]
The Father has decreed that every age excel
In deeds of courage and has barred no time of life,
According triumphs even to the crying babe.   745

'You must remember, for I told you many times,
When I amused you with old tales you would repeat
In prattling words, that Isaac was an only child,
Who, when he saw the sword and fire of sacrifice,
Stretched out his neck to meet his aged
    father's blow.[75]   750

'I told you, too, about that high and glorious strife
In which one mother's seven noble sons engaged,[76]
Mere infants in their years, but valiant men in deeds,
And how that mother urged them at its perilous close
To shed their blood and win the crown
    of martyrdom.   755

---

72. Cf. Matt. 20.22.
73. Cf. Matt. 2.16.
74. Cf. Vergil, *Aeneid* 1.664.
75. Cf. Gen. 22.6-10.
76. Cf. 2 Mach. 7.

'That mother saw before her eyes the instruments
Prepared to do her sons to death and was unmoved.
With joy she was filled when bath of hissing oil
Had seared and scorched a gallant lad, or fiery touch
Of red-hot metal plates had burned the tender flesh.   760

'The torturer tore off the scalp of one of them,[77]
So that the hideous skull, laid bare down to the neck,
Disgraced his noble head; the mother then cried out:
"Endure this shame, for soon a shining crown will clothe
This head with jewels of a kingly diadem."   765

'The tyrant ordered that the tongue of one brave youth
Should be cut out,[78] and then the mother calmly spoke:
"Sufficient glory now is ours, for lo, to God
Our body's noblest organ has been sacrificed;
The faithful tongue has now become a victim meet.   770

' "The soul's interpreter,[79] emotion's oracle,
The servant of the heart, the spirit's messenger,
Be it first offered in the sacred rite of death,
Of all the members first to pay the penalty;
Then their precursor all the rest will follow soon."   775

'The mother of the Maccabees thus urged her sons
And seven times subdued and overcame the foe,
As many triumphs winning as the sons she bore.
If through one child I shall achieve such great renown,
It lies this moment in your hands, my dearest life.   780

---
77. Cf. 2 Mach. 7.4.
78. Cf. *Ibid.*
79. Cf. Lucretius 6.1149.

'By this repository of my faithful womb,
This shrine which sheltered you for ten laborious
  months,
If nectar drawn from my full breasts was sweet to
  you,[80]
If soft you found my lap and childish toys pleased,
Be firm and praise the Author of these benefits.   785

'I know not how within me you began to live,
Or how from nothingness your body came to be;[81]
He only knows who made you and who gave you
  breath.
Hold dear your Maker by whose bounty you were
  born;
To render to the Giver what He gave is just.'   790

The child, encouraged by his mother's ringing words
Was laughing now at sounding rods and painful
  blows.
The cruel magistrate this judgment then
  pronounced:
'Confine the boy to a prison cell and wreak
Your vengeance on Romanus, author of his crime.'   795

The butchers plowed anew the paths of recent
  wounds,
And where a little while before the fiends had drawn
The piercing steel, they followed in the open tracks
And made the furrowed gashes flow again with
  blood.
The victor now upbraids them with their cowardice: 800

---
80. Cf. Vergil, *Aeneid* 4.316-319; 2 Mach. 7.27.
81. Cf. 2 Mach. 7.22.

'How feeble is your strength, how delicate your
   hands!
So long you have attempted to destroy this frame,
This poor decaying body, and your blows have failed.
It scarcely hangs together, yet it does not fall;
It thwarts the useless efforts of your sluggish arms. 805

'Dogs are more quick to tear a corpse with gnawing
   teeth,
And piercing beaks of vultures have far greater force
When they devour a shapeless mass of carrion flesh.
You are fatigued and faint from hunger
   unappeased,
You have the greed of beasts, but laggard appetite.' 810

These words aroused the violent anger of the judge,
And spurred him to pronounce the final penalty:
'If you are irked by these delays, a speedy end
Will now be yours: devouring flames will soon
   reduce
Your body to a little heap of ashen dust.' 815

As cruel lictors dragged the martyr from the court,
He looked intently on the judge, and thus he spoke:
'From this brutality of yours, O infidel,
I now appeal to Christ, not that I fear my doom,
But that your judgement may appear
   to all as nought.' 820

'Why this delay?' the prefect cried. 'Let both be slain,
The boy and the teacher, partners in this false belief.
Behead the child, who merits not the name of man,
And let avenging flames consume this impious
   knave.
Let both now die together, but in different ways.' 825

The place of execution soon was reached by them,
The mother clasping in her arms her precious child,
Like to the firstling of the flock that once was
   brought
By holy Abel as an offering unto God,
One chosen from the fold and whiter than the
   rest.[82]   830

The executioner then beckoned for the child,
And waiting not for tears, the mother gave him up,
As one last kiss she pressed upon his lips and said:
'Farewell, my dearest! When you enter Christ's
   blest realm,
Remember me as advocate and not as son.'   835

She spoke, and as the headsman struck the little neck,
The woman, who had learned the psalmody by heart,
Was heard to chant this hymn from David's holy
   book:
'The death of saints is precious in the sight of God;
He is Thy servant and the son of Thy handmaid.'[83]   840

As she intoned the verses, she unbound her robe
And stretched her hands out underneath
   the bleeding wound
To catch the ruddy stream that flowed from severed
   veins
And curly head, convulsed in agony of death,
Which she embraced and fondly to her bosom
   pressed.   845

---

82. Cf. Gen. 4.4.
83. Cf. Ps. 115.6-7.

A grimy overseer on the other side
Was building up from dry pinewood a massive pyre
And sprinkling with a sable shower of boiling pitch
The brushwood laid beneath and withered heaps of grass
That fed the crackling flames and made them
   brightly glow.[84]   850

And now Romanus, with his arms bound to the fork,
They brought, and as they placed him on the pyre,
   he cried:
'I know that I shall not be burned upon this wood.
This kind of passion is not destined to be mine.
A greater miracle is yet to be performed.'   855

These words of his were followed by a mighty crash
Of stormy clouds, from which the rain in torrents fell
And with a flood of ebon water quenched the fires.
In vain the servants fed the dying brands with oil,
For soaking rains had spoiled the sodden
   kindling wood.   860

The grim assassin, trembling at this prodigy,
Kept trying to revive the flames as best he could.
He stirred the firebrands with their embers cold and
   dank,
He nursed the living coals with wisps of flaxen tow,
And sought amid the water for the sparks of fire,[85]   865

When word of this came to the haughty prefect's ears
It roused in him a fit of bitter, vengeful ire:
'How long,' he roared, 'will this rank sorcerer
Make sport of us with his Thessalian trickery[86]
And canny gift of turning punishment to play?   870

---
84. Cf. Vergil, *Aeneid* 11.203; 6.214-219.
85. Cf. *Ibid.* 6.6.
86. Thessaly in Northern Greece was noted for witchcraft.

'Perhaps if I give orders that he yield his neck
To meet the keen-edged sword, he will forestall the
    blow;
Perhaps the cruel wound that cleaves the neck apart
Will heal, so that the severed parts will join again,
And once more will his head upon
    his shoulders stand.   875

'Let us begin, therefore, by cutting off some part
Of his still living body with the penal sword,
That by a single death this wretch of many crimes
May perish not, or fall beneath a single blow:
For every member I would have him die a death.   880

'I would make trial whether he puts forth new
    limbs[87]
That grow again, as told in Lerna's ancient myth,
Repairing thus the loss his body has sustained.
If so, a mighty Hercules will be at hand
Who is a veteran in burning Hydra's wounds.[88]   885

'Bring here a surgeon skilled in use of keen-edged
    knives,
Who can invade the narrow confines of the flesh
And sever all the fastenings of the ligaments.
Bring hither one who heals the dislocated bones
And mends and binds together all the
    fractured parts.   890

---

87. Cf. Seneca, *Octavia* 576.
88. One of the 'Labors' of Hercules was the destruction of the Hydra which infested the swamps of Lake Lerna in the Peloponnesus. The monster had many heads which grew again when cut off, but Hercules finally killed it by burning the stump with a firebrand.

'First let him pull the vicious tongue out by the roots,
Which is by far the body's basest instrument.
With shameless wagging it has scorned our mighty
    gods;
It has profaned our holy rites and ancient laws
And has not even spared the emperor himself.'   895

A certain doctor named Aristo now is called.
He comes at once and bids the saint put out his
    tongue.
The martyr puts it forth, exposing all his throat.
Aristo feels the palate, finds the vocal cords
With probing fingers as he seeks a place to stab.   900

He grasps the tongue and drawing it far from the
    mouth,
He thrusts his scalpel deep into the gaping throat.
As one by one the threads of flesh were cut apart,
The martyr never closed his mouth or clenched his
    teeth,
Nor swallowed any of the freely flowing blood.   905

Unmoved he stood with open jaws held wide apart
While streams of blood gushed forth
    and ran down, swift and red.
The noble scarlet emblem overspreads his chin,
And he beholds with joy his bosom's glorious stain
Like to the purple that adorns a kingly robe.   910

The prefect, thinking that he now could force the saint
To offer sacrifice, since tongueless he would lack
The words to prate against the worship of the gods,
Then ordered him to be brought back,
    now mute and weak,
Who once appalled his hearers by his stormy speech.   915

Again he placed an altar by the judgment seat,
Prepared the incense and the glowing coals of fire,
The entrails of a bull and belly of a sow.
Romanus, coming forward, saw these offerings
And breathed on them as if he saw
    demonic powers.[89]　　　　　　　　　　　　920

In better spirits, Asclepiades laughed him to scorn,
Then asked: 'Are you as brazen as you used to be,
Are you as quick to talk? Say all you have to say,
Hold forth at length and let us hear your arguments.
I give you leave to exercise your voice at will.'　　925

Romanus, sighing deeply, gave a long-drawn groan
Of sad complaint and thus began in ringing voice:
'A tongue has never failed the man who speaks of
    Christ,
Nor need you ask what organ is the source of words,
When He is praised who gave to us the gift of
    speech.　　　　　　　　　　　　　　　　930

'He who appointed that the lusty voice of man,
Arising from the lungs and thrust forth by the lips,
Should now reverberate against the palate's roof
And now be tempered by the sounding row of teeth,
Where plays the nimble tongue like quill of ivory,[90]　935

---

89. In addition to words, Christians from the earliest times employed symbolic actions, such as breathing, or laying on of hands, or making the sign of the cross, in exorcising evil spirits. Cf. Justin, 2 *Apology* 6 and Tertullian, *Apology* 23:15-16.
90. Cf. St. John Chrysostom, Homilies 1 and 2 on St. Romanus (PG 50.611;615).

'If He should bid the throat, like tuneful shepherd
    pipes,
To send forth as it breathes a blast of harmonies,
So that the passages themselves would utter words,
Or through the channel of the mouth the lips would
    speak
Like cymbals, now together pressed,
    now opened wide,   940

'Would you deny that nature's order could be
    changed
By Him who at the dawn of time established it?
The great Creator can at His good pleasure change
The laws He has established, make them and
    unmake,[91]
So that the tongue's support is not required
    for speech.   945

'Do you desire to know the power of our God?
He sets His foot upon the waters of the sea:[92]
Its limpid restless flood becomes a solid mass,
Contrary to its nature and its basic laws.
It stays up swimmers, now the feet that on it tread.   950

'To this great Deity belongs the certain power,
Which in the Father and in Christ we venerate,
To make the dumb to speak, the lame to walk again,
To grant the boon of hearing to the deafened ear,
And give the blind the unaccustomed light of day.[93] 955

---

91. Cf. Vergil, *Aeneid* 6.622.
92. Cf. Matt. 14.25. See also Damasus, *Epigram* 9.1 (Ihm, *op. cit.*
    p. 13).
93. Cf. Matt. 11.5.

'If any dullard thinks these miracles untrue,
Or you yourself have deemed them only idle tales
You may now witness proof of their veracity:
You have just heard him speak whose tongue
 you have cut out.
Yield your assent to this unquestioned miracle.' 960

With mortal fear the persecutor now is seized.
Dismay and wrath have so upset his darkened mind
He knows not whether he is dreaming or awake
And wonders, dazed, what kind of portent this
 may be.
Dread overcomes him while his anger spurs him on. 965

He cannot check the force of his unbridled will
And knows not where to turn the weapons of his
 wrath.
At last he fiercely summoned to the judgement seat
The unoffending doctor, whom he charged with
 fraud,
An underhand agreement to outwit the court 970
By doing nought but thrust a useless blunt-edged
 knife
Into the martyr's mouth and probe around in vain,
Or making with a certain skill a narrow wound
So that the tongue was injured only in one place,
And all the tendons were not wholly cut apart. 975

'It is impossible,' said he, 'for voice to sound
Or words to be expressed in mouth deprived of
 tongue,
Which is the instrument of vocal harmonies.
The breath may echo loudly in the empty vault,
But noise only comes therefrom, not human speech.' 980

The doctor thus refutes this calumny with truth:
'Examine for yourself the hollows of the throat
And pass your curious thumb around inside the teeth.
Look well and carefully into the open jaws
To find out what remains within to govern breath.   985

'If I had only pricked the tongue with lancet sharp,
Or if I had but grazed it with a petty wound,
Its pulsing would have ceased and speech
   would then have failed,
For when the mistress of the voice suffers injury,
The faculty of speech must also be impaired.   990

'If you desire, let us perform a test to see
What kind of growl a beast can make with tongue
   removed,
What kind of grunt a pig can make without a tongue;
I shall give proof that beasts with voice harsh and rude
Can make not even guttural sounds
   when they are dumb.   995

'I swear, O worthy judge, upon the emperor's head
That I have used the art of surgeon honestly
And faithfully obeyed the orders given me.
This man must know what god is helping him to
   speak.
I know not by what means the dumb
   can utter words.'   1000

Thus did Aristo plead and try to clear himself,
But on the impious wretch who hounded Christian
   souls
The words had no effect, and now his rage increased,
As he demanded whether it was alien blood
That stained the hero's breast, or that from
   his own wound.   1005

Romanus answered him: 'Behold me standing here:
The blood you see is truly mine, not that of ox.
Do you not understand, poor pagan, that I mean
The sacred ox in whose red gore you drench
    yourselves
When it is slaughtered for your sacrificial rite.[94]   1010

'Your high priest verily goes down into a trench,
Dug deep beneath the earth, to there be sanctified,
With strange head band and festal chaplets on his
    brow,
His perfumed hair restrained beneath a golden
    crown
And Gabine cincture holding up his silken robe.[95]   1015

'Above the trench they build a platform made of
    planks
Laid side by side, with ample crevices between,
And then by cutting or by boring through the floor
In many places with an auger or a saw,
They make a score of little openings in the wood.   1020

'Then to the place is led a bull of monstrous size,
With shaggy, threatening brow.[96] A flowery garland
    forms
A wreath around his shoulders and entwines his
    horns.
The victim's mighty head shines bright with
    burnished gold,
And glowing metal plates adorn his bushy hair.   1025

---

94. The pagan rite which Prudentius describes in lines 1011-1050 was called the *taurobolium* and was associated with the worship of Cybele. Prudentius is here the principal source for the details of the rite.
95. Cf. Vergil, *Aeneid* 7.612.
96. Cf. *Ibid.* 3.636.

'Above the trench the beast of sacrifice is placed.
With consecrated spear they open wide his heart,
And from the wound a stream of hot blood gushes out,
Which falls upon the bridge of wooden planks below
And spreads out over it, a heated billowing flood. 1030

'Then through the many channels of a thousand chinks
It filters in a gory shower of fetid rain
That falls upon the high priest in the pit below.
He holds his abject head to catch the dripping blood
That stains his robe and all his body with its filth. 1035

'And leaning back, he lifts his cheeks to meet the spray,
Beneath it holds his ears, his nostrils and his lips,
His very eyes subjecting to the laving stream,
And overlooking not the palate or the tongue,
Until his body wholly drinks the somber gore.[97] 1040

'When all the blood is spent, the flamens drag away
The bullock's rigid carcase from the bridge of planks,
And frightful to behold, the pontiff then comes forth,
With dripping head and beard all matted by the clots,
His fillets sodden and his vestments drenched with blood. 1045

'This man defiled by such impurity and filth,
Bespattered with the gore of recent sacrifice,
The crowd with reverential awe salutes and glorifies,
Because they think a dead ox's blood has hallowed him
As he was crouching in that dreadful cave below. 1050

---

97. Cf. *Ibid.* 11.803-804.

'Shall I remind you of that hecatomb of yours,
When by the sword a hundred animals are slain,
And from this carnage blood in such abundance flows
That scarce by swimming can the augurs make their
    way
Across the mighty sea of blood in front of them. 1055

'But why do I denounce the rich supply of meat
To feed the gods, or butchers all besmeared with gore
From cutting up the flesh of countless slaughtered
    herds?
Some rites there are in which you multilate
    yourselves
And maim your bodies in a painful offering. 1060

'A frenzied zealot thrusts a knife into his arms
And gashes them, the Mother goddess to appease.
Wild whirlings are regarded as her mystic rite.
The hand that spares the knife is deemed undutiful,
And cruel wounds deserving of divine reward. 1065

'Another to the goddess dedicates his sex;
He by the fiendish mutilation of his loins,
Unmans himself and offers her a shameful gift.
For her he cuts away the source of virile seed
And feeds her with the blood that issues
    from his veins. 1070

'Both sexes are displeasing to her holiness,
So he preserves the mean between the genders twain.
He ceases to be man, yet woman he is not.[98]
The happy Mother of the gods supplies herself
With beardless servants by a polished razor blade. 1075

---

98. Cf. Lactantius, *op. cit.* 1.21 (PL 6.234).

'Why speak of seals and marks of consecration here?
The pagans thrust fine needles into blazing fire
And when red hot they brand their members
   with the darts.
Whatever portion of the body thus is stamped,
This they believe is rendered holy by the mark.   1080

'When from his mortal frame the breath of life
   departs,
And to his sepulcher the sad procession moves,
On these same parts thin plates of metal are
   impressed.
A sheet of gold all shining overspreads the skin
And hides the portions by the fiery needles burned.   1085

'These sufferings the pagans are compelled to bear,
These rites the gods impose upon idolaters:
Thus Lucifer makes sport of those he has ensnared;
He teaches them to suffer vile indignities
And brand their wretched bodies with
   tormenting fires.   1090

'It is your cruelty that makes us shed our blood,
Your impious tyranny that lacerates our flesh
And racks the tender bodies of the innocent.
If you permit, we live in peace without bloodshed;
If we must shed our blood, we win the
   martyr's crown.   1095

'No further shall I speak; my destined end is near,
The end of all my woes, a glorious martyrdom.
No longer, wretch, will it be yours as heretofore
To torture me, to rend and tear my mortal flesh;
You must give up the bitter fight and own defeat.'   1100

'Indeed, the butcher and the torturer will give up,'
The prefect threatened, 'but the hangman's cruel hand
Will follow after them and quickly strangle you.
The tireless voice in that chattering mouth of yours
Will not be silent till I break the sounding reed.'   1105

He spoke, and ordered that the saint be dragged from court
And cast into the darkness of a prison foul.
There with a rope an impious lictor broke his neck.[99]
And so the martyr's passion ended, and his soul,
Freed from the chains of earth, took flight to heaven above.   1110

They say that to the emperor the prefect sent
A record of the acts, set forth in lengthy scrolls
And giving all the details of the tragic case.
The tyrant gladly placed in archives of the realm
The story of the crime on lasting parchment penned.   1115

But passing time destroys all these documents,
Smoke blackens them and dust envelops them with grime,
Age feeds on them or buries them beneath the ruins;
Immortal is the page inscribed by Christ's own hand:
In Heaven's register no letter is erased.[100]   1120

---

99. Cf. Horace, *Odes* 3.27.58-60.
100. Cf Luke 10.20; 16.17.

HYMNS

An angel standing at the foot of God's high throne[101]
Wrote all the martyr said and all the pain he bore,
Recording every word of his inspired discourse,
And with his stylus drawing pictures of the wounds
Inflicted on his sides, his face, his breast
   and throat.   1125

He noted down the quantity of blood from each,
The kind of furrows made by plowing instruments,
How deep and wide, how shallow and how long or
   short,
How violent the pain, how widespread were the
   wounds:
No drop of blood escaped his careful scrutiny.   1130

This volume is among celestial registers,
Where records of undying glory are preserved
To be reviewed by Heaven's everlasting judge,[102]
When one day in an equal balance He will place
The weight of suffering and the vastness
   of reward.[103]   1135

It is my wish that He may see me from afar,
When on His left I stand among the flock of goats,[104]
And at the martyr's prayer this mighty King may say:
'Romanus prays for him; go bring that goat to me
And let him stand, a fleecy lamb,
   on my right hand.'   1140

---

101. Cf. Matt. 18.10.
102. Cf. Apoc. 20.12.
103. Cf. 2 Cor. 4.17; Job 31.6.
104. Cf. Matt. 25.33. See also Paulinus of Nola, *Poema* 14.131-135 (PL 61.468).

11. TO BISHOP VALERIAN ON THE
PASSION OF THE MOST BLESSED
MARTYR HIPPOLYTUS[1]

Tombs of the saints without number I saw
   in the city of Romulus,
Holy Valerian, high priest and the servant of
   Christ.[2]

---

1. The identity of St. Hippolytus, schismatic bishop at Rome during the pontificates of Callistus, Urban, and Pontian, was established by the discovery in 1851 of the *Philosophumena,* a work now universally attributed to him. Legend has confused him with several martyrs of the same name, notably the soldier who was appointed to guard St. Lawrence and, converted with his whole household, was dragged to death by wild horses (BHL 3961-3964). See Allard, 'L'Hagiographie au IVe siècle,' *Revue des questions historiques* 37.369-379. Several documents of the fourth century contain references to the Roman presbyter celebrated in this hymn of Prudentius. Eusebius (*Ecclesiastical History* 6.20 and 22) refers to him as a bishop and mentions several of his works. St. Jerome (*De viris illustribus* 61) mentions him as the bishop of a church, the name of which he had not been able to discover, and lists his writings. In his Prologue to the Commentary on St. Matthew he confesses that he has read many previous commentaries, including that of the 'martyr Hippolytus'; and in a letter to Pammachius and Oceanus he declares that St. Ambrose was indebted to Hippolytus in compiling his *Hexaemeron.* With Pope Pontian, the martyr was banished to Sardinia and died there, reconciled to the Church, sometime after the year 235. Pope Fabian brought the bodies of the two to Rome and interred them with honors, Pontian in the papal crypt of Callistus and Hippolytus on the Via Tibur-

You would know the inscriptions engraved
   on the tombstones above them,
   Even the name of each one, not in my power to give,

For so vast was the throng of the just
   devoured by Rome's fury   5
   When she still worshipped the gods
      brought from her Trojan home.

Many a sepulcher tells in bright letters
   the name of the martyr,
   Or an inscription remains, lauding his valiant deeds.

There are marbles, however, enclosing the tombs
   with their silence,
   Or revealing to us only the number
      there shrined.[3]   10

You may learn that a number of bodies lie there
   together,[4]
   But the names of the saints do not appear on the
      tomb.

---

    tina near the tomb of St. Lawrence. (Cf. *Liber Pontificalis*, MGH 1.24). There Prudentius without doubt read the inscription which Pope Damasus placed on the tomb of St. Hippolytus. See Ihm, *Epigram* 37, *op. cit.* p. 64 and Ferrua, *Epigram* 35, *op. cit.* pp. 171-173. The hymn for the office of St. Hippolytus in the Mozarabic Breviary (PL 86.1183-1184) is based on the Acts of the legendary soldier converted by St. Lawrence.

2. Alamo ('Un texte du poète Prudence: Ad Valerianum episcopum,' *Revue d'histoire ecclésiastique* 35.750-756) finds evidence that Valerian, addressed in this hymn, was the bishop of Calahorra and not one of the Valerii of Saragossa as Allard assumes ('Prudence historien,' *Revue de questions historiques* 35) and Bergman repeats in his *Prologomena* X.
3. Cf. Damasus, *Epigram* 42.2 (Ihm, *op. cit.* p. 46); also Ferrua, *Epigram* 42.2, *op. cit.* p. 184.
4. Cf. *Ibid.* 12.1-2, p. 18; also Ferrua, *Epigram* 16.1-2, p. 120.

I remember finding that under one of the gravestones
   Ashes of sixty reposed, buried there deep in the
      ground.[5]

Only Christ knows surely the names
   of these militant heroes[6]   15
   Who have been joined to the great host
      of His intimate friends.

As my eyes wandered over the stones in my search
      for inscriptions
   Telling of time-honored deeds, which had
      escaped me before,

One I read of Hippolytus, who as a priest and an
      elder
   Once to Novatus adhered, claiming our faith to
      be false.[7]   20

Afterwards he was raised to the hallowed rank of a
      martyr,
   Winning that glorious meed by an ordeal of blood.

Nor is it strange that the aged man
      who was once an apostate
   Should be endowed with the rich boon of the
      Catholic faith.

---

5. Cf. *Ibid.* 43.2, p. 46; also Ferrua, *Epigram* 43.2, p. 185.
6. Cf. 2 Tim. 2.19.
7. Cf. Damasus, *Epigram* 37 (Ihm, *op. cit.* p. 42). If Hippolytus died shortly after the year 235, he could not have been an adherent of Novatus, antipope and founder of the Novatian sect during the pontificate of Cornelius (251-253). Hippolytus was antipope at the time of Callistus I and his successors (218-235), and Damasus may have associated the two schismatics, since both held rigorist views on the pardon of such sins as adultery and apostasy.

HYMNS 243

When, triumphant and joyful in spirit,
   he was being conducted   25
By the unmerciful foe onward to death of
   the flesh,

He was attended by loving throngs
   of his faithful adherents.
Thus he replied when they asked
   whether his doctrine was sound:

'Leave, O unhappy souls,[8] the infernal schism of
   Novatus;
Rally again to the true fold
   of the Catholic Church.[9]   30

'Let the one faith of ancient times in our temples
   now flourish,
Doctrines by Paul and the high Chair of Peter
   maintained.

'I repent of my teachings and witness as worthy
   of reverence
What I once hated and thought alien to worship
   of God.'

With these words he directed his flock away from
   that devious pathway,   35
Bidding them walk in the road beckoning them
   to the right.[10]

---

8. Cf. Vergil, *Aeneid* 3.639.
9. Cf. Damasus, *Epigram* 37.5-6 (Ihm, *op. cit.* p. 42; also Ferrua, *op. cit.* pp. 171-172).
10. Cf. Claudian, *Carmina minora* 18.13.

And by the spurning of error, he who had caused
    them to wander
  Offered himself as their guide showing the way
    to the truth.

Then he was brought before a ruler bereft of all
    reason
  Who was harassing Christ's heroes by the Tiber's
    wide mouth.[11]   40

That very day he had left the city of Rome
    bent on striking
  People who lived on the outskirts with his
    dreadful decrees,[12]

Not content with bedewing the earth within Rome's
    mighty ramparts[13]
  With the blood of the just slain in this merciless
    war.

When he beheld the Janiculum, rostrums, squares
    and Subura   45
  Drenched now and flooded with red torrents
    of Christian blood,

He extended his fury as far as Tyrrhenian beaches[14]
  And to the regions that lay next to the maritime
    port.

With his staff of officials and executioners round him
  Proudly he sat there in state, high on his
    judgement seat,   50

---
11. Cf. Vergil, *Aeneid* 1.13-14.
12. Cf. Horace, *Epistles* 2.2.84.
13. Cf. Vergil, *Aeneid* 1.7.
14. Cf. Claudian, *De bello Gildonico* 482-483.

And on fire to wrest the denial of faith from disciples
>Who were rebelling against worship of devilish
>gods.

Throngs with their hair grown long in the hideous
>prisons he summoned
>Into the court to be doomed, tortured,
>and put to death.

One could hear the creaking of chains and the hiss
>of the lashes,[15] 55
>Or the loud crash of the rods splintered by
>deafening blows.

Into the hollow framework of their ribs the claws
>were inserted,
>Opening cavities deep, tearing their innermost
>parts.

When the butchers grew weary, the judge gave way
>to his anger,
>Driven to fury and rage at his abortive inquest, 60

For not one of the servants of Christ in the midst
>of these torments
>Was to be found who would dare suffer
>the loss of his soul.

Then the prefect cried out in his fury: 'Have done,
>you tormentors!
>If your fierce blows and the iron hooks are in vain,
>let them die.

---
15. Cf. Vergil, *Aeneid* 6.557-558.

'Cut off the head of this man, let the cross to the sky
    lift the other,[16] 65
  Offering up to the grim vultures his quivering eyes.

'Quickly lay hold of these and cast them into a
    furnace
  Where the one fire may devour all the culprits
    at once.

'These you see here you may place at once on a leaking
    old vessel[17]
  And then put out to the high seas where the waters
    are deep. 70

'When the hazardous craft has borne them through
    furious billows
  And it is ready to sink under the force of the waves,

'Then its framework will part and the rotten hull
    will be broken,
  So that the water will pour in and engulf
    the frail ship.

'Soon a scaly monster will furnish a grave
    for the wretches 75
  Deep in its cavernous maw, gorged with the
    bodies consumed.'

As he was haughtily giving these orders,
    before his tribunal
  All of a sudden an old man was brought forward
    in chains,

---

16. Cf. *Ibid.* 11.455.
17. Cf. *Ibid.* 6.413-414.

And the throng of young men who crowded around
    him were shouting
That the one they accused led the adorers
    of Christ: 80

If the head should be promptly destroyed the hearts
    of the people
Freely would turn to the gods honored and
    worshipped by Rome.

Then they cry out for his death by unwonted
    and different torture,
As an example that would frighten and warn
    all the rest.

Taking his seat, the prefect threw back his head
    and demanded: 85
    'What is his name?' They replied, 'It is Hippolytus.'

'Let him be a Hippolytus,[18] then. Let a team
    of wild horses,
Goaded to madness by fright tear his whole
    body apart.'

Scarcely had he spoken these words, when they forced
    two wild coursers
Who till then had never known bridle, to bend
    to the yoke.   90

---

18. A play on the etymology of the word Hippolytus, from the Greek *hippos*, horse, and *lutos*, that may be loosed or dissolved. In lines 87-136 Prudentius is clearly indebted to Seneca's *Phaedra* (11.1000-1114), a tragedy based on the Greek myth of Hippolytus, son of Theseus and Hippolyte, who was dragged to death by frightened horses. See Sixt, 'Des Prudentius abhängigkeit von Seneca und Lucan,' *Philologus* 51.501-506.

They were unused to the stall or a master's gentle
    caressing,[19]
  And they had never before suffered a rider's
    control.

Beasts of the field and untamed, they were from
    the drove just impounded,
  And a timorous dread quickened their mettlesome
    spirits.

Then despite their resistance, the twain they
    harnessed together   95
  And their belligerent heads joined in an
    odious league.

Keeping their bodies apart a rope instead of a timber
  Moved to and fro between them, striking the flanks
    of the two.

From the yoke extending, it was dragged along far
    behind them,
  Under their clattering hoofs, trailing in wake
    of their tracks.[20]   100

At the end of the rope, where the ruts in the
    powdery surface
  Followed the galloping beasts in their capricious
    course,

Was a noose that fastened the legs of the hero
    together,
  Tying his feet to the cord with a tenacious knot.

---
19. Cf. Vergil, *Georgics* 3.184-186.
20. Cf. Vergil, *Aeneid* 9.392.

Now that all was prepared for shedding the blood
    of the martyr,   105
  Cudgels of leather and ropes, wild and ferocious
    steeds,

Forthwith they spurred the animals on with whips
    and with shouting,[21]
  Urging them forward with goads piercing their
    quivering flanks.

These were the final words the venerable patriarch
    uttered:
  'Let these destroy this frame, but, O Christ,
    take Thou my soul.'   110

Off go the furious horses, running in every direction,
  Blindly led on by the din and by their frenzy and
    fear.

They are fired by their fury, impelled by the race
    and the noise,
  Wholly unconscious of that pitiful burden
    they bear.[22]

Through the forests they rush, across the streams
    and the headlands,   115
  Stayed by no river's high bank nor by the torrent's
    swift flood.[23]

They surmount all the hedges and every barrier
    break through;
  Over the uplands they go, leaping down crags
    and high cliffs.

---

21. Cf. *Ibid.* 5.227-228.
22. Cf. Claudian, *De consulatu Stilichonis* 3.321.
23. Cf. Claudian, *De bello Gildonico* 472-473.

Little by little the martyr's body is broken and
   shattered,
  Torn by the briers and thorns covering the
   rocky terrain.   120

Parts of it hang from the cliffs and others cling
   to the bushes,
  Some of it reddens the boughs, some of it
   moistens the earth.

Painted on a wall is a picture describing this
   outrage,[24]
  Showing in myriad hues all the details of the
   crime.

Over the tomb is a vivid scene depicting the martyr   125
  Dragged by the steeds with his torn body
   all covered with blood.

Rocks that were wet with this gore, I saw,
   O Reverend Father,
  And the bright roseate stains dyeing the
   thorny shrubs.

There a hand that was skilled in painting the green
   of the brambles,
  Had in vermilion portrayed all the red hues
   of the blood.   130

---

24. Though many commentators have expressed doubts as to the existence of the fresco described in lines 123-144, recent writers see no reason to doubt that Prudentius actually saw the picture he describes. Cf. Allard, 'Rome au IVe siécle d'apres les poemes de Prudence,' *Revue des questions historiques* 36. 48-61; Ermini, *Peristephanon* pp. 78-79; and Vives, 'Veracidad historica en Prudencio,' *Analecta Tarraconensia* 17.200-202. There is some evidence that Damasus may have adorned the shrines of the martyrs with paintings as well as inscriptions. See Ferrua, *op. cit.* pp. 168 and 188.

One could see the members, torn asunder and
    scattered,[25]
  Lying about here and there over the devious
    route.

Painted there, too, in tears, was the loving flock
    of the martyr
  Following wherever the ruts showed them
    his roundabout way.[26]

Dazed by their sorrow, they walked along as they
    searched for his relics   135
  And in their togas' broad folds gathered his
    mangled flesh.

One of them lovingly presses the snowy head to his
    bosom,
  Fondly caressing the white hair with a reverent
    touch.

While another takes up the hands and the arms
    and the shoulders,
  Also the elbows and knees and the bare fragments
    of legs.   140

Even the blood that bespatters the sands they soak up
    with their garments,
  So that no drop may be left there to discolor the
    dust.

And wherever the warm rosy dew besprinkles
    the brambles
  With a soft sponge they remove it and take it away.

---

25. Cf. Vergil, *Aeneid* 6.596-597.
26. Cf. *Ibid.* 1.418.

Now the thick woodland no longer held any part
   of his body,   145
  Nor to the sacred remains was fit interment denied.

When they took account of the parts it was found
   that the number
  Rendered the body complete that had been
   mangled and torn.

When they had combed the devious track and the
   rocks and the branches
  Nothing remained of his flesh left in that pathless
   domain.   150

Now a place for his tomb must be found and the port
   was abandoned:
  Rome alone offered a site meet for the holy
   remains.

Near the surrounding belt of gardens,[27] not far
   from the ramparts,
  Yawns a dark cave that extends deep in the bowels
   of the earth.[28]

---

27. *pomeria*. The pomerium was a line demarcating an augurally constituted city. The term was later applied to the strip between the wall and urban property and also to a cultivated belt outside the wall.
28. The crypt was discovered by Armellini and Marucchi in 1881 on the Via Tiburtina. Prudentius visited it at the beginning of the fifth century and saw the tomb with the inscription of Pope Damasus mentioned in note 7 above. The sanctuary was destroyed by the Goths in the sixth century, and an inscription (Ihm, *Epigram* 83, *op. cit.* pp. 85-96) records its restoration during the pontificate of Vigilius 537-555). Adrian I (772-785) again restored the cemetery of St. Hippolytus. See *Vita Adriani* I, (PL 96.1199): *coemeterium beati Hippolyti martyris iuxta sanctum Laurentium, quae a priscis marcuerant temporibus, a nova renovavit.*

HYMNS 253

Into its shadowy depths a winding stairway leads
    downward, 155
And a glimmer of light guides the descending step.

Sunlight that enters the door as far as the top of the
    chasm
Only illumines the threshold of the vestibule.

Then as with careful step you descend, it slowly
    grows darker,[29]
And the dense shadows of night fill the mysterious
    cave. 160

Presently openings appear above you, high in the
    ceiling,
Shedding down into the crypt radiant beams of
    light.

Though here and there narrow chambers are formed
    in the murky recesses
That extend back on each side under the somber
    arcades,

Many a ray of light finds its way through the holes
    in the ceiling 165
Into the cavernous vault piercing the side of the
    hill.

Thus one beholds the light of the sun in the
    underground hallways
And enjoys the beams shed from its distant orb.[30]

---

29. Lines 159-166 are reminiscent of a passage in Jerome in which he describes his visits to the catacombs while a student in Rome about the year 365. See his *Commentary on Ezechiel* 12.40.
30. Cf. Damasus, *Epigram* 83.7-8 (Ihm, *op. cit.* p. 85).

Such is the hidden retreat where Hippolytus' body
    is buried
  Next to an altar nearby, built for the worship
    of God.   170

Table from which the sacrament all holy is given,[31]
  Close to the martyr it stands, set as a faithful
    guard,

Shielding his bones in the tomb to await their eternal
    avenger,
  Feeding with sacred repast dwellers on Tiber's
    broad shores.

Holiness reigns in this place, and the altar is ever
    propitious,   175
  Giving to suppliant men hope of God's bounty
    and grace.

Never was help denied me, one sick in mind and in
    body
  When at this shrine I prayed, prostrate upon
    the ground.

That I was blest with a happy home-coming; that,
    Reverend Father,
  I have been granted the good fortune to embrace
    you again;   180

That I am writing these words: to Hippolytus I owe
    all these favors
  Who has received from our Lord, power to grant
    our requests.

---
31. The Holy Eucharist.

HYMNS 255

His remains, sloughed off by the soul, now repose
  in a chapel
  Gleaming with fretwork of pure silver skillfully
  wrought.

Plaques that shine like concave mirrors, dazzling
  in brightness,   185
  In the facade have been set by a generous hand.

Not content with adorning the entrance with Parian
  marbles,
  He has enriched it with bright panels of silver
  and gold.

In the morning men hasten to offer up prayers
  to the martyr,[32]
  Coming and going from dawn, even to set
  of the sun.   190

Love of the shrine brings together a motley
  concourse of people,
  Mingling together as one, Latins and strangers
  alike.

Rapturous kisses they imprint on the luminous
  metal
  Faces all wet with their tears as they bestrew
  it with balm.[33]

Then when the months have passed, and the year
  recommences its cycle,   195
  Bringing the day of his birth,[34] feast of his
  martyrdom blest,

---
32. Cf. Vergil, *Georgics* 2.462.
33. Cf. Vergil, *Aeneid* 6.699.
34. *Natalem diem*, the anniversary of the death of a martyr, the day of his entry into heavenly life. Cf. Tertullian, *De Corona* 3.

What a multitude flocks to the shrine in zealous
　　devotion,
　What a full chorus of prayer renders due glory
　　to God![35]

Mighty Rome in a constant stream disgorges her
　　citizens;
　Lords and plebeians unite, urged by the selfsame
　　resolve,   200

Legions in sundry array advancing shoulder to
　　shoulder,[36]
　Every distinction of rank banished by reverent
　　faith.

Out from the gates of Alba a white-robed army
　　deploys,
　Which in continuous file eagerly marches along.

Shouts of joy resound on the roads in every
　　direction;   205
　Folk of Picenum come, those of Etruria too.

Samnites fierce meet those who dwell in Campanian
　　Capua,
　People of Nola arrive joining the gathering throng.

---

35. Cf. Jerome, *Commentary on the Epistle to the Galatians* 2 (PL 26.381): *Romanae plebis laudatur fides. Ubi alibi tanto studio et frequentia, ad ecclesias et ad martyrum sepulchra concurritur? Ubi sic ad similitudinem coelestis tonitrui 'Amen' reboat, et vacua idolorum templa quatiuntur? Non quod aliam habeant Romani fidem, nisi hanc quam omnes Christi Ecclesiae; sed quod devotio in eis major sit, et simplicitas ad credendum.*
36. Cf. Juvenal, *Satires* 2.46; also Claudian, *De nuptiis Honorii* 200.

HYMNS 257

All in the company of their wives and innocent
  children
Joyfully hasten along, eager to reach the spot.   210

Scarce can the broad expanses of prairie hold the
  rejoicing cohorts,[37]
  Packed close together though they are on the
  limitless plain.

One can see that the crypt is too small for this
  concourse of pilgrims,
  Wide though the entrance may be into its
  shadowy depths.

Near it, however, stands a temple renowned
  for its beauty,[38]   215
  Where the vast throngs may then go who have
  come thither to pray.

Proudly it lifts its magnificent dome, majestic in
  splendor,
  Gleaming with precious stones generous pilgrims
  have brought.

---

37. Cf. Claudian, *De Raptu Proserpinae* 1.221; *De sexto Cons. Honorii* 515.
38. Cf. Vergil, *Aeneid* 1.446-449. Ermini (*op. cit* p. 252) cites the opinion of Ruggeri that the temple referred to here was the basilica of St. Lawrence erected by Constantine on the Via Tiburtina (*Liber Pontificalis* MGH 1.63). An epigraph discovered in 1882 records the adornment of the basilica of St. Hippolytus by Pope Damasus (Ferrua, *op. cit.* pp. 173-174). William of Malmsbury includes in his *Gesta Regum Anglorum* a seventh century itinerary in which mention is made of the Church of St. Lawrence and immediately afterwards of the basilica of St. Hippolytus: *Et ibi, non longe, basilica sancti Ipoliti, ubi ipse cum familia pausat, id est, decem et octo* (PL 179.1355). See Vives, *op. cit.* pp. 203-204.

Columns in double rows, set under the aureate rafters,
    Hold up the ceiling above shining with fretwork
        of gold.[39]   220

Lower of roof, the slender aisles on both sides
    of the temple
    Stretch the full length of the nave, making more
        room within.

But in the center there looms an aisle of broader
    dimension
    With its bright ceiling above raised to a loftier
        height.

Facing the entrance, with steps leading up to it,
    stands the tribunal[40]   225
    Raised for the use of the priest offering praises
        to God.

Scarce is there room in the church for the turbulent
    waves of the faithful,
    And at the portal they crowd, surging in
        through the doors,[41]

As she opens wide her motherly arms to her children,
    Tenderly clasping them all close to her life-giving
        breast.   230

If I remember, illustrious Rome[42] on the thirteenth
    of August
    Honors the saint with a feast after the custom
        of old.

---

39. Cf. Claudian, *De nuptiis Honorii* 88-89.
40. The high altar. Cf. Vergil, *Aeneid* 1.166; Claudian, *In Rufinum* 2.382.
41. Cf. Vergil, *Georgics* 2.461-462.
42. *pulcherrima Roma.* Cf. *Ibid.* 2.534.

And I wish that you, too, would honor him,
   Reverend Bishop,
Counting his feast among those yearly observed
   in our land.

Blessings, believe me, he will obtain for all who
   invoke him   235
Here at the dawn of his day, meed for their
   homage and love.

With the feast of Eulalia, Chelidonius and Cyprian
Let this solemnity come round for you year after
   year.

So may Christ, the all-powerful, hear your prayers
   for the people
Whose salvation and life have been entrusted
   to you;[43]   240

So may the ravening wolf from your full sheepfold
   be excluded
That not a lamb may be lost, seized by him
   from your flock.[44]

So may you as a fond shepherd bring me home to
   your folding
When, a sick sheep, I am lost deep in the grass
   of the field.

Finally, when with milk-white lambs you have filled
   all your sheepfolds,   245
May you in Heaven above holy Hippolytus join.

---

43. Cf. Claudian, *Carmina minora* 50.3-14. Lines 239-245 are similar to this passage of Claudian in which *sic* introduces six successive couplets.
44. Cf. Vergil, *Aeneid* 9.59; John 10-12.

12. THE PASSION OF THE APOSTLES PETER AND PAUL

'More than their wont do the people flock hither
   today; my friend pray tell me
Why do they hurry throughout Rome rejoicing?

'Once more has come round the triumphal feast day
   of two apostles,[1]
By blood of Peter and of Paul made sacred.

'One and the same day with space of a year intervening
   was the witness   5
Of laurels won by glorious death in battle.[2]

'Well does the Tiberine marsh that is washed by the
   river flowing through it
Know that its soil by these twin crowns was
   hallowed.

'For it was witness to victories by cross and by sword,
   which twice poured showers
Of crimson rain upon its grassy meadows.[3]   10

---

1. Cf. Augustine, *Sermon* 298.2 (PL 38.1365). As early as the year 255 the feast of the two Apostles was celebrated on June 29. See the Martyrology of St. Jerome.
2. Cf. Augustine, *Sermon* 381 (PL 39.1683).
3. St. Peter and St. Paul suffered martyrdom at Rome during the persecution of Nero (64-69), but the exact dates are not known.

'Sentence fell first upon Peter, condemned by the laws
    of cruel Nero
To die, upon a lofty tree suspended.

'Fearing, however, to rival the glory won by his
    Lord and Master
By death upon a towering wooden gibbet,

'He was resolved to be nailed with his feet in the air
    and head bent downward[4]   15
So that the crown unto the base extended.

'Straightway his hands were then fastened below and
    his feet turned toward the summit,
His soul more noble as his frame was humbled.

'Mindful that heaven is wont to be reached from a
    lowly place more quickly,[5]
He bowed his head in giving up his spirit.   20

'When the bright car of the sun had completed the
    journey round its orbit,
And that day dawned again on earth's horizon,

'Nero unleashed all his ire on the neck of the Doctor
    of the Gentiles[6]
And straightway ordered Paul to be beheaded.

    According to well-founded traditions, St. Peter was crucified at Nero's Circus on the Vatican Hill, and St. Paul was beheaded on the Ostian Way. See Eusebius. *Ecclesiastical History* 2.25 and 3.1. (Trans. in Vol. 19, this series, pp. 132 and 138); also Tertullian, *De praescriptione* 36 and *Liber Pontificalis* (MGH 1.4-5).
4. Cf. Eusebius, *op. cit.* 3.1.
5. Cf. Job 22.29; Luke 18.14.
6. Cf. 2 Tim. 1.11.

'That his release from this life was at hand the Apostle
    had predicted: 25
  "I long to be with Christ, my course is finished."[7]

'Without delay he was seized and to death by the
    sword was rudely sentenced.
  The hour and day were those of his foretelling.

'Flowing between the blest tombs of the martyrs, the
    Tiber separates them,
  Both banks made holy by their sacred ashes.[8]   30

'On the right bank in a golden basilica lie the bones
    of Peter,[9]
  Mid olives gray and near a purling fountain.

'Water that trickles from springs on the hilltop
    sustains this lively streamlet,[10]
  Forever fruitful of the holy chrism.

---

7. Cf. Phil. 1.23; 2 Tim. 4.6.
8. Cf. Eusebius, *op. cit.* 2.25.
9. This was the basilica erected by Constantine over the tomb of St. Peter. Cf. *Liber Pontificalis* (MGH 1.56-57). Excavations carried out by archeologists at St. Peter's since 1939 tend to establish the fact that the tomb of the Apostle was actually located on the spot where the Constantinian basilica was built. See the official report published by the Pontifical Commission, *Esplorazioni sotto la Confessione di San Pietro in Vaticano eseguite neglianni 1940-1949*, citta del Vaticano, 1951.
10. In lines 33-44 Prudentius describes the aqueduct on Vatican Hill and the baptistery adjoining the basilica of St. Peter, which were constructed by Pope Damasus. Two epigrams of Damasus record these operations. See Ferrua, *op. cit.* pp. 88-96. The aqueduct is still in use and is fed by springs about twelve hundred yards west of St. Peter's.

'Now through a channel of marble it rushes and
  moistens all the hillside,   35
At last emerging in a verdant basin.

'Down in the lowermost part of the underground
  crypt the stream falls loudly
Into a deep and icy pool of water.

'Bright-hued mosaics above are reflected upon its
  glassy surface,
The gold is tinged with green from shining
  mosses,   40

'While in the shades of the water is mirrored the
  overhanging purple;
The ceiling seems to dance upon the billows.

'There the great Shepherd now laves in this icy
  cold pool of living waters
The sheep that thirst for Christ's eternal
  fountains.[11]

'Opposite, near the left bank of the Tiber,[12] the
  Ostian Way now treasures   45
The temple that to Paul is dedicated.

---

11. Cf. Apoc. 21.6; also Damasus, *Epigram* 1.2 (Ihm, *op. cit.* p. 1). The allusion here is without doubt to the font in which the Popes as shepherds of their flocks baptized the Christian neophytes. Cf. Damasus, *Epigram* 4 (Ferrua, *op. cit.* p. 94). Some commentators have thought that the passage refers to a fresco of Christ as the Good Shepherd.
12. Cf. Vergil, *Aeneid* 8.63-64.

'Regal in style is this shrine that our dutiful sovereign
    has embellished
And poured upon its walls his boundless riches.[13]

'Plates of bright gold he affixed to the beams, and the
    light within is ruddy
As is the morning sun at its first rising.   50

'Columns of Parian marble upholding the rich
    gold-paneled ceiling
Adorn the central aisle in fourfold order.

'Then with mosaics of many bright hues he inlaid
    the vaulted arches,[14]
Which shine like meadows gay with flowers
    in springtime.[15]

'Lo, you behold the twin dowers of Faith by the
    Heavenly Father given   55
To be revered by togaed Rome forever.

'Mark how the people of Romulus surge through
    the streets in both directions,
For two feasts on this day are celebrated.[16]

---

13. The basilica erected by Constantine over the tomb of St. Paul (*Liber Pontificalis,* MGH 1.60-61) was rebuilt by the emperors Theodosius and Honorius toward the end of the fourth century.
14. Cf. Vergil, *Georgics* 4.334.
15. Cf. Claudian, *De consulatu Stilichonis* 1.86.
16. In a hymn attributed to St. Ambrose (PL 17.1253), mention is made of the celebration of the feast of the Apostles at three stations. According to the Philocalian Calendar and the Martyrology of St. Jerome a third station was celebrated on the

'Now with glad steps let us hasten to visit these
    holy sanctuaries,
And there let us unite in hymns of joy. 60

'First we shall go by the road that leads over the
    mighty bridge of Hadrian,
And later we will seek the stream's left margin.

'After the vigil the Pontiff officiates first across the
    Tiber,[17]
Then thither hastens to renew the offering.[18]

'Let it suffice that at Rome you have learned of these
    feasts; in your own country, 65
Remember thus to keep this double feast day.'

    Appian Way at the Catacomb of St. Sebastian, where according to an ancient Roman tradition the bodies of St. Peter and St. Paul were hidden during the persecution of Valerian. An inscription of Pope Damasus (Ihm, 26; Ferrua, 20) confirms this tradition. See Ferrua, *op. cit.* pp. 139-144.

17. *Transtiberina prius soluit sacra pervigil sacerdos.* The poet here refers to the nocturnal vigil on the eve of the feast, which was concluded by the celebration of the Sacrifice of the Mass at dawn at St. Peter's and afterwards at St. Paul's.

18. Cf. Vergil, *Aeneid* 8.556.

13. THE PASSION OF CYPRIAN[1]

Punic soil bore the martyr who everywhere
  enlightens mankind;
There is the birthplace of Cyprian, glorious guide
  of all the nations.
As a martyr his native land claims him, by speech
  and love we own him.
Though his blood waters the Libyan shores, in all
  realms his tongue is mighty.
Now of his body it only remains, it alone can
  never perish,   5
While Christ suffers the race of mankind to exist
  and earth to flourish.
Long as one volume shall last and collections of
  sacred books be treasured,
All who love Christ will peruse thee, O Cyprian,
  and will learn thy teachings.

---

1. St. Cyprian (Thascius Caecilius Cyprianus) was bishop of Carthage from 248 or 249 to 258, when he suffered martyrdom during the persecution of Valerian and Gallienus. The date and place of his birth are unknown. He was converted from paganism a few years before his election to the episcopate and thereafter led a zealous Christian life as his writings testify. Prudentius in this hymn and St. Gregory Nazienzen (*Oratio* 24) have identified him with the legendary Cyprian of Antioch, the magician converted by St. Justina (BHL 2047-2051). The works of St. Cyprian were influential in the development of Christian thought and were everywhere known and acclaimed in the third and fourth centuries. The story of his martyrdom is

God's Spirit flowing before on the prophets with
  holy inspiration[2]
Watered thee, too, from the heavenly fountains with
  lucid streams of discourse.   10
O how chaste is thy eloquence, purer than snow
  and full of sweetness!
Like an ambrosial liquor it softens the heart
  and gives joy to the palate,
Piercing the soul and enkindling the spirit as it spreads
  through all the members,
Till the indwelling of God is felt in the inmost depths
  of our being.

Show us, O Father, the source of this singular boon
  to every nation.   15
When there was need for a brilliant expounder of
  apostolic writings,
One was chosen, endowed with rare eloquence, to
  instruct all mankind,
One who would serve as the faithful polemic of Paul's
  surpassing volumes,
Who would whet the dull minds of men with desire
  to know more fully
Both the work of God's fear and the mystical depths
  of Christ's glad tidings.[3]   20

---

recorded in two early documents; the biography written by Pontius shortly after his death (Trans. in Vol. 15, this series), and the *Acta Proconsularia,* an official account of the trial classed among the acts of the martyrs as having a certain degree of authenticity (PL 3.1557-1566). St. Augustine in one of his several sermons on St. Cyprian shows that he was acquainted with the latter document (*Sermon* 309, PL 38.1410-1412).

2. Cf. Heb. 1.1.
3. Probably a reference to the Old and New Testaments. Cf. Lactantius, *Div. inst.* 5.1.

'Mongst the youth of that land was one versed in
   the ways of evildoing,
Ravishing virtue by artful intrigues and regarding
   nothing sacred,
Often in cemeteries resorting to magic incantations
That he might rouse the passions of women and
   break the law of wedlock.[4]
Christ of a sudden arrested this frenzy of wanton
   indulgence,   25
Scattered the darkness within his heart and cast out
   its raging madness,[5]
Filling it with His love, with faith, and with shame
   for past misdoing.

Changed henceforth were his face and the garb
   that of yore was so replendent:
Gone was the smooth-shaven look, now transformed
   to an air of grave composure;
Long curling ringlets were shorn and his head
   was deprived of all its glory.   30
Now he was chaste in his speech and secure in his hope
   and rule of living,
Seeking only the justice of Christ and a knowledge
   of our doctrine.
Thus by his virtues meriting highest esteem,
   this holy Doctor
Soon was advanced to the bishop's throne, where
   he held supreme dominion.

Ruling imperial Rome at the time were Valerian
   and haughty Gallienus: 35
Jointly they passed a decree, condemning to death
   all God's confessors.

---

4. Cf. Gregory of Nazianzen, *Oratio* 24.9.
5. Cf. Seneca, *Thyestes* 899.

Thousands of idols born of the earth they commanded
   them to worship.
Cyprian with pastoral zeal exhorted the people
   to oppose them,
Urging his followers not to forfeit the badge
   of lofty courage,
Nor to abandon through fear the promised reward
   of all the faithful.   40

'Light are the pangs,' he said, 'when compared with
   the everlasting joy,
Recompense God himself has promised to His
   intrepid soldiers.
Pain is the price that we pay for hope of the dawn
   of life eternal,
And on the fleet wings of time every suffering soon will
   pass and vanish.
Nothing is heavy to bear if the end brings us rest
   and crowning glory.   45
I will go first in the long procession of glorious
   death and bloodshed,
I will surrender my head to the sword as a
   sacrificial offering.
Who so aspires to union with Christ, let him follow
   in my footsteps.'

When by these words he had kindled men's hearts
   with sure hope and Christian ardor,[6]
Him first of all the raging proconsul condemned
   to chains and prison.   50
Hidden away at a distance from Tyrian Carthage
   is a dungeon,
Filled with Tartarean gloom and wholly deserted
   by the sunlight.

---

6. Cf. Vergil, *Aeneid* 12.269.

Mured in this cavern, both hands with fetters
   encircled, holy Cyprian
Prayed to the Heavenly Father, invoking His name
   in humble worship:

'Father of Christ, almighty God and the Author of
   creation,   55
Christ, the Redeemer of men, whom Thou lovest
   and willest not to perish,[7]
I am he whom Thou, in Thy goodness and merciful
   compassion,
Didst once cleanse from the stains of sin and the
   Serpent's deadly venom,
Bidding me, as another Cyprian, to be Thy faithful
   servant,
Put on the new man, put off the old, and abjure
   my past offenses.[8]   60
If by Thy powerful grace Thou didst purge
   my foul heart of its uncleanness,
Deign now to visit this prison house and dispel
   its gloomy shadows.
Loose my soul from the chains of the flesh,
   set it free from earthly bondage.[9]
Let me pour out my blood for Thee
   as a victim immolated.[10]
Suffer no feeling of pity to soften my cruel
   persecutor,   65
Nor let the wrath of the tyrant grow cool and so rob
   me of my glory.
Grant that none of the flock I have ruled as Thy own
   may be inconstant,

---

7. Cf. Ezech. 18.23; 1 Tim. 2.3-4.
8. Cf. Col 3.9-10; also Cyprian, *Epistles* 1.3-4.
9. Cf. Vergil, *Aeneid* 1.54.
10. Cf. *Ibid.* 12.690-691.

That not one of Thy servants may stumble and fall
   beneath his burden,
So I may render to Thee the full number and
   pay the debt I owe Thee.'

By these words he won favor with God; straightway
   the Spirit descended   70
On the Christian people of Carthage, inspiring in
   them a lofty courage,
So that their hearts, illumed by His grace, might be
   filled with burning ardor[11]
To attain at the price of their blood the celestial crown
   of glory,[12]
Urging them not to give way to fear nor to yield
   to cruel torments,
But of one mind with Christ to stand fast in the Faith
   for love of Heaven.[13]   75

History relates[14] that in midst of a field by command
   a pit was hollowed
And was filled well nigh to the margin with hot and
   seething limestone.
Fire rose up from the heated stones and the snow-white
   dust smoked grimly,
Burning all that it touched and dealing quick death
   with noisome vapors.
It is said that beside the pit a high altar was erected,   80
Where the Christians were forced to offer a grain of
   salt or entrails,

---

11. Cf. *Ibid.* 6.101.
12. Cf. Claudian, *Carmina minora* 11.4.
13. Cf. Horace, *Epistles* 1.1.36; Phil. 4.1-2.
14. *Fama refert.* Cf. Damasus, *Epigram* 40.1 and 52.1 (Ihm, *op. cit.*
   pp. 43 and 54).

Or to leap headforemost into that deep infernal
 crater.
Eager for glory, three hundred quickly sprang forward
 all together,
And as they sank in the powdery maelstrom,
 the arid flood devoured them,
Whelming the daring band that flung itself headlong
 to the bottom.[15]
Whiteness takes hold of their bodies, whiteness uplifts
 their souls to Heaven,   85
And they justly are named the 'White Throng'[16]
 henceforth for all the ages.

Thascius rejoicing meanwhile at the sight of
 the triumph of his people,
Now was summoned before the raging proconsul's
 high tribunal.
When he was asked to make known his way,
 he replied, 'One God I worship,   90
And I proclaim the holy mysteries revealed by
 Christ our Savior.'[17]
Thereupon the prefect cried out: 'We have here
 sufficient witness.
Thascius himself confesses his crime; he denies
 Jove's mighty thunder.

---

15. Cf. Vergil, *Aeneid* 6.581.
16. *Candida massa.* In his sermon, *In natali martyrum Massae Candidae* (PL 38.1400), St. Augustine explains these words as referring to the large number of these martyrs and the splendor of their cause, but he does not indicate the manner of their death. Elsewhere he says that they numbered more than one hundred and fifty-three (*Enarr. in psalm* 49), and that they suffered martyrdom at Utica (*Sermon* 311.10, PL 38.1417). Prudentius indicates that his account is based on tradition (*fama refert*).
17. Cf. *Acta Proconsularia* 1 (PL 3.1599).

Headsmen, draw your steel: let him die by the sword,
   who scorns our idols.'
Giving due thanks to the Lord,[18] the martyr intoned
   a hymn of triumph.   95

Sorrowful Africa mourned the loss of this hero,
   by whose doctrine
She was reformed, by whose words she gloried
   in having been enlightened.
Then still weeping she reared a shrine where his blest
   remains were hallowed.

Cease to mourn for this saint; in heaven above
   he now is reigning,
Yet he still hovers over the world and on earth
   is always present,   100
Ever discoursing, exhorting, expounding, instructing,
   prophesying.
Nor does he guide the Libyan peoples alone,
   but presses onward
To the East and the West, enkindling the faith
   of Gauls and Britons,
Guarding Italian lands[19] and making Christ known
   on Spain's far borders.
Finally, he is our teacher on earth and a martyr too
   in heaven.   105
Here he enlightens mankind; as our advocate
   there he grants us blessings.

---
18. Cf. *Ibid.* 4 (PL 3.1563).
19. *praesidet Hesperiae.* Cf. Vergil, *Aeneid* 1.530-533.

14. THE PASSION OF AGNES[1]

The native home of Romulus now enshrines
The tomb of Agnes, virgin and martyr blest.[2]
Reposing there in sight of its lofty towers,[3]
The maiden watches over the sons of Rome,
And pilgrims, too, enjoy here protecting care,   5

---

1. According to the best authorities St. Agnes suffered martyrdom at Rome about the year 304 during the persecution of Diocletian. The Latin Fathers of the Church in the fourth century give testimony to the widespread popularity of the cult of the virgin martyr. St. Jerome mentions her in his letter to Demetrias, and St. Augustine refers to her in one of his sermons (*Sermon* 273.6, PL 38.1250). Pope Damasus composed an epigraph in her honor, which Prudentius probably read during his visit to Rome (*Epigram* 40, Ihm, *op. cit.* p. 44; *Epigram* 37, Ferrua, *op. cit.* pp. 175-178). In his *De virginibus* (PL 16.200-202) St. Ambrose gives a brief account of her martyrdom, with which Prudentius seems to have been acquainted. He also wrote a hymn in her honor, now recognized as genuine (PL 17.1249) and made incidental mention of her in his *De officiis ministrorum* (PL 16.90). The Acts attributed to St. Ambrose (BHL 156-158) are now regarded as belonging to the fifth century. St. Agnes is listed in the Martyrology of St. Jerome on January 21 and January 28, feasts also observed at present according to the Roman Martyrology. The entire hymn of Prudentius is used for the Vespers and Lauds of the feast in the Mozarabic Breviary, observed in that rite on January 20 (PL 86.1050-1054).
2. Cf. Damasus, *Epigram* 40.10 (Ihm, *op. cit.* p. 44); also Ferrua, notes 4 and 10, *op. cit.* p. 178.
3. Constantia, the daughter of Constantine, caused a basilica to be erected at the tomb of St. Agnes on the Via Nomentana (*Liber*

Who pray to her with pure and believing hearts.
With splendid twofold diadem she is crowned:[4]
Virginity unmarred by the stain of sin
And glory won by freely embracing death.[5]

That maiden, they relate, who was not yet ripe   10
For marriage vows and still but a child in years,[6]
Her soul aflame with rapturous love of Christ,
Withstood the impious edict to sacrifice
To idols and abandon her holy Faith.

Assailed at first by every art and wile,   15
Now by the coaxing words of a fawning judge,
Now by the butcher's sinister threats of doom,[7]
Dauntless she stood, nor shrank from her stern
    resolve,
Willing to give her body to torments sore,
Nor quailing from the threat of a cruel death.   20

Then spoke the angry tyrant:[8] 'If she can face
The thought of grinding torture and woeful pangs,[9]

    Pontificalis MGH 1.62). Pope Symmachus (498-514) renovated the church and its apse then falling into ruin *(Ibid.* 1.125). The basilica remains today as restored and embellished by Pope Honorius I between the years 625 and 638 *(Ibid.* 1.171). For a discussion of the inscription placed there by Pope Damasus and the pseudo-Damasian acrostic, *Constantina Deo,* see Ihm, *op. cit.* pp. 44 and 88, and Ferrua, *op. cit.* pp. 175-178 and 246-250.
4. Cf. Ambrose, *De virginibus* 1.2.9; *De officiis* 41.203.
5. Cf. Horace, *Odes* 4.14.18.
6. Cf. Ambrose, *Hymn* 65.6 (PL 17.1249); Jerome, *Epistle* 120.5. St. Ambrose *(De virginibus* 1.2.7) gives the age of Agnes as twelve, and St. Augustine *(Sermon* 273.6, PL 38.1251) says that she was thirteen.
7. Cf. Ambrose, *De virginibus* 1.2.9.
8. Cf. Damasus, *Epigram* 40.4 (Ihm, p. 44); Ferrua, *Epigram* 37, p. 176 and note, p. 178.
9. Cf. Horace, *Odes* 2.5.1.

And sets at naught her life as of little worth,
Her consecrated chastity she holds dear.[10]
Into a common den of impurity   25
I am resolved to cast her unless she bows
Before Minerva's altar and begs her grace,
That virgin she, a virgin, has dared despise.
There all the youths in wanton delight will rush,[11]
To seek this newest slave of their lustful sport.'   30

Then Agnes answered: 'Never will Christ forget
His own nor let our precious virginity
Be snatched from us. He will not abandon us.
He ever shields the chaste and will not permit
The gift of holy purity to be soiled.   35
My blood may dye your sword, if it is your will,
But never will my body be stained with lust.'

So spoke the maid; the prefect then gave command
That she should stand exposed in the public square.
As there she stood, the pitying throngs fell back   40
And turned their eyes away in respectful awe,
None daring to regard her with brazen look.

It chanced that one was forward enough to fix
His gaze upon the maiden and did not fear
To look with lustful eye on her sacred form.   45
But lo, a flame as swift as a lightning flash[12]
Quick struck his wanton eyes with its trembling dart.
The youth fell down and, blinded by glaring light,
Lay panting in the dust of the crowded street.
His fellows lifted him from the ground, half-dead,   50
Bewailing him with clamorous words and tears.

---
10. Cf. Tertullian, *Apology* 20.12; also Ambrose, *De virginibus* 2.4.23.
11. Cf. Vergil, *Aeneid* 2.63-64.
12. Cf. Horace, *Odes* 4.4.1.

The virgin went forth singing a hymn of praise
In thanks to God the Father and Christ, His Son,
That when exposed to peril of vilest stain,
Her chastity had triumphed, and she had found   55
The den of squalid infamy clean and pure.
Some tell that Agnes, asked to implore of Christ
That He restore the sight of the guilty wretch,
Poured forth a fervent prayer, and the prostrate youth
Regained the breath of life and his vision whole.   60

In her ascent to heaven the saint had passed
But the first step; a second was yet to come.
The bloody tryant burned with revengeful ire.
'I am outdone,' he groaned. 'Go, unsheathe your sword,
You soldier there, and carry into effect   65
The laws our prince and sovereign lord decreed.'

When Agnes saw the furious headsman stand
With weapon drawn, in transports of joy she cried:
'Far happier am I that a swordsman comes,
A wild uncouth barbarian, fierce and grim,   70
Than that a languid suitor pays court to me,
A lovesick creature, scented with rare perfumes,
Who would destroy my soul with my chastity.[13]
This butcher is the lover who pleases me:
His bold advances I shall go forth to meet   75
And will not try to hinder his ardent suit.[14]
I gladly bare my breast to his cruel steel
And deep into my heart I will draw his blade.
Thus as the bride of Christ I shall mount above
The darkness of the world to the realms of light.   80

---
13. Cf. Lucan, *De bello civili* 4.231-232.
14. Cf. Juvenal, *Satires* 14.250; Ovid, *Metamorphoses* 8.71.

Eternal King, unfasten the gates of heaven
That till of late were closed to the sons of earth,
And call Thy virgin spouse to Thyself, O Christ,
A victim to the Father now sacrificed.'

As Agnes spoke these words, she inclined her head   85
In humble prayer to Christ, that her gentle neck
Might readier be to suffer the threatened wound.[15]
Thus was her ardent longing fulfilled at last,
For with one blow[16] the soldier struck off her head
And speedy death prevented all sense of pain.[17]   90

Then putting off the garment of flesh, her soul
Flies forth and speeds untrammelled into the skies,[18]
Her shining path surrounded by angel choirs.
In wonder she looks down on the world below;[19]
On high she views the darkness beneath her feet,   95
And at the circling wheel of the sun she laughs[20]
As round its orb the heavenly spheres revolve.
She sees the raging whirlwind of human life[21]
And all the vanities of the fickle world:
Despots and kings, imperial power and rank,   100

---

15. Cf. Ambrose, *De virginibus* 1.2.9: *stetit, oravit, cervicem inflexit.*
16. Cf. Lucan, *op. cit.* 6.613.
17. St. Ambrose also implies that Agnes was beheaded (*De virginibus* 1.2.7,9). Damasus (Ihm, *Epigram* 40.5) says that she was condemned to death by fire. According to the Acts, wrongly attributed to St. Ambrose, she was decapitated after remaining untouched by the flames (PL 17.818-819).
18. Cf. Lucan, *op. cit.* 9.3-4; Damasus, *Epigram* 11.11-12 (Ferrua, *op. cit.* pp. 108-110).
19. Cf. Vergil, *Eclogues* 5.56-57.
20. Cf. Lucan, *op. cit.* 9.12-14.
21. Cf. Seneca, *Agamemnon* 1.198.

The pageantry of honor and foolish pride,
The thirst for gold and silver, which all men seek
And gain by every species of wickedness,
The stately palaces with their gilded walls,
The vain display of richly embroidered robes,[22]   105
The hatreds, fears, desires and impending woes,
The long enduring griefs and the fleeting joys,
Black envy with its smoking firebrands that blight
The hopes of men and tarnish all human fame,
And last, but worse than every other ill,   110
The sordid clouds and darkness of pagan rites.

All these things Agnes tramples beneath her feet,[23]
And with her heel she crushes the dragon's head,[24]
That monster vile who poisons all things of time
And plunges them into the infernal pit.   115
But vanquished now and under the virgin's foot
He lies crestfallen, prone in the dust of earth,
His fiery head not daring to lift again.[25]
Meanwhile the virgin martyr's unsullied brow
God circles with a glorious twofold crown: 120
One glowing with the rays of eternal light,
A sixty-fold reward, and the other fruit,
Increased a hundred-fold, of celestial grace.[26]

O happy virgin,[27] glory but lately dawned,
O noble dweller in the celestial courts,   125

---

22. Cf. Vergil, *Georgics* 2.464.
23. Cf. Damasus, *Epigram* 37.4 (Ferrua, *op. cit.* pp. 176-178).
24. Cf. Gen. 3.15.
25. Horace, *Odes* 3.16.19.
26. Cf. Matt 13.8.
27. Cf. Vergil, *Aeneid* 3.321; Damasus, *Epigram* 71.14 (Ferrua, *op. cit.* p. 248).

Adorned with thy resplendent twin diadem,
Deign now to turn thy face on our miseries.
To thee alone the Father of all has given
Power to make pure the dwelling of sin itself.
I, too, shall be made clean by thy radiant glance   130
If thou wilt fill my heart with its gracious light.
All is pure where thou deignest in love to dwell,
Or where thine own immaculate foot may tread.

THE FATHERS OF THE CHURCH

(A series of approximately 100 volumes when completed)

Volume 1:   THE APOSTOLIC FATHERS   (1947)
    The Letter of St. Clement of Rome to the Corinthians
    The So-called Second Letter of St. Clement
    The Letter of St. Polycarp to the Philippians
    The Martyrdom of St. Polycarp
    The Didache or Teaching of the Twelve Apostles
        translated by F. Glimm
    The Letters of St. Ignatius of Antioch
    Letter to Diognetus
        translated by G. Walsh
    The Shepherd of Hermas
    The Fragments of Papias (first printing only)
        translated by J. Marique
                          OCLC 367814

Volume 2:   SAINT AUGUSTINE   (1947)
    Christian Instruction
        translated by J. Gavigan
    Admonition and Grace
        translated by John Courtney Murray
    The Christian Combat
        translated by R. Russell
    Faith, Hope and Charity *(Enchiridion)*
        translated by B. Peebles
                          OCLC 728405

Volume 3: THE WRITINGS OF SALVIAN THE PRESBYTER (1947)
    The Governance of God
    Letters
    The Four Books of Timothy to the Church
        translated by J. O'Sullivan
                          OCLC 806839

Volume 4:   SAINT AUGUSTINE   (1947)
    The Immortality of the Soul

         translated by L. Schopp
        The Magnitude of the Soul
         translated by J. McMahon
        On Music
         translated by R. Taliaferro
        The Advantage of Believing
         translated by L. Meagher
        On Faith in Things Unseen
         translated by R. Deferrari, M–F. McDonald
                                    OCLC 856032

Volume 5:   SAINT AUGUSTINE   (1948)
        The Happy Life
         translated by L. Schopp
        Answer to Skeptics *(Contra Academicos)*
         translated by D. Kavanagh
        Divine Providence and the Problem of Evil
         translated by R. Russell
        The Soliloquies
         translated by T. Gilligan
                                    OCLC 728405

Volume 6:   WRITINGS OF SAINT JUSTIN MARTYR   (1948)
        The First Apology
        The Second Apology
        The Dialogue with Trypho
        Exhortation to the Greeks
        Discourse to the Greeks
        The Monarchy or Rule of God
         translated by T. Falls
                                    OCLC 807077

Volume 7:   NICETA OF REMESIANA   (1949)
        Writings of Niceta of Remesiana
         translated by G. Walsh
        Prosper of Aquitaine: Grace and Free Will
         translated by J. O'Donnell
        Writings of Sulpicius Severus
         translated by B. Peebles
        Vincent of Lerins: The Commonitories
         translated by R. Morris
                                    OCLC 807068

Volume 8:   SAINT AUGUSTINE   (1950)

        The City of God (books 1–7)
        translated by D. Zema, G. Walsh
                                       OCLC 807084

Volume 9:   SAINT BASIL ASCETICAL WORKS   (1950)
        translated by M. Wagner
                                       OCLC 856020

Volume 10:   TERTULLIAN APOLOGETICAL WORKS   (1950)
        Tertullian Apology
        translated by E–J. Daly
        On the Soul
        translated by E. Quain
        The Testimony of the Soul
        To Scapula
        translated by R. Arbesmann
        Minucius Felix: Octavius
        translated by R. Arbesmann
                                     OCLC 1037264

Volume 11:   SAINT AUGUSTINE   (1957)
        Commentary on the Lord's Sermon on the Mount
        Selected Sermons (17)
        translated by D. Kavanagh
                                   OCLC 2210742

Volume 12:   SAINT AUGUSTINE   (1951)
        Letters (1–82)
        translated by W. Parsons
                                   OCLC 807061

Volume 13:   SAINT BASIL   (1951)
        Letters (1–185)
        translated by A–C. Way
                                   OCLC 2276183

Volume 14:   SAINT AUGUSTINE   (1952)
        The City of God (books 8–16)
        translated by G. Walsh, G. Monahan
                                   OCLC 807084

Volume 15:   EARLY CHRISTIAN BIOGRAPHIES   (1952)
        Life of St. Ambrose by Paulinus
        translated by J. Lacy
        Life of St. Augustine by Bishop Possidius

Life of St. Cyprian by Pontius
translated by M. M. Mueller, R. Deferrari
Life of St. Epiphanius by Ennodius
translated by G. Cook
Life of St. Paul the First Hermit
Life of St. Hilarion by St. Jerome
Life of Malchus by St. Jerome
translated by L. Ewald
Life of St. Anthony by St. Athanasius
translated by E. Keenan
A Sermon on the Life of St. Honoratus by St. Hilary
translated by R. Deferrari
OCLC 806775

Volume 16:   SAINT AUGUSTINE   (1952)
The Christian Life
Lying
The Work of Monks
The Usefulness of Fasting
translated by S. Muldowney
Against Lying
translated by H. Jaffe
Continence
translated by M-F. McDonald
Patience
translated by L. Meagher
The Excellence of Widowhood
translated by C. Eagan
The Eight Questions of Dulcitius
translated by M. Deferrari
OCLC 806731

Volume 17:   SAINT PETER CHRYSOLOGUS   (1953)
Selected Sermons
Letter to Eutyches
          SAINT VALERIAN
Homilies
Letter to the Monks
translated by G. Ganss
OCLC 806783

Volume 18:   SAINT AUGUSTINE   (1953)

Letters (83–130)
translated by W. Parsons
OCLC 807061

Volume 19:   EUSEBIUS PAMPHILI   (1953)
Ecclesiastical History (books 1–5)
translated by R. Deferrari
OCLC 708651

Volume 20:   SAINT AUGUSTINE   (1953)
Letters (131–164)
translated by W. Parsons
OCLC 807061

Volume 21:   SAINT AUGUSTINE   (1953)
Confessions
translated by V. Bourke
OCLC 2210845

Volume 22:   FUNERAL ORATIONS   (1953)
Saint Gregory Nazianzen: Four Funeral Orations
translated by L. McCauley
Saint Ambrose: On the Death of His Brother Satyrus I & II
translated by J. Sullivan, M. McGuire
Saint Ambrose: Consolation on the Death of Emperor Valentinian
Funeral Oration on the Death of Emperor Theodosius
translated by R. Deferrari
OCLC 806797

Volume 23:   CLEMENT OF ALEXANDRIA   (1954)
Christ the Educator
translated by S. Wood
OCLC 2200024

Volume 24:   SAINT AUGUSTINE   (1954)
The City of God (books 17-22)
translated by G. Walsh, D. Honan
OCLC 807084

Volume 25:   SAINT HILARY OF POITIERS   (1954)
The Trinity
translated by S. McKenna
OCLC 806781

Volume 26:   SAINT AMBROSE   (1954)

Letters (1–91)
  translated by M. Beyenka
            OCLC 806836

Volume 27:   SAINT AUGUSTINE (1955)
 The Divination of Demons
  translated by R. Brown
 Faith and Works
 The Creed
 In Answer to the Jews
  translated by L. Ewald
 Adulterous Marriages
  translated by C. Huegelmeyer
 The Care to be Taken for the Dead
  translated by J. Lacy
 Holy Virginity
  translated by J. McQuade
 Faith and the Creed
  translated by R. Russell
 The Good of Marriage
  translated by C. Wilcox
            OCLC 855069

Volume 28:   SAINT BASIL (1955)
 Letters (186–368)
  translated by A–C. Way
            OCLC 2276183

Volume 29:   EUSEBIUS PAMPHILI (1955)
 Ecclesiastical History
  translated by R. Deferrari
            OCLC 708651

Volume 30:   SAINT AUGUSTINE (1955)
 Letters (165–203)
  translated by W. Parsons
            OCLC 807061

Volume 31: SAINT CAESARIUS OF ARLES I (1956)
 Sermons (1–8)
  translated by M–M. Mueller
            OCLC 806828

Volume 32:   SAINT AUGUSTINE (1956)

  Letters (204–270)
    translated by W. Parsons
                   OCLC 807061
Volume 33:   SAINT JOHN CHRYSOSTOM (1957)
  Commentary on St. John The Apostle and Evangelist
  Homilies (1–47)
    translated by T. Goggin
                   OCLC 2210926
Volume 34:   SAINT LEO THE GREAT (1957)
  Letters
    translated by E. Hunt
                   OCLC 825765
Volume 35:   SAINT AUGUSTINE   (1957)
  Against Julian
    translated by M. Schumacher
                   OCLC 3255620
Volume 36:   SAINT CYPRIAN   (1958)
  To Donatus
  The Lapsed
  The Unity of the Church
  The Lord's Prayer
  To Demetrian
  Mortality
  Works and Almsgiving
  Jealousy and Envy
  Exhortation to Martyrdom to Fortunatus
  That Idols Are Not Gods
    translated by R. Deferrari
  The Dress of Virgins
    translated by A. Keenan
  The Good of Patience
    translated by G. Conway
                   OCLC 3894637
Volume 37:   SAINT JOHN OF DAMASCUS (1958)
  The Fount of Knowledge
  On Heresies
  The Orthodox Faith (4 books)
    translated by F. Chase, Jr.
                   OCLC 810002

Volume 38:	SAINT AUGUSTINE	(1959)

Sermons on the Liturgical Seasons
translated by S. Muldowney

OCLC 810000

Volume 39:	SAINT GREGORY THE GREAT	(1959)

Dialogues
translated by O. Zimmermann

OCLC 3713482

Volume 40:	TERTULLIAN	(1959)

To the Martyrs
Spectacles
translated by R. Arbesmann
The Apparel of Women
The Chaplet
Flight in Time of Persecution
translated by E. Quain
Prayer
Patience
translated by E. Daly

OCLC 810006;804160

Volume 41:	SAINT JOHN CHRYSOSTOM	(1960)

Commentary on St. John the Apostle and Evangelist
Homilies 48–88
translated by T. Goggin

OCLC 2210926

Volume 42:	SAINT AMBROSE	(1961)

Hexameron
Paradise
Cain and Abel
translated by J. Savage

OCLC 806739

Volume 43:	THE POEMS OF PRUDENTIUS	(1962)

The Book of Hymns for Every Day
The Book of the Martyrs' Crowns
translated by C. Eagan

OCLC 806750

Volume 44:	SAINT AMBROSE	(1963)

The Mysteries
The Holy Spirit

        The Sacrament of the Incarnation of Our Lord
        The Sacraments
           translated by R. Deferrari
                                                OCLC 2316634

Volume 45:   SAINT AUGUSTINE   (1963)
        The Trinity
           translated by S. McKenna
                                                OCLC 784847

Volume 46:   SAINT BASIL   (1963)
        Exegetic Homilies
           translated by A-C. Way
                                                OCLC 806743

Volume 47:   SAINT CAESARIUS OF ARLES II   (1963)
        Sermons (81–186)
           translated by M. M. Mueller
                                               OCLC 2494636

Volume 48:   THE HOMILIES OF SAINT JEROME   (1964)
        Homilies 1–59
           translated by L. Ewald
                                               OCLC 412009

Volume 49:   LACTANTIUS   (1964)
        The Divine Institutes
           translated by M-F. McDonald
                                               OCLC 711211

Volume 50:   PAULUS OROSIUS   (1964)
        The Seven Books of History Against the Pagans
           translated by R. Deferrari
                                             OCLC 711212

Volume 51:   SAINT CYPRIAN   (1964)
        Letters (1–81)
           translated by R. Donna
                                             OCLC 806738

Volume 52:   THE POEMS OF PRUDENTIUS   (1965)
        The Divinity of Christ
        The Origin of Sin
        The Spiritual Combat
        Against Symmachus (two books)
        Scenes from Sacred History Or Twofold Nourishment
           translated by C. Eagan

		OCLC 806750
Volume 53:	SAINT JEROME	(1965)

On the Perpetual Virginity of the Blessed Mary Against Helvidius
The Apology Against the Books of Rufinus
The Dialogue Against the Pelagians
   translated by J. Hritzu

		OCLC 806757
Volume 54:	LACTANTIUS	(1965)

The Workmanship of God
The Wrath of God
The Deaths of the Persecutors
The Phoenix
Appendix
   translated by M–F. McDonald

		OCLC 806760
Volume 55:	EUGIPPIUS	(1965)

The Life of Saint Severin
   translated by L. Bieler, L. Krestan

		OCLC 806735
Volume 56:	SAINT AUGUSTINE	(1966)

The Catholic and Manichaean Ways of Life
The Way of Life of the Catholic Church
The Way of Life of the Manichaeans
   translated by D. Gallagher, I. Gallagher

		OCLC 295838
Volume 57:	THE HOMILIES OF SAINT JEROME	(1966)

Homilies 60–96
   translated by L. Ewald

		OCLC 412009
Volume 58:	SAINT GREGORY OF NYSSA	(1967)

On Virginity
On What It Means to Call Oneself a Christian
On Perfection
On the Christian Mode of Life
The Life of Saint Macrina
On the Soul and the Resurrection
   translated by V. Callahan

OCLC 806734

Volume 59:   SAINT AUGUSTINE   (1968)
    The Teacher
    The Free Choice of the Will
    Grace and Free Will
        translated by R. Russell
                OCLC 712674

Volume 60:   SAINT AUGUSTINE   (1968)
    The Retractations
        translated by I. Bogan
                OCLC 712676

Volume 61: THE WORKS OF SAINT CYRIL OF JERUSALEM I (1969)
    Procatechesis
        translated by A. Stephenson
    Lenten Lectures 1–12 (Catecheses)
        translated by L. McCauley
                OCLC 21885

Volume 62:   IBERIAN FATHERS I   (1969)
    Writings of Martin of Braga
        Sayings of the Egyptian Fathers
        Driving Away Vanity
        Exhortation to Humility
        Anger
        Reforming the Rustics
        Rules For An Honest Life
        Triple Immersion
        Easter
    Paschasius of Dumium
        Questions and Answers of the Greek Fathers
    Writings of Leander of Seville
        The Training of Nuns and the Contempt of the World
        Sermon on the Triumph of the Church for the Conversion of the Goths
        translated by C. Barlow
                OCLC 718095

Volume 63:   IBERIAN FATHERS II   (1969)
    Braulio of Saragossa
        Letters of Braulio
        Life of St. Emilian
        List of the Books of Isidore of Seville
    Writings of Fructuosus of Braga

                Rule for the Monastery of Compludo
                General Rule for Monasteries
                Pact
                Monastic Agreement
                translated by C. Barlow
                                                    OCLC 718095

Volume 64:   THE WORKS OF SAINT CYRIL   (1970)
                    OF JERUSALEM II
                Lenten Lectures (Catcheses) 13–18
                    translated by L. McCauley
                The Mystagogical Lectures
                Sermon on the Paralytic
                Letter to Constantius
                    translated by A. Stephenson
                                             OCLC 21885

Volume 65   SAINT AMBROSE   (1972)
              Seven Exegetical Works
                  Isaac or the Soul
                  Death as a Good
                  Jacob and the Happy Life
                  Joseph
                  The Patriarchs
                  Flight from the World
                  The Prayer of Job and David
                  translated by M. McHugh
                                           OCLC 314148

Volume 66:   SAINT CAESARIUS OF ARLES III   (1973)
              Sermons 187–238
                  translated by M. M. Mueller
                              OCLC 1035149; 2494636

Volume 67:   NOVATIAN   (1974)
              The Trinity
              The Spectacles
              Jewish Foods
              In Praise of Purity
              Letters
                  translated by R. DeSimone
                                                   OCLC 662181

Volume 68:   SAINT JOHN CHRYSOSTOM   (1978)
Discourses Against Judaizing Christians
translated by P. Harkins

OCLC 3003009

Volume 69:   MARIUS VICTORINUS   (1981)
Theological Treatises on the Trinity
Letter of Candidus the Arian to Marius Victorinus Rhetor On the Divine Begetting
Letter of Marius Victorinus Rhetor of the City of Rome to Candidus the Arian
Letter of Candidus the Arian to the Most Illustrious Marius Victorinus
Against Arius Book I A
Against Arius Book I B
Against Arius Book II
Against Arius Book III
Against Arius Book IV
On the Necessity of Accepting the Term *Homoousios*
Hymns on the Trinity
translated by M. T. Clark

OCLC 5029056

www.ingramcontent.com/pod-product-compliance
Lightning Source LLC
Chambersburg PA
CBHW030527010526
44110CB00048B/707